T0321172

THE
KNOWLEDGE
GRID

THE
KNOWLEDGE
GRID

Hai Zhuge
Chinese Academy of Sciences, China

 **World Scientific**

NEW JERSEY · LONDON · SINGAPORE · BEIJING · SHANGHAI · HONG KONG · TAIPEI · CHENNAI

Published by

World Scientific Publishing Co. Pte. Ltd.

5 Toh Tuck Link, Singapore 596224

USA office: 27 Warren Street, Suite 401-402, Hackensack, NJ 07601

UK office: 57 Shelton Street, Covent Garden, London WC2H 9HE

British Library Cataloguing-in-Publication Data
A catalogue record for this book is available from the British Library.

THE KNOWLEDGE GRID

ISBN-13 978-981-256-140-4
ISBN-10 981-256-140-4

Typeset by Stallion Press
Email: enquiries@stallionpress.com

Printed in Singapore

Foreword

The history of long-distance communication, from message sticks, smoke signals, pony riders, semaphore (with the world's first Internet in western Europe two centuries ago), telegraph, telephone, and radio, has led to the modern Internet. This history has converged with that of the knowledge repository, from cave drawings, clay tablet collections, manuscript libraries (notably the famous library at Alexandria), university libraries, the lending libraries associated with the rise of popular literacy, to the very recent World Wide Web and its parasitic search engines, which are based on the Internet.

Now the Net and its Web are being extended by mobile telephones and commercialized by media companies. Will all this become just an extension of the telephone, newspaper and television industries?

There are those who hope not, among them Professor Hai Zhuge who, with his China Knowledge Grid Research Group, is aiming to show that formal knowledge classification and storage combined with disciplined knowledge sharing is possible, practical and beneficial.

This book gives a view of their broad ideas about a future interconnection environment, and a description of the methods and models they are already using at this early stage of development of the Knowledge Grid.

I can only wish for the Group, and for this book, the success they deserve.

Neville Holmes
September 27, 2004

Foreword

Preface

The Internet connects computers all around the world to support e-document transmission. The World Wide Web makes informative Web pages conveniently available to Internet users everywhere. The aim of the Knowledge Grid is to provide effective knowledge services by connecting globally distributed resources. It goes beyond the scope of the current Web and Grid computing.

The Knowledge Grid is to be a large-scale human-machine environment, where people, machines, society and nature can productively coexist and harmoniously evolve. It stands for the human ideal of a living, wise, systematic, and optimal social environment.

Recognizing the nature, source and principles of knowledge is essential to realizing effective information services and knowledge sharing. The Knowledge Grid bases its methodology on epistemology and ontology as well as on multi-disciplinary approaches.

Established in July 2000, the China Knowledge Grid Research Group (http://kg.ict.ac.cn) has been exploring this field. The group has rapidly developed from the initial three members to the current thirty members. It leads the China Semantic Grid Project, a $US 3 million project supported by the National Grand Fundamental Research 973 Program. Developing applications in the areas of e-science and culture heritage protection, the group has evolved into the Knowledge Grid Center (http://www.knowledgegrid.net) that includes research groups and laboratories co-sponsored by universities and institutions in many parts of China.

The research work in this book was supported by the National Grand Fundamental Research 973 Program (2003CB317001), the National

Science Foundation of China (Grants 60273020 and 70271007), and the Innovation Fund of Institute of Computing Technology, Chinese Academy of Sciences.

I would like to take this opportunity to thank my wife for her consistent support in every stage of my academic career.

I sincerely thank all the members of the China Knowledge Grid Research Group for their cooperative spirit and diligent work, especially my students Jie Liu, Xiang Li, Xue Chen, Erlin Yao, Yunpeng Xing, Ruixiang Jia, Yunchuan Sun and Weiyu Guo, who provided useful materials and helped check the manuscript.

Finally, I hope this book will help in promoting the development of this promising area.

Hai Zhuge
September 20, 2004

Contents

Chapter 1

The Knowledge Grid Methodology

The development of science and technology has extended human behavior and sensation, accelerated the progress of society, and enabled people to understand the objective world and themselves more profoundly. But we still have much to find out, especially about machine-enabled knowledge creation, evolution, inheritance and sharing.

Knowledge in nature is a product of society. It evolves and endures throughout the life of a culture rather than that of an individual as mentioned in "As We May Think" (V. Bush, *The Atlantic Monthly*, 1945, vol.176, no.1, pp.101-108). Modern communication facilities like the Internet provide people with unprecedented social opportunities for knowledge generation and sharing. However, our increasing computing power and communication bandwidth does not of itself improve this knowledge generation and sharing. To do this, the semantic ability of the facilities that transmit and store knowledge must be improved. Improving our social interaction in this way would help enrich knowledge in our society by supporting social activities at different levels (both the physical and the mental level) and in different environmental spaces (entity space, semantic space and knowledge space).

The ideal of the Knowledge Grid is to foster worldwide knowledge creation, evolution, inheritance, and sharing in a world of humans, roles and machines as stated in "China's e-Science Knowledge Grid Environment" (H. Zhuge, *IEEE Intelligent Systems*, 2004, vol.19, no.1, pp.13-17; the Knowledge Grid forum, center and community portal http://www.knowledgegrid.net).

The capturing and expressing of semantics involves complex psychological and cognitive processes. The exploitation of psychology, cognitive science and philosophy plays an important role in studying semantics—the basis for knowledge sharing.

The Knowledge Grid methodology is a multi-disciplinary system methodology for establishing a global knowledge world that obeys the principles and laws of economics, nature, society, psychology and information technology.

Implementation of the Knowledge Grid will speed up the development of human civilization.

1.1 Towards The Next-Generation Web

The Internet and the World Wide Web are milestones of information technology. People have become increasingly reliant on them for supporting modern work and life. For example, scientists can communicate with each other using net forums and email, share their experimental data and research results by posting them in Web pages on personal or corporate websites, and retrieve technical reports and academic papers of interest to them from online digital libraries or from less formal websites using general-purpose search engines.

But the exponential growth and intrinsic characteristics of the Web and its pages prevent people from effectively and efficiently sharing information. Much effort has been put into solving this problem with but limited success. In any case it is hard for the Web to provide intelligent services because the representation used by the current Web does not support the inclusion of semantic information.

With the development of communication facilities and Web applications, computing is struggling to extend its support from individual to group and social behavior, from closed to open systems, from simple and centralized to complex and distributed computing, and from static computing to dynamic and mobile information, computing and knowledge services.

To overcome the deficiencies of the current Web, scientists and developers are working towards a next-generation Web. These efforts lie in three main categories: the first includes the *Semantic Web, Web Service* and *Web Intelligence*, which aim to improve the current Web, the second is the *Grid* (http://www.gridforum.org), which aims at a new application platform of the Internet, and the third is *Peer-to-Peer Computing*, which enables resource sharing in an egalitarian, large-scale and dynamic network as discussed in "Peer-to-peer Prospects" (D. Schoder and K. Fischbach, *Communications of the ACM,* 2003, vol.46, no.2, pp.27-29). Recent reports indicate that all are indeed moving closer to their targets.

The aim of the *Semantic Web* (http://www.semanticweb.org) is to support cooperation between Web resources by establishing ontological and logical mechanisms by using standard markup languages like XML (eXtensible Markup Language, http://www.w3.org/XML), RDF (Resource Description Framework, http://wwww.w3.org/RDF), OIL (Ontology Interchange Language) and DAML (DARPA Agent Markup Language) to replace HTML (HyperText Markup Language, http://www.w3.org/MarkUp) and to allow Web pages to hold descriptions of their content.

The aim of *Web Service* is to provide an open platform for the development, deployment, interaction, and management of globally distributed e-services based on Web standards like UDDI (Universal Definition Discovery and Integration) and WSDL (Web Service Description Language, www.w3.org/TR/wsdl). It enables the integration of services residing and running in different places. Using intelligent agents is an important technique that can be used to implement active Web Service.

The aim of *Web Intelligence* is to improve the current Web by using artificial intelligence (especially distributed intelligence) and information processing technologies such as symbolic reasoning, text mining, information extraction and information retrieval.

The aim of the global *Grid* is to share, manage, coordinate, schedule and control distributed computing resources, which could be machines, networks, data, and any types of devices. The ideal of the Grid is that any compatible device could be plugged in anywhere on the Grid and be guaranteed the required services regardless of their locations, just like the electrical power grid. Grid computing does not use Web technologies.

The *Semantic Grid* (http://www.semanticgrid.org) attempts to incorporate the advantages of the Grid, Semantic Web and Web Service approaches. The Grid architecture has become the service-oriented Open Grid Services Architecture (OGSA) (I.Foster, C.Kesselman, J.M.Nick, and S.Tuecke, "Grid Services for Distributed System Integration", *Computer*, 2002, vol.35, no.6, pp.37-46), in which some features of Web Service can be plainly seen.

By defining standard mechanisms for creating, naming, and locating services, the Semantic Grid can incorporate peer-to-peer technology under OGSA, and so enable autonomous computing objects to cooperate in a network of equals and with scalability.

Peer-to-peer networking should work not only at the computing level but also at the semantic level. How to automatically map from a semantically rich space into a peer-to-peer network is an important research problem that must be solved before the gap between the peer-to-peer network and high-level intelligent applications can be bridged.

1.2 Challenges and Opportunities

The development of operating systems, advanced languages, and database systems were crucial events in computing history, and were also very important to the success of personal computing. The Internet and its applications are now moving computing towards an open and socialized service environment. But it is still difficult for the current Internet application platform (based on client/server architecture) to support complex and intelligent applications, especially under large-scale and dynamic conditions.

Demanding application requirements provide researchers with many challenges and opportunities. Complex and intelligent applications require the support of completely new databases, programming languages, and operating systems to support distributed sharing, coordination, deployment, execution and management of services and resources, and the implementation of applications that are beyond the ability of the current Web. Fig. 1.1 depicts the evolutionary trend of computing.

The Knowledge Grid is a newly proposed computing platform, which supports new resource organization models, new computing models, and new networks such as sensor, mobile and wireless networks.

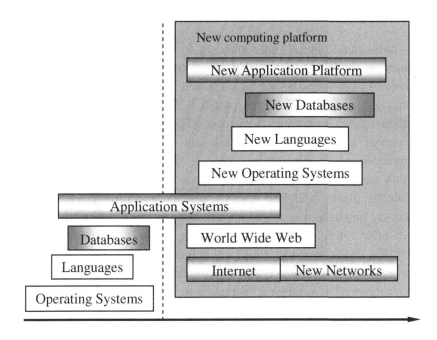

Fig. 1.1 The evolution of computing environments.

1.3 Towards the Knowledge Grid

Acquiring knowledge is the basis for intelligent services. Fran Berman pointed out the challenge of extracting knowledge from terabytes of data in her essay "From TeraGrid to Knowledge Grid" (*Communications of the ACM*, 2001, vol.44, no.11, pp.27-28). She commented that the "Knowledge Grid" has to synthesize knowledge from data by means of mining and reference, and to enable search engines to make references, answer questions, and draw conclusions from masses of data. Recent understanding and development of the Knowledge Grid has gone beyond the scope of Fran Berman's proposal.

1.3.1 *Virtual characteristics*

Many computer scientists are exploring ideal computing and resource organization models for the next-generation Web. The editorial of the first special issue on Semantic Grid and Knowledge Grid for the *Future Generation Computer Systems* journal (2004, vol.20, no.1, pp.1-5) described the following scenario: The future interconnection environment will be a platform-irrelevant *Virtual Grid* consisting of requirements, roles and resources.

With machine-understandable semantics, a resource can actively and dynamically cluster and fuse relevant resources to provide on-demand services by understanding requirements and functions and relating them to each other. Versatile resources are encapsulated to provide services by way of a *single semantic image* within the uniform resource model. A resource can intelligently assist people to accomplish complex tasks and solve problems by employing versatile resource flow cycles through virtual roles to use appropriate knowledge, information, and computing resources.

With the development of society and science, people have a more profound understanding of nature, society, and themselves than ever before. So appropriate rules and principles of nature, society and economics should be adopted when we develop the next-generation Web.

1.3.2 *Social characteristics*

The Knowledge Grid has social characteristics. In the real world, people live and work in a *social grid* obeying social and economic rules and laws. The Knowledge Grid is a *virtual social grid*, where people enjoy and provide services through versatile flow cycles like control flows, material flows, energy flows, information flows and knowledge flows.

People can communicate and gain knowledge from each other through mutually understandable semantics.

An artificial interconnection environment can only be effective when it works harmoniously with its social grids. For example, an effective e-business environment requires harmonious cooperation between information flows, knowledge flows, material flows, e-services and social services. The e-services belong to e-business platforms. The material flows and social services belong to society. The information flows and knowledge flows belong to both society and the platforms. The proper semantic representation supports mutual understanding between the social grid and the artificial interconnection environment. In future, different artificial interconnection environments will co-exist and compete with each other for survival, rights and reputation, and will harmoniously evolve with the social grid (H.Zhuge and X.Shi, "Eco-grid: A Harmoniously Evolved Interconnection Environment", *Communications of the ACM*, 2004, vol.47, no.9, pp79-83).

1.3.3 *Adaptive characteristics*

"On-demand services" is a fashionable catchphrase in the context of the future Web. But there is no limit to demand. So, to provide all participants with services on demand is impossible and unreasonable as long as service generation and service provision carry a significant cost and services themselves differ in quality.

Economics is concerned with three kinds of entity: participants, markets and economic systems. The market is an important mechanism for automatically and reasonably adjusting the decisions and behaviors of market participants, for example, agents and soft-devices (H.Zhuge, "Clustering Soft-Devices in Semantic Grid", *IEEE Computing in Science and Engineering*, 2002, vol.4, no.6, pp.60-63). Besides the influence of the market, participants' behaviors and decisions can be adjusted by negotiation. Governments, organizations and social rights also play important roles in influencing market participants' behavior and decision making. Market participants, producers and consumers, look for satisfactory rather than optimal exchanges through agreement (the evaluation of "satisfactory" involves psychological factors). Being based on simple principles, the market mechanism adapts by avoiding complex computation.

The natural ecological system establishes a balance among natural species through energy flow, material flow and information flow. These flows in their turn influence the social system (H. Zhuge and X. Shi, "Fighting Epidemics in the Information and Knowledge Age", *Computer*, 2003, vol.36, no.10, pp.114-116). Different species evolve together as parts of the entire ecological system.

The Knowledge Grid also supports three major roles: producers, consumers and a market mechanism for adapting to the behavior of different participants. It should adopt economic and ecological principles to balance the interests of knowledge producers and knowledge consumers, and adapt to knowledge evolution and expansion.

1.3.4 *Semantic characteristics*

Research on semantic information processing has a long history in the computing field (M.L. Minsky, ed., *Semantic Information Processing*, MIT Press, 1968). Knowledge representation approaches such as frame theory (Minsky, 1975), the Knowledge Representation Language KRL (D.G. Bobrow, 1979) and the Semantic Network (M.R. Quillian; H.A. Simon, 1970) are approaches to expressing semantics. Before the emergence of the Internet interchange standard XML and the Resource Description Framework RDF (http://www.w3.org/RDF/), the Knowledge Interchange Format KIF (http://www.logic.stanford.edu/kif) and Open Knowledge Base Connectivity OKBC (http://www.ai.sri.com/~okbc) were two standards for knowledge sharing.

Knowledge acquisition is the bottleneck of knowledge engineering. Data mining approaches help a bit by automatically discovering knowledge (association rules) in large-scale databases. These approaches can also be used to discover semantic relationships within and between texts.

Why were the symbolic approaches, especially the KIF and OKBC of AI, and ODBC in the database area, not widely adopted in the Internet age?

One cause is the success of HTML, which is easy to use both for a writer and, in cooperation with a browser, for a reader. Its main advantage is that "anything can link to anything" (T. Berners-Lee, J. Hendler and O. Lassila, Semantic Web, *Scientific American*, vol.284, no.5, 2001, pp.34-43).

A second cause is that traditional AI's knowledge representation approaches try to explicate human knowledge, while the Web focuses on structuring Web resources and the relationship between resources, that is, it is more concerned with semantics.

A third cause is that cooperation between machines (applications) has become the dominant aim in realizing intelligent Web applications, while traditional knowledge engineering focuses on cooperation between human and machine.

A fourth cause is the cross-platform requirement. Consequently XML has been adopted as the information exchange standard of the Web.

What are the semantic problems of the Internet age?

The first is the acquisition problem — to automatically acquire semantic relationships within and between resources.

The second is the representation problem — but the focus is on expressing the semantic relationships between Web resources (just as in the ER model in the relational data model, the focus is on expressing semantic relationships between entities), on establishing an appropriate semantic computing model, and on seeking an approach that synthesizes the semantics expressed within different semantic spaces. Prior research into expressing the internal semantics of resources helps solve this problem.

The third is the normal organization problem — to properly organize semantic information under semantic normal forms and integrity constraints so that the correctness and efficiency of semantic operations is guaranteed. If we can solve this problem, Web resources can be correctly used in light of their semantics.

The fourth is the problem of processing semantics — to refine, abstract and synthesize large-scale semantic information to provide appropriate and succinct semantic information.

The fifth is the maintenance problem — to maintain correct semantics in large-scale and dynamic semantic resource spaces.

Solving the above problems is beyond the scope of current research on the Semantic Web. The RDF would be a less than ideal approach to expressing the semantics of Web resources because it does not directly address the semantic problems of the Internet age.

At a high level, the Knowledge Grid is a "world" of requirements, roles and services. Services are provided by resources that are implemented on the basis of a uniform resource model. Services can actively find and advertise requirements. People can play the roles of services, and enjoy services provided by others. Requirements and services are organized into conglomerations that belong to different communities. Some services can play the broker role and be responsible for dynamically integrating services to meet varying requirements.

At a low level, a Semantic Resource Space organizes and uses resources by way of a *single semantic image*, that is, various resources are mapped onto a single semantic space to expose their commonality. The single semantic image can be realized by semantic relationship models like orthogonal classification and semantic linking. Normalization theory guarantees the correctness and effectiveness of resource operations (H.Zhuge, "Semantics, Resources and Grid", *Future Generation Computer Systems*, 2003, vol.20, no.1, pp.1-5). The Semantic Resource Space requires a semantic browser that enables not only people but also services to exploit the semantics of a resource being browsed, to extract from the resource and reason from the extract, to explain the display, and to anticipate subsequent browsing.

A huge gap exists between low-level semantics and high-level semantics as shown in Fig. 1.2. Current Web application software technologies and tools only use low-level semantics such as keywords and surface content (texture, color, and so on). Users have to search an enormous name space to find what they need within huge and expanding Web resources.

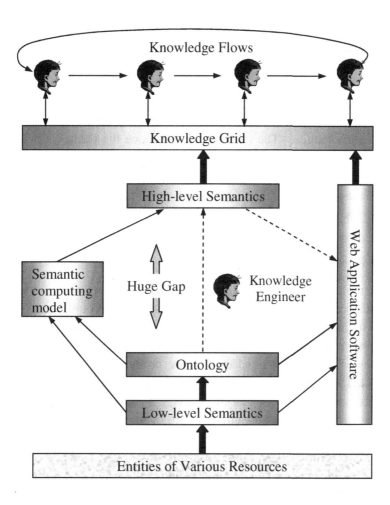

Fig. 1.2 Gap between low-level semantics and high-level semantics.

Complex cognitive and psychological processes are involved in this huge gap. Some computer scientists seek to obtain high-level semantics by establishing domain ontology mechanisms for explaining the semantics of resources and their ties. Building tools and finding methods for creating ontologies are becoming popular in the Semantic Web area. Ontology can reflect people's consensus on semantics in name spaces or symbolic spaces to a certain extent. But it is hard to cope with the complexity of human cognitive processes.

A *semantic computing model* that could at least partly bridge this huge gap must be found. The model should go beyond the scope of traditional formal semantics, which has been extensively investigated in computer science in the past with success that is significant in theory but limited in practice. The model should balance the formal and informal and reflect human cognitive characteristics.

Epistemology, which has been neglected in previous efforts towards the next-generation Web, plays the key role in human cognitive processes.

1.4 Epistemology

Epistemology is a branch of philosophy. It concerns the nature, scope and source of knowledge. Computer scientists could improve their understanding of computing by studying the history and variety of epistemology.

Empiricism sees knowledge as the product of sensory perception. Knowledge results from a kind of mapping or reflection of external objects, from our sensory organs, possibly assisted by some observational instruments, into our brain to be used by our mind.

Rationalism considers knowledge to be the product of rational reflection. Knowledge results from the organization of perceptual data on the basis of cognitive structures called *categories*. Categories include *space*, *time*, *objects* and *causality*.

Pragmatism holds that knowledge consists of mental models that simplify our perception of the real world. It is assumed that a model only reflects the main characteristics of the real world. Otherwise, it would be too complicated to be of any practical use. Thus different or even seemingly contradictory models for solving the same problem could co-exist. Problem solving is a process of developing and selecting useful models. Mathematical modeling plays an important role in scientific problem solving.

Individual constructivism sees the individual as trying to build coherence between different pieces of knowledge. In the mental construction process, knowledge that succeeded in integrating previously incoherent pieces of knowledge will be kept, and knowledge that is inconsistent with the bulk of other knowledge that the individual has will tend to be rejected.

Social constructivism regards consensus on different subjects as the ultimate criterion for judging knowledge. Truth or reality will be accorded only to those constructions on which most people of a social group agree. Karl Marx's theory of ideology can be regarded as a type of social epistemology. An ideology is a set of beliefs, a world view, or a form of consciousness that is in some fashion false or delusive. The cause of these beliefs and their delusiveness is the social situation and interests of the believers. The theory of ideology is concerned with the truth and falsity of beliefs, so it is a kind of *classical social epistemology.* *Feminist epistemology and philosophy of science* studies the ways in which gender influences, and ought to influence, our conceptions of knowledge, the knowing subject, and practices of inquiry and justification.

Evolutionary epistemology assumes that knowledge is constructed by a subject or group of subjects in order to adapt to their environment in the broad sense. That construction is a process going on at different levels—at biological as well as psychological or social levels. Construction happens through blind variation of existing pieces of knowledge, and the selective retention of those new combinations that somehow contribute more to the survival and reproduction of the subjects within their given environment. Knowledge is regarded as an instrument questing for survival. Evolutionary epistemology emphasizes the importance of natural selection. Selection is the generator and maintainer of the reliability of our sensory and cognitive mechanisms, as well as of the *fit* between those mechanisms and the world. Trial and error learning and the development of scientific theories can be explained as evolutionary selection processes.

A recent evolutionary view is that knowledge can actively pursue goals of its own. It notes that knowledge can be transmitted from one individual to another, and thereby lose its dependence on any particular individual. A piece of knowledge may be successful even though its predictions may be totally wrong, as long as it is sufficiently convincing to new carriers. In this theory, the individual having knowledge has lost his primacy, and knowledge becomes a force in its own right with proper goals and ways of developing itself. This emphasizes communication and social processes in the development of knowledge, but instead of regarding knowledge as the object constructed by the social system, it rather views social systems as constructed by knowledge processes. Indeed, a social group can be seen as organized by members sharing the same types of knowledge. *To keep evolution sustainable, knowledge should have the characteristic of diversity.*

The following references can help readers learn more about epistemology:

(1) F. Heylighen (1993), "Epistemology Introduction", in:
     F. Heylighen, C. Joslyn and V. Turchin (editors): *Principia Cybernetica Web*, http://pespmc1.vub.ac.be/epistemology.html.
(2) P.D. Klein, (1998). "Epistemology". In E. Craig (ed.), *Routledge Encyclopedia of Philosophy*. London: Routledge.
     http://www.rep.routledge.com/article/P059.
(3) E. Anderson, "Feminist Epistemology and Philosophy of Science", *Stanford Encyclopedia of Philosophy*,
     http://plato.stanford.edu/entries/feminism-epistemology/.
(4) M. Brady and W. Harms, "Evolutionary Epistemology", *Stanford Encyclopedia of Philosophy*,
     http://plato.stanford.edu/entries/epistemology-evolutionary/.
(5) R. Feldman, *Stanford Encyclopedia of Philosophy* article,
     "Naturalized Epistemology".
(6) A. Goldman, "Social Epistemology", *Stanford Encyclopedia of Philosophy*, http://plato.stanford.edu/entries/epistemology-social/.

1.5 Ontology

Ontology — another branch of philosophy — is the science of what is, and of the kinds and structures of the objects, properties and relations in every area of reality. Ontology in this sense is often used in such a way as to be synonymous with metaphysics. In simple terms, it seeks to classify entities. Each scientific field has its own preferred ontology, defined by the field's vocabulary and by the canonical formulations of its theories.

Traditional ontologists tend to model scientific ontologies by producing theories, organizing them and clarifying their foundations. Ontologists are concerned not only with the world as studied by sciences, but also with the domains of practical activities such as law, medicine, engineering, and commerce. They seek to apply the tools of ontology to solving problems that arise in these domains.

In the field of information processing, different groups of data-gatherers have their own idiosyncratic terms and concepts that guide how they represent the information they receive. When an attempt is made to put information together from different groups, methods must be found to resolve terminological and conceptual incompatibilities. At first such incompatibilities were resolved case by case. Then people gradually came to realize that providing once and for all a common backbone taxonomy of entities relevant to an application domain would have significant advantages over resolving incompatibilities case by case. This common backbone taxonomy is called an *ontology mechanism* by information scientists.

In the context of knowledge sharing and reuse, an ontology mechanism establishes a terminology for members of a community of interest. These members can be humans, application software, or automated agents. An ontology can be represented as a formal vocabulary organized in taxonomic hierarchies of classes, whose semantics is independent of both user and context. Readers can obtain more information about ontology from the Semantic Web website (http://www.semanticweb.org).

1.6 System Methodology

Web and Grid computing have not yet made use of the principles and methods of system methodology.

Darwin's theory of evolution holds time to be an "arrow" of evolution. The subjects of the evolutionary process evolve as time progresses, so the overall process is irreversible, just like time. Life evolves from the simple to the complex, from a single-celled ameba to a multi-celled human being.

The second law of thermodynamics (R.J.E. Clausius and L. Boltzmann) tells us of a degenerate arrow: all processes manifest a tendency toward decay and disintegration, with a net increase in what is called the *entropy*, or state of randomness or disorder, of the overall system.

The theory of dissipative structure was created against the background of the collision between the two arrows.

1.6.1 *The theory of dissipative structure*

A system with dissipative structure is an open system that exists far from thermodynamic equilibrium, efficiently dissipates the heat generated to sustain it, and has the capacity to change to higher levels of orderliness.

According to Prigogine's theory, systems contain subsystems that continually fluctuate. At times a single fluctuation or a combination of them may become so magnified by positive feedback that it shatters the existing organization. At such revolutionary moments, it is impossible to determine in advance whether the system will disintegrate into chaos or leap to a new, more differentiated, higher level of order. The latter case is called a dissipative structure, so termed because it needs more energy to sustain itself than the simpler structure it replaces and is limited in growth by the amount of heat it is able to dissipate.

According to the theory of dissipative structure, the exponential growth of Web resources tends to disorder. The current efforts towards the future Web are trying to establish a new kind of order — the order of diverse resources. But how such an order can be prevented from becoming disordered again is a critical issue that needs to be considered as we work towards the future Web.

Here is a very interesting question: *Can we design a dissipative structure for the future Web?*

1.6.2 Synergetic theory

Synergetics is a theory of pattern formation in complex systems. It tries to explain structures that develop spontaneously in nature. Readers can obtain more information from H. Haken's works (*Synergetics, An Introduction: Nonequilibrium Phase-Transitions and Self-Organization in Physics, Chemistry and Biology*, Springer, 1977; *Synergetics of Cognition*, Springer-Verlag, 1990 (with M.Stadler); *Principles of Brain Functioning: A Synergetic Approach to Brain Activity, Behavior, and Cognition*, Springer-Verlag, 1995).

The purpose of introducing the relevant concepts here is to provoke constructive thought about their possible influence on the future Web.

How order emerges out of chaos is not well defined, so synergetics employs the ideas of probability (to describe uncertainty) and information (to describe approximation). Entropy is a central concept relating physics to information theory. Synergetics concerns the following three key concepts: compression of the degrees of freedom of a complex system into dynamic patterns that can be expressed as a collective variable; behavioral attractors of changing stabilities; and the appearance of new forms as nonequilibrium phase transitions.

Systems at instability points are driven by a *slaving principle*: long-lasting quantities can enslave short-lasting quantities (that is, they can act as order parameters). Close to instability, stable motions (or "modes") are enslaved by unstable modes and can be ignored, thereby reducing the degrees of freedom of the system. The macroscopic behavior of the system is determined by the unstable modes. The dynamic equations of the system reflect the interplay between stochastic forces ("chance") and deterministic forces ("necessity").

Synergetics deals with self-organization, how collections of parts can produce structures. Synergetics applies to systems driven far from equilibrium, where the classic concepts of thermodynamics are no longer adequate. Order can arise from chaos and can be maintained by flows of energy or matter.

Synergetics has wide applications in physics, chemistry, sociology and biology (population dynamics, evolution, and morphogenesis). Completely different systems exhibit surprising analogies as they pass through an instability. Biological systems are unique in that they exhibit an interplay between structure and function that is embodied in structure and latent in form.

The ideas introduced above imply that synergetics can help us explore the intrinsic self-organization principle of the future Web and its resources (for example, how the components such as services can form a well behaved structure to provide an appropriate service), and find better approaches to solve existing problems in information processing.

1.6.3 *The hypercycle — a principle of natural self-organization*

A living system has three features: *self-reproduction*, *metabolism*, and *evolution*. A *hypercycle* is a system that consists of self-reproducing macro-molecular species that are linked cyclically by catalysis. It is interesting to investigate pre-biotic evolution since it might explain how molecular species having a small number of molecules could evolve into entities with a great amount of genetic information. The idea of the hypercycle, introduced by Eigen in 1971, has been experimentally and theoretically verified by Gebinoga in 1995. The purpose of introducing here the concept of the hypercycle is to provoke some rethinking about work towards the future Web.

The following example explains the concept of the hypercycle. Living cells contain both nucleic acids and proteins, and molecules of the two classes interact. Genetic information controls the production of polypeptide chains, that is, proteins. Data encoded in nucleic acids ensure that certain proteins can be produced. Information about proteins helps the replication of nucleic acids and enables information transmission. A system of nucleic acids and proteins helping to replicate each other is an important basis for evolution as evolution can occur only when the state information can be obtained, maintained and extended.

M. Eigen and P. Schuster consider hypercycles to be predecessors of protocells (primitive unicellular biological organisms). As quasispecies, hypercycles have also been mathematically analyzed in detail.

The self-reproducing automaton was investigated early on by John von Neumann.

A similar system of catalytically interacting macromolecules called a *syser* is comprised of a polynucleotide matrix and several proteins. There are two obligatory proteins: the replication enzyme and the translation enzyme. A *syser* can also include some structural proteins and additional enzymes. The polynucleotide matrix encodes the composition of proteins, and the replication enzyme controls the matrix replication process. The translation enzyme controls the protein synthesis according to the data encoded in the matrix. Structural proteins and additional enzymes can provide optional functions. Different *sysers* should be inserted into different organisms for effective competition.

Compared to hypercycles, *sysers* are more like simple biological organisms. The concept of *sysers* makes it possible to analyze evolutionary stages starting from a mini-*syser*, which contains only a matrix and replication and translation enzymes. An adaptive *syser* includes a simple molecular control system, which "turns on" and "turns off" synthesis by some enzyme in response to change in the external medium.

Readers can learn more about the hypercycle from M. Eigen and P. Schuster, *The Hypercycle: A principle of natural self-organization*, Springer, Berlin, 1979.

The notion of a *soft-device*, the uniform resource model of the future Web, is introduced in "Clustering Soft-Devices in Semantic Grid" (H.Zhuge, *IEEE Computing in Science and Engineering*, 2002, vol.4, no.6, pp.60-63) and envisions that the future Web will be a world of versatile soft-devices and roles. Ideal soft-devices have the same function as *sysers*.

Hypercycle theory will give us some useful notions for when we explore the organization mode of the future Web. For example, the future Web can be imagined as a living system or environment, which consists of resource species in the form of soft-devices and versatile flow cycles. Resources could be dynamically organized into diverse flows such as knowledge flows, information flows, and service flows to provide users or applications with on-demand services. Once a requirement is confirmed, all relevant flows could be formed automatically (H.Zhuge and X.Shi, "Eco-Grid: A Harmoniously Evolved Interconnection Environment", *Communications of the ACM*, 2004, vol.47, no.9, pp.79-83).

The future Web can be imagined as a quasihuman body, which has knowledge and intelligence and operates with special hypercycles. It can cooperate with people in a humanized way and provide appropriate, up-to-date, on-demand and just-in-time services.

1.6.4 *Principles and strategies*

The Knowledge Grid methodology should adopt the principles and rules of social science, economics, psychology, biology, ecology and physics, and inherit the fundamental ideas, views, rules and principles of system science.

Principles

(1) *Integrity and uniformity principles* — The idea of integrity requires us to resolve the issue of correctness (for example, the correctness of operations). The idea of uniformity requires us to resolve the issue of simplicity, that is, to simplify a system. The integrity theory of the relational database model is a good example of integrity and it could give us useful ideas for developing the theory and system of a Knowledge Grid, especially in resource management.

(2) *The hierarchical principle* — H.A. Simon unveils the hierarchical principle of artificial systems in his book (*The Sciences of the Artificial*, Cambridge, MA: The MIT Press, 1969). The construction of a Knowledge Grid should follow this principle. Furthermore, different levels of a system could work in different semantic spaces. Consistency should be maintained between multiple semantic spaces,

such as between the semantic space of logic and the semantic space of algebra.

(3) *The open principle* — This principle would keep the Knowledge Grid away from the equilibrium state. Standards are a critical criterion for open systems. The Knowledge Grid could make use of the standards of the Internet, the World Wide Web and the Grid. For example, XML could be the basis for knowledge expression and transformation.

(4) *The self-organization principle* — Resources including systems themselves can actively collaborate with each other according to some principle (for example, the economic principle) and common regulations.

(5) *The principle of competition and cooperation* — Resources including systems (multiple systems or environments could coexist) evolve through competition and cooperation so that competitive resources or systems could play a more important role.

(6) *The optimization principle* — Optimization means making a system more effective. Information flow, knowledge flow and service flow can be optimized to achieve efficiency in logistic processes.

(7) *The principle of sustainable development* — Sustainable development requires individuals and communities, the interconnection environment and its human-machine interfaces, the human-machine society, and even the natural environment to harmoniously coexist and coevolve.

Strategies

The following strategies could help develop the Knowledge Grid as a future interconnection environment.

The fusion of inheritance and innovation — the Knowledge Grid environment should absorb the advantages of the Grid, the Semantic Web, and Web Services. Current Web applications should be able to work in the new environment. Smooth development would enable the future Web to exploit research on the current Web.

The fusion of centralization and decentralization — Advantage should be taken of both centralization and decentralization. On the one hand, an ideal system should be able to dynamically cluster and fuse relevant resources to provide complete and on-demand services for applications. On the other hand, it should be able to deploy the appropriate resources into the appropriate locations to achieve optimized computing.

The fusion of abstraction and specialization — On the one hand, we need to abstract a variety of resources to investigate common rules, and on the other hand, to investigate the special rules of different resources to properly integrate and couple resources.

The fusion of mobility and correctness — On the one hand, the Knowledge Grid should support mobile applications to meet the needs of ubiquitous applications. On the other hand, we should guarantee the quality of services and the means of verification.

The fusion of symbolic and connectionist approaches — Current ontology only uses the symbolic approach, which is very similar to traditional knowledge base construction. The combination of the symbolic approach and the connectionist approach would help find better solutions for intelligent applications.

The incremental strategy — As a worldwide interconnection environment, the Knowledge Grid will undergo a development process similar to that of the World Wide Web — from simple to complex, from immature to mature, from a small community to a large-scale human-machine environment with an exponential expansion of developers, users, and demands. So the Knowledge Grid development methodology should support an incremental strategy.

Adoption of new computing models — The functions of new computing models will go beyond the abilities of the Grid and of peer-to-peer and client/server networks. It is hard for any single model to yield an ideal solution. An ideal computing model should incorporate the advantages of various models or even be a set of collaborative models.

Cross-disciplinary research — Compared to natural and social systems, the artificial interconnection environment is only at a very primitive stage. The principles and rules of natural and social systems will give us useful guidelines for establishing the ideal Knowledge Grid.

1.7 Knowledge Management

Early in 1880, the American engineer F.W. Taylor investigated workers' efficiency, and formulated a scientific management method for raising productivity by standardizing operations and work. He published his authoritative book *The Principles of Scientific Management* in 1911. With increasing industrial productivity and social development, scientific management methods nowadays pay increasing attention to production processes, social changes, psychological factors, and so on.

With the development of information technology, enterprises more and more become knowledge organizations, which leads to great changes in decision processes, management methods and working conditions. P.F. Drucker pointed out that existing knowledge organizations, such as the symphony orchestra, can inspire us to develop new management approaches to knowledge organizations (*Harvard Business Review on Knowledge Management*, Boston, MA: Harvard Business School Press, 1998). After all, a large-scale orchestra can perform very well with just one conductor. Organizational learning and knowledge innovation become the key competitive abilities of a knowledge organization (I. Nonaka, "A dynamic theory of organizational knowledge creation", *Organization Science*, 1994, vol.5, no.1, pp.14-37).

The multi-dimensional knowledge space has been used by M.E. Nissen to explain organizational learning ("An extended model for knowledge-flow dynamics", *Communications of the Association for Information Systems*, 2002, vol.8, pp.251-266). An epistemological dimension is used to classify knowledge into explicit knowledge and tacit knowledge. An ontological dimension is used to describe knowledge that is shared between members of an organization. Knowledge flow within dimensions is of four types: 1) social flow, in which knowledge moves from creation by an individual to acceptance by the organization (from small to large); 2) externalization flow, in which knowledge moves from tacit form to explicit; 3) combination flow, in which the knowledge of small teams is combined and coordinated to generate the knowledge of a large team; and 4) internalization flow, in which explicit knowledge of the organization becomes tacit.

A peer-to-peer knowledge flow refers to the propagation of external and explicit knowledge that can be formalized, transmitted via communication media, and stored in computing machinery as discussed in "A knowledge flow model for peer-to-peer team knowledge sharing and management" (H. Zhuge, *Expert Systems with Applications*, 2002, vol.23, no.1, pp.23-30). The planning of a knowledge flow network seeks to formalize and optimize knowledge flows.

A knowledge flow network is in itself a kind of organizational knowledge that is more relevant to the roles of the organization and less focused on individuals. It is more concerned with the content of knowledge and with effective knowledge sharing in distributed cooperative teams especially the agent-based virtual organization. Knowledge content can be layered as concepts, axioms, rules and methods, can be classified according to its application domains, and can be organized in a knowledge space of three dimensions: the knowledge category dimension, the knowledge level dimension, and the knowledge location dimension.

Epistemology plays the key role in the process of generating knowledge. In the context of knowledge sharing and the future Web, we are aiming at a kind of semantic description and generation mechanism that reflects human cognition. Different people may see a different epistemology in the same object or event. Epistemological mechanisms help humans and agents understand, generate and describe new knowledge when they share resources. An easy way to implement an epistemological mechanism in the current Web would be to develop an epistemological appendage, generated and used in conjunction with the original resources.

Some researchers are interested in mining Web usage logs. These logs record data about the Web's users. The researchers are striving to use the results of mining Web usage logs to support personalized Web services. However, the Web logs only reflect a small portion of users' behavior, and they are unable to capture users' actual intentions, thinking or understanding.

A personalized epistemological appendage together with a domain ontology could improve the current Web's keyword-based approaches and ontology-only approaches. The form of the appendage could be a kind of semantic representation like the semantic link network, which will be introduced later.

1.8 Definition, Characteristics and Strategies of the Knowledge Grid

1.8.1 *Definition*

We first explain what is *not* the major concern of the Knowledge Grid. Traditional natural language processing, recognition of human speech and handwriting, and formal semantics are not the major concern of the Knowledge Grid. Security and scientific computing are not its key issues. The Knowledge Grid will go beyond the traditional and will look to improved information retrieval, filtering, mining and question answering techniques.

The Knowledge Grid is an intelligent and sustainable Internet application environment that enables people or virtual roles (mechanisms that facilitate interoperation among users, applications, and resources) to effectively capture, coordinate, publish, understand, share and manage knowledge resources. It provides on-demand and robust services to support innovation, cooperative teamwork, problem solving and decision making in a distributed environment, which varies in scale and stability. It incorporates epistemology and ontology to reflect human cognition characteristics; exploits social, ecological and economic principles; and adopts the techniques and standards developed during work toward the future web (H. Zhuge, "China's e-Science Knowledge Grid Environment", *IEEE Intelligent Systems*, 2004, vol.19, no.1, pp.13-17).

Efforts towards the future Web supply the Knowledge Grid with several candidate techniques and implementation platforms. *The Grid is not the only platform for realizing the Knowledge Grid, and the Knowledge Grid should absorb the ideal and some ideas of the Grid.*

The meaning of the term *grid* in the Knowledge Grid is broader than it is in Grid computing. Actually, people have a long history of using the word "grid" in drawing and mapping, geodetic surveying, and mathematics. The word was borrowed from the power grid to refer to clustered computing power when the concept of Grid computing appeared in 1995.

Fig. 1.3 depicts the relationships among the Internet, the Grid, the Semantic Web, the Semantic Grid, and the Knowledge Grid. We can see that the Semantic Grid is the direct basis of the Knowledge Grid.

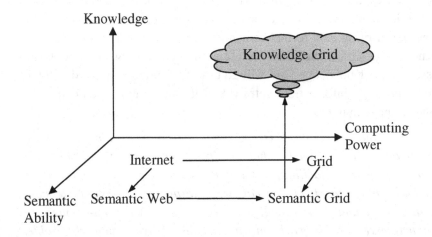

Fig.1.3   Relationships between the Knowledge Grid, the Semantic Grid, the Semantic Web, the Grid and the Internet.

In the long run, a Knowledge Grid should be established on the *future interconnection environment*, which should be a large-scale, autonomous, living, sustainable and intelligent network where society and nature can develop together, functioning and evolving cooperatively. It would collect useful resources from the environment, transform and organize them into semantically rich forms that could be used easily by both machine and human. Geographically dispersed people and resources could work together to accomplish tasks and solve problems by using the network to actively promote the flow of material, energy, techniques, information, knowledge and services through roles and machines, improving both the natural and the artificial environment.

Intelligence, Grid, peer-to-peer and environment represent humanity's four aspirations for the future working and living environment. The intelligence reflects humanity's pursuit of recognizing themselves and the society. The Grid reflects humanity's pursuit of optimization and system. The peer-to-peer reflects humanity's pursuit of freedom and equality. The environment reflects humanity's pursuit of understanding of nature and its harmony.

1.8.2 Parameters

As a large-scale dynamic human-machine system, a Knowledge Grid environment will be characterized by five parameters:

1. *Space* — the capacity to hold a great variety of both individual and shared knowledge resources.
2. *Time* — the arrow of evolution.
3. *Structure* — the construction of the environment and resources in the environment.
4. *Relation* — relationships among parameters and among resources.
5. *Measurement* — the evaluation of the status of, and the prospects for, resources, processes and their relationships.

   Einstein's general theory of relativity reveals the relationship between space and time in physical world: space and time are malleable entities. On the largest scales, space is naturally dynamic, expanding or contracting over time.
   A Knowledge Grid environment will foster the growth of knowledge by supporting social activities at different levels (from the simple physical level to the complex human-machine community level) and in different disciplines. As a product of society in nature, it evolves and endures throughout the life of the race rather than the life of an individual.

Human social activities generate and develop the semantics of natural languages. Human-machine social activities will need to be based on a kind of human-machine semantics, to establish an "understanding" between inanimate resources and humans. Such semantics will be needed so that the services and knowledge of future machines can be beneficially used and protectively regulated by humans.

1.8.3 Distinctive characteristics of the Knowledge Grid

(1) *Single semantic entry point access to worldwide knowledge.* In the Knowledge Grid environment, people could access knowledge distributed around the world from a single semantic access entry point without needing to know where the required knowledge is.

(2) *Intelligently clustered, fused and distributed knowledge.* In the Knowledge Grid environment, related knowledge distributed around the world could intelligently cluster together and fuse to provide appropriate on-demand knowledge services with underlying reasoning and explanation. So knowledge providers should include meta-knowledge (knowledge about how to use knowledge), and could use a kind of uniform resource model to encapsulate the provided knowledge and meta-knowledge to realize active and clustered knowledge services.

(3) *Single semantic image.* The Knowledge Grid environment could enable people to share knowledge and to enjoy reasoning services in a single semantic space where there are no barriers to mutual understanding and pervasive knowledge sharing.

(4) *Worldwide complete knowledge service.* The Knowledge Grid could gather knowledge from all regions of the world and provide succinct and complete knowledge relevant to the solution of particular problems. To achieve this goal, we need to create a new knowledge organization model.

(5) *Dynamic evolution of knowledge.* In the Knowledge Grid environment, knowledge would not be just statically stored, but would evolve to keep up-to-date.

1.8.4 *The Knowledge Grid's general research issues*

(1) *Theories, models, methods and mechanisms for supporting knowledge capture and representation.* The Knowledge Grid should be able to help people or virtual roles effectively capture, and conveniently publish knowledge in a machine-processable form that could directly, or after simple transformation, be understood by humans. We should build an open set of semantic primitives to help knowledge representation. These primitives should be able to represent multi-granular knowledge. The capture of knowledge here has two meanings: one is when people learn from each other directly, or from the resources published by others, and then publish new knowledge on the Knowledge Grid; the other is when the Knowledge Grid gets knowledge from numeric, textual or image resources by mining, induction, analogy, deduction, synthesizing, and so on.

(2) *Knowledge display and creation.* These come mainly through an intelligent user interface (for example, a semantic or knowledge browser) that enables people to share knowledge with each other in a visual way. The semantic link network and the cognitive map are two ways to depict knowledge. The interface should implement the distinctive characteristics of the Knowledge Grid and be able to inspire people's discovery of knowledge through analogy and induction.

(3) *Propagation and management of knowledge within virtual organizations.* This could eliminate redundant communication between team members to achieve effective knowledge management in a cooperative virtual team. Knowledge flow management is a way to achieve knowledge sharing in a virtual team.

(4) *Knowledge organization, evaluation, refinement and derivation.* Knowledge should be organized normally to obtain high retrieval efficiency and ensure the correctness of operations. The Knowledge Grid should be able to eliminate redundant knowledge and refine knowledge so that useful knowledge can be increased. It can also

derive new knowledge from existing well-represented knowledge, from case histories, and from raw knowledge material like text.

(5) *Knowledge integration.*   Integrating knowledge resources at different levels and in different domains could support cross-domain analogies, problem solving, and scientific discovery.

(6) *Abstraction.* It is a challenge to automatically capture semantics from a variety of resources, to make abstractions, and to reason and explain in a uniform semantic space. The semantic constraints and rules of abstraction ensure the validity of resource usage at the semantic level.

(7) *Scalable network platform.* The Knowledge Grid should enable a user, a machine or a local network to freely join in and leave without affecting its performance and services. It is a challenging task to organize and integrate knowledge within a dynamic network platform.

1.8.5 *Differences between the Web and the Knowledge Grid*

Here we use examples to make a brief comparison between the Web and the Knowledge Grid. With the current Web, people with an illness can use search engines to retrieve relevant medical information, and browse hospital or health websites to find suitable hospitals and doctors, depending on what URLs they can remember. As there are more than 82 million health websites, ill people are often annoyed by the large amount of useless information in a search result and by the time consumed in browsing through many websites. They may be further confused by the various opinions of different doctors. They may also worry about whether the result of their searching is based on up-to-date knowledge. Entering related symptoms, they can usually only obtain results for separate symptoms. Further, the whole searching process may overlook some experts, especially those who specialize in uncommon diseases.

Such searches will be improved by the Knowledge Grid, which can accurately and completely locate all relevant knowledge, cluster and synthesize the search result and then actively present it to ill people according to their illness profiles. The ill people can get an explanation of the search result with underlying reasoning based on the clustered knowledge. The relationship between the symptoms of a disease will be considered during reasoning. The search results can adapt to change in illness profiles. Knowledge provided by different doctors worldwide will be refined, checked and evaluated as to usefulness, consistency and time-effectiveness.

In the Knowledge Grid, new knowledge can be derived from: existing knowledge, patients' feedback, and mining in medical textbooks, papers and other related sources. Ill people can also choose to provide symptoms of their disease through a single semantic entry point when accessing the Knowledge Grid to obtain instant consulting service. The result may include several candidate treatments selected by considering such factors as cost, waiting time, skill level, transportation, and so on.

Similar advantages of the Knowledge Grid also exist in scientific research, business, education and other application domains.

1.8.6 *The technological basis of the Knowledge Grid*

The Knowledge Grid is not pie in the sky. It is based on existing methods and technologies such as the Grid, the Semantic Web, Web Services, Peer-to-Peer, AI, proper data modeling, information processing technologies (for example, data and text mining, information filtering, extraction, fusion and retrieval), and system methodology as shown in Fig. 1.4.

The adoption of a new system methodology, a new organization model, a new computing model, and the principles of relevant disciplines will further challenge current software methodology. The implementation of the ideal Knowledge Grid requires a new software methodology that can cope with evolution, fuse resources, and support competition and sustainable development.

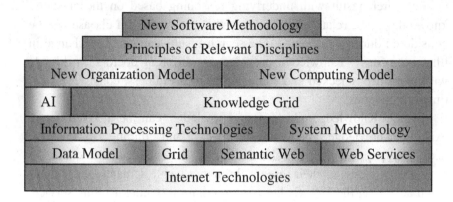

Fig. 1.4 The technologies of the Knowledge Grid.

1.8.7 *The dream and the strategy*

James Gray summed up computing history in his 1999 Turing Award Lecture: the dream of Charles Babbage (1791-1871, the father of the computer) has been largely realized, and the dream of Vannevar Bush has almost become reality, but it is still difficult for computer systems to pass the Turing Test — computing systems still do not have human intelligence although significant progress has been made. Gray extended Babbage's dream: computers should be highly secure and available, and they should be able to program, manage, and replicate themselves.

Scientists have made significant progress towards establishing highly secure and available systems — the goal of the Grid. But so far, we are still far from the goal of self-programming, self-managing and self-replicating. Gray extended Bush's Memex vision to an ideal that automatically organizes indexes, digests, evaluates, and summarizes information, and indeed scientists in the information processing area are making efforts towards this goal. He proposed three more Turing Tests: prosthetic hearing, speech, and vision (*Journal of the ACM*, January 2003, vol.50, no.1, pp.41-57).

What modern society needs from the future computing environment has gone far beyond the scope of the Turing Test and other automatic machine intelligence problems such as self-programming. Computing has evolved from mainframe computers to personal computers, to locally networked computers, and to the Internet. People now primarily use computers interactively on a large scale, so that the *dynamics, evolution, cooperation, fusion, sustainability*, and *social effects* of computer use have become major concerns.

Fig. 1.5 shows the evolution of the computing environment. The Knowledge Grid is the platform that will support the large-scale human-computer environment.

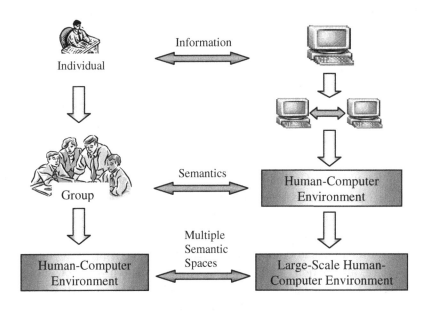

Fig. 1.5 The evolution of the computing environment.

Communication in human society is carried out in multiple semantic spaces, such as the emotional, cultural, artistic, scientific, and that of daily life, which establish the basis for mutual understanding. Loosely or tightly coupled rules could be used to coordinate between these semantic spaces. Traditional research on natural language processing only focuses on one semantic space — the text space, where some information has inevitably been lost in the writing process. This is one reason why different people have different understandings of the same text. So it is impossible to realize the dream of automatically processing natural language if only text analysis is used.

We need an incremental strategy to develop the Knowledge Grid. A worldwide Knowledge Grid is a long-term target. A preliminary stage developing a medium-sized Knowledge Grid based on an institution's intranet would be an appropriate step in the long march towards the long-term target. It could support more effective knowledge management within institutions of various kinds. *Institutional Knowledge Grids* could then become components of the worldwide Knowledge Grid.

A *Micro Knowledge Grid* could be the basic component of a medium-sized Knowledge Grid and thus the basic component of the worldwide Knowledge Grid. It would be useful in helping individual knowledge management — managing raw knowledge (expressed in natural language text) and refined knowledge (expressed in a knowledge representation code), and transforming tacit knowledge into explicit knowledge. *However, a worldwide Knowledge Grid should be more powerful than the sum of its components.*

A Knowledge Grid should support more semantic spaces than just one text space. Knowledge sharing in a Knowledge Grid depends on a correct understanding of the semantics of its resources. But these semantics are not the same as traditional formal semantics. These should be a kind of informal computable semantics, which supports computing, reasoning, abstraction, integration and transformation between semantic spaces. The semantics of the Knowledge Grid should be easily understood by humans and readily processed by machines.

The internal structure of resources that express the same semantics could be completely different. So finding effective ways (for example, markup languages) to express the internal structure will be much more complex than finding ways to express the external semantics — the semantic relationships between resources. Since no object in the world exists in isolation, the semantics of a resource could be determined or roughly reflected by the semantics of the resources related to it and the relationships between them.

Symbolic systems are elegant computing models. Artificial intelligence was regarded as evidenced by the behavior of working symbolic systems. However, symbolic systems have their own particular scope of ability. Non-symbolic systems also have their particular scope of ability. The Knowledge Grid should combine the approach of symbolic systems with the approach of non-symbolic systems (this still needs much work).

Billions of years of natural evolution have created a natural environment and an intelligent species that has evolved into human society.

If we draw an analogy between the future interconnection environment and the world of nature, a challenging question arises: what is the field theory of the interconnection environment? As its basic material, the various resources in the interconnection environment exist in a special field, where resources flow from higher intensity nodes to lower intensity nodes. But the duplication and generation of resources does not cause the loss of any other resource, and the flow of resources also does not mean the loss of any resource. This means that the law of energy conservation in the physical world does not hold in the abstract world of knowledge. The laws and principles in this special field will become the basic theory of the future interconnection environment.

If we draw an analogy between the future interconnection environment and human society, a challenging question arises: what is the market and what the price of services in the future interconnection environment?

If we draw an analogy between the future interconnection environment and the human body, some further challenging questions arise:

(1)   What is the circulatory system of the future interconnection environment? This question impels us to investigate and establish a flow model for information, knowledge and services.

(2)   What is the immune system of the future interconnection environment? This question impels us to investigate the principles of resource clustering and security.

(3)   What is the digestive system? This question impels us to investigate the principles of generation and understanding of resources.

(4)   What is the nervous system? This question impels us to investigate the principles of the control flow within the future interconnection environment.

(5)   What is the ecology? What are the rules of evolution? Will the environment degrade and its species diversity decrease? To answer these questions requires us to carry out research relating ecology to the future interconnection environment.

(6)   What are the sustainable development principles and the rules of the future interconnection environment that could evolve harmoniously with human society? This question impels us to carry out research relating the following areas: our society, its economy and the future interconnection environment.

So far, we can assert that both the notion and the ideal of the Knowledge Grid are understandable, useful and challenging. The methodology of the Knowledge Grid should also include the testable and incremental aspects that James Gray mentioned in his Turing Award Lecture.

The incremental aspect would make our short-term target modest. We believe that the major characteristics of the Knowledge Grid will be realized by a medium-sized Knowledge Grid in some application area, such as e-science and e-government, based on the current Web and Grid technologies.

As for the testable aspect, we can use the following basic criteria to evaluate whether it is a Knowledge Grid or a knowledge based system within the prior art:

(1) The effectiveness of knowledge/information services, for example, the response time;

(2) The quality of knowledge/information services, for example, users' degree of satisfaction with the use and the content of services; and

(3) The improvement of services, for example, whether the services can be improved during use.

On average, a Knowledge Grid should perform better than other systems in 70% of tests.

The following chapters concern detailed research and practice — some preliminary attempts to fulfill the ideal of the Knowledge Grid. The methodology of the Knowledge Grid is guiding the China Knowledge Grid Research Group (http://kg.ict.ac.cn) in its continuing research and development.

Chapter 2

The Semantic Link Network

2.1 The Idea of Mapping

The idea of geographical mapping helps in exploring the future interconnection environment. A geographical map is an abstract pictorial representation of a region's physical or social properties. People can use certain features of such a map to accurately and efficiently locate or identify places or regions.

(1)   *Coordinate location.* Lines are drawn on maps to connect points of equal latitude (distance from the equator) and points of equal longitude (angle from a standard straight line joining the two poles, usually the Greenwich meridian). These enable people to locate a surface feature on a map if they know its coordinates— the latitude and longitude.

(2)   *Referential location.* People can locate a surface feature on a map even if they don't know its coordinates, provided they know its distance and direction from a known point or feature on the map. For example, a town about twenty kilometers to the west of the center of Beijing can be found indirectly on a map by referring to the location of the center of Beijing.

(3)   *Regional partition.* Maps often have lines drawn on them to mark the boundaries of different social or climatic regions. Where there is a hierarchy of regions, different kinds of lines are used to mark the boundaries at different levels of the hierarchy. Knowing what region, such as country or district, a surface

feature is in can make it easier to find on a map.

(4)   *Color.* When regions are marked on a map, neighboring regions are usually filled in with contrasting colors. This makes it much easier to see the extent of any particular region of search.

(5)   *Overlays.* To map information of different kinds, such as traffic, climate, and ecological data, onto the same area, transparent overlays with boundary markings are sometimes used. The distribution of properties such as traffic and population density, rainfall and temperature, and cropping, can then be conveniently compared.

(6)   *Legends.* A legend is used to explain aspects of a map, such as its name, its scale, and the meaning of the symbols and labeling.

If we can create a semantic map for the Web, then users will be able to use the map to effectively browse its contents. Such a semantic map would bring us much closer to the ideal Knowledge Grid.

Location by coordinates, the most important aid in geographical mapping, can be adapted to Web mapping by using semantic classification. This approach requires Web page providers to encode semantic categories when adding resources. A well-defined semantic classification scheme will help both providers and users.

Referential location of a kind has been the purpose of Web hyperlinks from their beginning, as they enable users to browse from page to page. However, they do not entail semantic relationships, and we cannot accurately locate a resource by just referring to a known resource and giving the semantic relationship.

Regional partition of the Web is provided by the names in the URL (Uniform Resource Locator) of each of its pages. Each URL identifies exactly where in the Web a resource is stored, much like a postal address.

So far the use of color on the Web is quite arbitrary. There are no regulations for using color to convey semantic properties. And there are no semantic overlays on the Web and no semantic legends.

2.2 Overview

A *semantic link network* (SLN) is a directed network consisting of *semantic nodes* and *semantic links* between nodes. A semantic node can be a piece of text, a concept, a general resource, or even an SLN. A semantic link directed from one node (predecessor) to another (successor) can be represented as a pointer labeled with a semantic property.

The SLN is an extension of the hyperlink network, where hyperlinks connect Web pages to allow for Web browsing. Attaching semantic properties to the hyperlinks means an SLN can gain the following distinct advantages:

(1) Semantic-based resource organization and retrieval. Simple hyperlinking as in the current Web basically supports ad hoc retrieval, and various search engines provide keyword retrieval. Neither approach is well suited to semantic retrieval. By adding semantic qualification, the SLN can make retrieval more effective.
(2) Semantic-based reasoning and browsing. The semantic relationships encoded in the links of SLNs support coarse semantic reasoning, which enables intelligent browsing.
(3) Semantic overlaying. An SLN can be a semantic overlay for the Web. Its semantic properties support intelligent applications.

What are the main challenges in realizing an SLN?

The first is to construct a mathematical model of the SLN that can support effective semantic-based retrieval and reasoning. The second is to normalize the SLN to ensure the correctness and effectiveness of SLN management. The third is to develop algorithms and theorems for the SLN relevant to supporting intelligent applications. The fourth is to automatically construct the SLN.

Why are SLNs relevant to the Knowledge Grid?

Semantics is the basis of understanding and sharing knowledge. An SLN embodies a kind of coarse semantics and has some of the characteristics of the Web. Given a formal structure and a well developed theory, an SLN can be used as a semantic interconnection overlay of the Knowledge Grid. However, the Knowledge Grid should have multiple semantic overlays for different semantic scales.

In general, it is reasonable to assume that there exists a set of primitive semantic properties Ω in a given domain, such that any semantic relationship between two resources can be described by a property or combination of properties in Ω.

Definition 2.2.1 A semantic link, a directed relationship between two nodes, is denoted by X—α→Y, where X and Y are the nodes, α belongs to or can be derived from Ω, and —α→ is called an α-link.

(1) If at least one α-link, or a link that can be derived from existing links, points from X to Y, we say that Y is semantically reachable from X, and we say that X and Y are mutually reachable in browsing (regardless of direction).

(2) If we have X—α→Y, Y—α→Z ⇒ X—α→Z (⇒ stands for implication), then we say that α or the α-link is transitive, and that there exists a semantic chain from X to Z.

(3) If X—α→Y ⇒ X—β→Y, then we say that α implies β, denoted by α→β.

(4) We say that X is semantically equivalent to Y, denoted by $X = Y$, if they can substitute for each other wherever they occur.

The following is a set of semantic link primitives:

(1) The *cause-effect link*, denoted by ce as in r—ce→r', for which the predecessor is a cause of its successor, and the successor is an effect of its predecessor. The cause-effect link is transitive, that is, r—ce→r', r'—ce→r'' ⇒ r—ce→r''. Cause-effect reasoning can chain along cause-effect links because of this transitivity.

(2) The *implication link*, denoted by *imp* as in r—*imp*$\rightarrow r'$, for which the semantics of the predecessor implies that of its successor. The implication link is transitive, that is, r—*imp*$\rightarrow r'$, r'—*imp*$\rightarrow r'' \Rightarrow r$—*imp*$\rightarrow r''$. Implication links can help a reasoning process find semantic relationships between documents.

(3) The *subtype link*, denoted by *st* in as r—*st*$\rightarrow r'$, for which the successor is a part of its predecessor. The subtype link is transitive, that is, r—*st*$\rightarrow r'$, r'—*st*$\rightarrow r'' \Rightarrow r$—*st*$\rightarrow r''$.

(4) The *similar-to link*, denoted by *(sim, sd)* as in r—*(sim, sd)*$\rightarrow r'$, for which the semantics of the successor is similar to that of its predecessor, and where *sd* is the degree of similarity between r and r'. Like the partial-inheritance relationship (H. Zhuge, "Inheritance rules for flexible model retrieval", *Decision Support Systems*, 1998, vol.22, no.4, pp.397-390), the similar-to link is intransitive.

(5) The *instance link*, denoted by *ins* as in r—*ins*$\rightarrow r'$, for which the successor is an instance of the predecessor.

(6) The *sequential link*, denoted by *seq* as in r—*seq*$\rightarrow r'$, which requires that r be browsed before r'. In other words, the content of r' is a successor of the content of r. The sequential link is transitive, that is, r—*seq*$\rightarrow r'$, r'—*seq*$\rightarrow r'' \Rightarrow r$—*seq*$\rightarrow r''$. The transitivity enables relevant links to be connected in a sequential chain.

(7) The *reference link*, denoted by *ref* as in r—*ref*$\rightarrow r'$, for which r' is a further explanation of r. The reference link is transitive, that is, r—*ref*$\rightarrow r'$, r'—*ref*$\rightarrow r'' \Rightarrow r$—*ref*$\rightarrow r''$.

(8) The *equal-to link*, denoted by *e* as in r—*e*$\rightarrow r'$, for which r and r' are identical in meaning. Clearly, any resource is equal to itself.

(9) The *empty link*, denoted by ϕ as in r—$\phi$$\rightarrow r'$, for which r and r' are completely irrelevant to each other.

(10) The *null or unknown link*, denoted by *Null* or *N* as in r—*N*$\rightarrow r'$, for which the semantic relation between two resources is unknown or uncertain. The *Null* relation means that there might be a semantic relationship, but we do not yet know what it is. A null link can be replaced by a provider or by a computed link.

(11) The *non-α relation*, denoted by *Non* (α) or α^N as in r—α^N→r', for which there is no α relationship between r and r'. It is sometimes useful in the reasoning process to know that a particular semantic relationship between two resources is absent.

(12) The *reverse relation operation*, denoted by *Reverse* (α) or α^R as in r—α^R→r'. If there is a semantic relation α from r to r', then there is a reverse semantic relationship from r' to r, that is, r'—α→r ⇒ r—α^R→r'. A semantic relation and its reverse declare the same thing, but the reverse relationship is useful in reasoning.

The semantic link primitives should open up new application domains.

Characteristic 2.2.1 For α, β and $\gamma \in \Omega$, we have: α→β→γ ⇒ α→γ.

For example, with the *cause-effect link*, denoted by X—ce→Y, the predecessor is a cause of its successor, and the successor is an effect of its predecessor. The cause-effect link is transitive, that is, X—ce→Y, Y—ce→Z ⇒ X—ce→Z. Cause-effect reasoning can be done by chaining cause-effect links, relying on their transitivity.

Definition 2.2.2 Let X, Y and Z be different resources, and α and β be two semantic properties. We say that α is orthogonal to β, denoted by $\alpha \perp \beta$, if and only if X—α→Z and Y—β→Z can uniquely determine Z, that is, if there exists Z' such that X—α→Z' and Y—β→Z' then Z is semantically equivalent to Z'.

Orthogonal semantic relationships play an important role in some applications especially those that are relevant to layout. For transitive semantic links, we have the following lemma.

Lemma 2.2.1 If two chains of semantic links X_1—α_1→X_2—α_2→X_3—α_3→X_4 ... X_{n-1}—α_{n-1}→X_n and Y_1—α_1→Y_2—α_2→Y_3—α_3→Y_4 ... Y_{m-1}—α_{m-1}→Y_m are both transitive, and $X_n = Y_m$ can be uniquely determined, then the two chains imply two orthogonal semantic links.

Like latitudes and longitudes, orthogonal semantic links help us accurately locate a node. For example, if we want to find the destination X and know that A—*is-south-of*→X and B—*is-east-of*→X, then we can locate X at the meeting point of the two links.

Definition 2.2.3 Let SLN_1 and SLN_2 be two SLNs. We say that SLN_1 implies SLN_2 (that is, $SLN_1 \to SLN_2$) if there exists a graph isomorphism φ between a subgraph of SLN_1 and SLN_2 such that: (1) for any node n in SLN_1, we have $n = \varphi(n)$ or $n \to \varphi(n)$; and (2) for any semantic link l in SLN_1, we have $l = \varphi(l)$ or $l \to \varphi(l)$.

Definition 2.2.4 Two SLNs are semantically equivalent to each other if there exists an isomorphism between them such that corresponding nodes are the same or semantically equivalent to each other and the semantic properties of the corresponding links imply each other.

Definition 2.2.5 Let SLN_1 and SLN_2 be two SLNs. If there is a subgraph of SLN_2 that is semantically equivalent to SLN_1, we say that SLN_2 semantically includes SLN_1, denoted by $SLN_1 \subseteq SLN_2$ or $SLN_2 \supseteq SLN_1$.

The notion of minimal cover of an SLN introduced in section 2.4 provides an effective approach for determining the relationship between SLNs. Section 2.8 will discuss the implementation of operations on SLNs.

Characteristic 2.2.2 The semantic inclusion relationship is transitive, that is, $SLN_1 \subseteq SLN_2$, $SLN_2 \subseteq SLN_3 \Rightarrow SLN_1 \subseteq SLN_3$.

Characteristic 2.2.3 $SLN_1 \supseteq SLN_2$, $SLN_2 \to SLN_3 \Rightarrow SLN_1 \to SLN_3$.

2.3 Semantic Reasoning Rules

Semantic reasoning rules are rules for chaining related semantic links to obtain a reasoned result. For example, if we have two links r—ce→r' and r'—ce→r'', we get the reasoned result r—ce→r'' because the cause-effect link is transitive.

Reasoning acts through rules, as for example r—ce→r', r'—ce→r'' ⇒ r—ce→r''. A rule for reasoning can also be represented as $\alpha \bullet \beta \Rightarrow \gamma$, where α, β, $\gamma \in \Omega$, and the rule above can be represented as $ce \bullet ce \Rightarrow ce$.

A simple case of reasoning is where all the semantic links have the same type, that is, single-type reasoning. For transitive semantic links we have the reasoning rule: r_1—α→r_2, r_2—α→r_3, ..., r_{n-1}—α→r_n ⇒ r_1—α→r_n, where $\alpha \in \{ce, imp, st, ref, e\}$.

Table 2.1 shows some heuristic reasoning rules. Rules 1–4 are for connecting cause-effect links to others. Rules 5–8 are for connecting implication links to others. Rules 9–12 are for connecting sub-type links to others. Rules 13–15 are for connecting instance links to others. Rules 16–22 show that sequential connection is *additive*, that is, any two links with the same type can be added by sequentially connecting their predecessors and successors respectively. (H.Zhuge, "Retrieve Images by Understanding Semantic Links and Clustering Image Fragments", *Journal of Systems & Software*, 2004, vol. 73, no.3, pp.455-466).

An order relationship ≤ can be defined on semantic links < Ω, ≤ >, for example, $ref \le ins \le st \le ce \le e$, where stronger relationships are on the right. To obtain a well reasoned result, the reasoning mechanism should find the strongest link among its candidates.

Semantic links can also be inexact. An inexact semantic link represents an uncertainty for its relationship, and is denoted by: r—(α, cd)→r', where $\alpha \in \Omega$ and cd is the degree of certainty.

Inexact single-type reasoning is of the following form:

$$r_1\text{—}(\alpha, cd_1)\text{→}r_2, r_2\text{—}(\alpha, cd_2)\text{→}r_3, \ldots\ldots, r_n\text{—}(\alpha, cd_n)\text{→}r_{n+1}$$

$$\Rightarrow r_1\text{---}(\alpha, cd)\text{---}r_{n+1}, \text{ where } cd = min\ (cd_1, \ldots, cd_n)$$

Table 2.1 Heuristic reasoning rules for semantic links.

No.	Rules	Summary
1	$r\text{---}ce\rightarrow r'$, $r'\text{---}imp\rightarrow r'' \Rightarrow r\text{---}ce\rightarrow r''$	$ce \bullet \beta \Rightarrow ce$
2	$r\text{---}ce\rightarrow r'$, $r'\text{---}st\rightarrow r'' \Rightarrow r\text{---}ce\rightarrow r''$	$ce \bullet \beta \Rightarrow ce$
3	$r\text{---}ce\rightarrow r'$, $r'\text{---}sim\rightarrow r'' \Rightarrow r\text{---}ce\rightarrow r''$	$ce \bullet \beta \Rightarrow ce$
4	$r\text{---}ce\rightarrow r'$, $r\text{---}ins\rightarrow r'' \Rightarrow r''\text{---}ce\rightarrow r'$	$ce \bullet \beta \Rightarrow ce$
5	$r\text{---}imp\rightarrow r'$, $r'\text{---}st\rightarrow r'' \Rightarrow r\text{---}imp\rightarrow r''$	$imp \bullet st \Rightarrow imp$
6	$r\text{---}imp\rightarrow r'$, $r'\text{---}ins\rightarrow r'' \Rightarrow r\text{---}ins\rightarrow r''$	$imp \bullet ins \Rightarrow ins$
7	$r\text{---}imp\rightarrow r'$, $r'\text{---}ce\rightarrow r'' \Rightarrow r\text{---}ce\rightarrow r''$	$imp \bullet ce \Rightarrow ce$
8	$r\text{---}imp\rightarrow r'$, $r'\text{---}ref\rightarrow r'' \Rightarrow r\text{---}ref\rightarrow r''$	$imp \bullet ref \Rightarrow ref$
9	$r\text{---}st\rightarrow r'$, $r'\text{---}ce\rightarrow r'' \Rightarrow r\text{---}ce\rightarrow r''$	$st \bullet ce \Rightarrow ce$
10	$r\text{---}st\rightarrow r'$, $r'\text{---}imp\rightarrow r'' \Rightarrow r\text{---}imp\rightarrow r''$	$st \bullet imp \Rightarrow imp$
11	$r\text{---}st\rightarrow r'$, $r'\text{---}ref\rightarrow r'' \Rightarrow r\text{---}ref\rightarrow r''$	$st \bullet ref \Rightarrow ref$
12	$r\text{---}st\rightarrow r'$, $r'\text{---}ins\rightarrow r'' \Rightarrow r\text{---}ins\rightarrow r''$	$st \bullet ins \Rightarrow ins$
13	$r\text{---}ins\rightarrow r'$, $r'\text{---}ce\rightarrow r'' \Rightarrow r\text{---}ce\rightarrow r''$	$ins \bullet ce \Rightarrow ce$
14	$r\text{---}ins\rightarrow r'$, $r'\text{---}imp\rightarrow r'' \Rightarrow r\text{---}imp\rightarrow r''$	$ins \bullet imp \Rightarrow imp$
15	$r\text{---}ins\rightarrow r'$, $r'\text{---}ref\rightarrow r'' \Rightarrow r\text{---}ref\rightarrow r''$	$ins \bullet ref \Rightarrow ref$
16	$r\text{---}ins\rightarrow r'$, $r_1\text{---}ins\rightarrow r_1' \Rightarrow$ $(r\text{---}seq\rightarrow r_1)\text{---}ins\rightarrow(r'\text{---}seq\rightarrow r_1')$	$r\text{---}\beta\rightarrow r'$, $r_1\text{---}\beta\rightarrow r_1'$ $\Rightarrow (r\text{---}seq\rightarrow r_1)$ $\text{---}\beta\rightarrow(r'\text{---}seq\rightarrow r_1')$
17	$r\text{---}ref\rightarrow r'$, $r_1\text{---}ref\rightarrow r_1' \Rightarrow$ $(r\text{---}seq\rightarrow r_1)\text{---}ref\rightarrow(r'\text{---}seq\rightarrow r_1')$	ditto
18	$r\text{---}seq\rightarrow r'$, $r_1\text{---}seq\rightarrow r_1' \Rightarrow$ $(r\text{---}seq\rightarrow r_1)\text{---}seq\rightarrow(r'\text{---}seq\rightarrow r_1')$	ditto
19	$r\text{---}ce\rightarrow r'$, $r_1\text{---}ce\rightarrow r_1' \Rightarrow (r\text{---}seq\rightarrow r_1)$ $\text{---}ce\rightarrow(r'\text{---}seq\rightarrow r_1')$	ditto
20	$r\text{---}imp\rightarrow r'$, $r_1\text{---}imp\rightarrow r_1' \Rightarrow (r\text{---}seq\rightarrow r_1)\text{---}imp\rightarrow(r'\text{---}seq\rightarrow r_1')$	ditto
21	$r\text{---}st\rightarrow r'$, $r_1\text{---}st\rightarrow r_1' \Rightarrow (r\text{---}seq\rightarrow r_1)$ $\text{---}st\rightarrow(r'\text{---}seq\rightarrow r_1')$	ditto
22	$r\text{---}sim\rightarrow r'$, $r_1\text{---}sim\rightarrow r_1' \Rightarrow$ $(r\text{---}seq\rightarrow r_1)\text{---}sim\rightarrow(r'\text{---}seq\rightarrow r_1')$	ditto

Different types of inexact semantic links can be also chained according to the rules in Table 2.1. For example, Rule 1 can be extended using the following inexact rule:

$$r\text{—}(ce, cd_1)\to r', r'\text{—}(imp, cd_2)\to r'' \Rightarrow r\text{—}(ce, min\,(cd_1, cd_2))\to r''$$

Another kind of inexactness is associated with the similar-to link. For example, connecting the cause-effect link to the similar-to link can give the following inexact reasoning rules:

$$r\text{—}ce\to r', r'\text{—}(sim, sd)\to r'' \Rightarrow r\text{—}(ce, cd)\to r'',$$
$$\text{where } cd \text{ is derived from } sd \;(cd = sd \text{ is a simple choice}).$$

More reasoning rules are given in "A Computing Model for Semantic Link Network" (H. Zhuge, et al., *Proceedings of the 2nd International Workshop on Grid and Cooperative Computing*, Dec. 2003, LNCS 3033, pp.795-802).

2.4 An Algebraic Model of the SLN

Operations such as reversal, addition and multiplication can be defined for transforming and composing semantic links. These operations take one or two semantic properties in and put one semantic property out.

Semantic properties and the operations on them constitute an algebraic system. This section investigates the SLN's algebraic model and its characteristics. By representing an SLN as a semantic matrix, reasoning can be carried out by the self-multiplication of the matrix.

Definition 2.4.1 If there is a semantic relation α from node r_1 to node r_2, then there is a reverse semantic relationship from r_2 to r_1 called the reversal relationship, denoted by *Reverse* (α) or α^R.

Example. A cause-effect link from r_1 to r_2 signifies that r_1 is a cause of r_2 and that r_2 is an effect of r_1, that is, it implies a *Reverse* (*ce*) or ce^R link from r_2 to r_1.

A semantic relation and its reverse are equivalent, but the reverse relationship is useful in reasoning. The following operational laws are clearly true:

(1) $e^R = e$

(2) $N^R = N$

(3) $\phi^R = \phi$

(4) $sim^R = sim$

(5) $(\alpha^R)^R = \alpha$

Definition 2.4.2   If there exist two semantic links with properties α and β from r_1 to r_2, then the two links can be merged into one with the semantic property $\alpha + \beta$. Merging is termed the addition of α and β.

Certain laws and characteristics of addition follow from this definition.

Laws of Addition

(1) $\alpha + \alpha = \alpha$ (Idempotency)

(2) $\alpha + \beta = \beta + \alpha$ (Commutativity)

(3) $(\alpha + \beta) + \gamma = \alpha + (\beta + \gamma)$ (Associative Addition)

(4) $\alpha + Null = \alpha = Null + \alpha$

(5)   If $\alpha' \leqslant \alpha$, then $\alpha + \alpha' = \alpha$. In particular, $e + \alpha = e$, where α is a semantic property that is compatible with e.

(6) $(\alpha + \beta)^R = \alpha^R + \beta^R$

Characteristic 2.4.1 For any two semantic properties α and β in a consistent SLN, we have $\alpha \leqslant \alpha + \beta$ and $\beta \leqslant \alpha + \beta$.

Characteristic 2.4.2 For any three semantic properties α, β and γ in a consistent SLN, if $\alpha \geqslant \beta$ and $\alpha \geqslant \gamma$, then $\alpha \geqslant \beta + \gamma$.

Definition 2.4.3 If there are two semantic relations, α from r_1 to r_2, and β from r_2 to r_3, in a consistent SLN, and if we can get the semantic properties γ_1, γ_2, ..., and γ_k from r_1 to r_3 by reasoning, then we call the reasoning process multiplication, denoted by $\alpha \times \beta = \gamma$ where $\gamma = \gamma_1 + \gamma_2 + ... + \gamma_k$.

Laws of multiplication

(1) $\alpha \times e = \alpha = e \times \alpha$

(2) $\alpha \times N = N = N \times \alpha$

(3) $\alpha \times \phi = N = \phi \times \alpha$ (note that $\phi \times \phi = N$)

(4) $(\alpha + \beta) \times \gamma = \alpha \times \gamma + \beta \times \gamma$ and $\alpha \times (\beta + \gamma) = \alpha \times \beta + \alpha \times \gamma$

(5) $(\alpha \times \beta)^R = \beta^R \times \alpha^R$

Lemma 2.4.1 For any semantic relations $r_1 \!-\!\alpha\!\rightarrow\! r_2$, $r_1 \!-\!\beta\!\rightarrow\! r_2$, and $r_2 \!-\!\gamma\!\rightarrow\! r_3$ in a consistent SLN, if $\alpha \geqslant \beta$, then the semantic relation from r_1 to r_3 is $\alpha \times \gamma$ ($\alpha \times \gamma \geqslant \beta \times \gamma$).

Definition 2.4.4 The *closure* of an SLN $S = (V, E)$ is a new network $S^+ = (V, E')$, where E' is constructed as follows:

(1) All semantic links included in E are included in E'; and,

(2) A semantic link from one node to another is copied to E' if the relation between two nodes is available via reasoning on E.

The closure has the following characteristics:

(1) $S \subseteq S^+$.

(2) An SLN is equivalent to its closure.

(3) Two SLNs are equivalent if and only if their closures are the same or equivalent.

(4) The equivalence relationship is reflexive, symmetric and transitive.

Lemma 2.4.2 For two SLNs S and T, S is equivalent to T if and only if $T \subseteq S^+$ and $S \subseteq T^+$.

A *minimal cover* is obtained by removing all redundant semantic links from an SLN.

Definition 2.4.5 An SLN M is the minimal cover of another SLN S, if M and S satisfy the following conditions.

(1) $M = S^+$; and
(2) no semantic link l exists in M such that $(M - l)^+ = M^+$.

The minimal cover of an SLN involves the fewest possible semantic links and keeps the semantics unchanged. The minimal cover of an SLN is unique.

Matrix representation. An SLN can be represented by an adjacency matrix called the semantic relationship matrix (SRM). Given an SLN with n nodes $r_1, r_2, ..., r_n$, it can be represented by an SRM as follows, where α_{ij} represents the semantic property from r_i to r_j.

$$\begin{bmatrix} \alpha_{11} & \alpha_{12} & \cdots & \alpha_{1n} \\ \alpha_{21} & \alpha_{22} & \cdots & \alpha_{2n} \\ \cdots & \cdots & \cdots & \cdots \\ \alpha_{n1} & \alpha_{n2} & \cdots & \alpha_{nn} \end{bmatrix}$$

where $\alpha_{ii} = e$ and $\alpha_{ij} = \alpha_{ji}^R$. If there are no semantic relations between r_i and r_j, then $\alpha_{ij} = \alpha_{ji} = Null$. The SRM of any SLN is unique if the allocation of nodes is fixed.

Reasoning on an SLN derives relations between nodes by semantic link reasoning. Suppose a consistent SLN has n nodes: $r_1, r_2, ..., r_n$, and its SRM is *mat*. Can we reliably derive the semantic relations of any two nodes from the SRM? Clearly, we can get α_{ij} as the semantic relation between r_i and r_j if the link is in the matrix. However, α_{ij} is sometimes *Null* even though there may in fact be a relationship that can be computed. In such cases the reliable semantic relation, denoted by $\alpha_{ij}^{\#}$, is derived by reasoning.

Theorem 2.4.1 In a consistent SLN, a reliable semantic relation can be computed as $\alpha_{ij}^{\#} = mat_{i*} \times mat^{n-2} \times mat_{*j}$, where mat_{i*} is the ith row vector and mat_{*j} is the jth column vector.

Corollary 2.4.1 In a consistent SLN, we have $\alpha_{ij}^{\#} \geqslant \alpha_{ij}$.

If we compute the semantic relationships of all pairs of nodes in a consistent SLN, then we can get a new SRM, called the full SRM (FSRM), denoted by mat_f. An FSRM is the SLN matrix of the closure of the original SLN. We can get the reliable semantic relationship between any two nodes in the SLN from the FSRM. Of course, some of these semantic relationships are in the original SLN, and some are derived. Any semantic reasoning can be done by self-multiplication of the SLN matrix.

The FSRM is an efficient tool for semantic reasoning because there is a reliable semantic relationship between every pair of nodes. It is also useful for detecting inconsistency and so for keeping an SLN consistent.

Corollary 2.4.2 For a semantic relationship matrix *mat* and its FSRM *mat$_f$*, we have:

(1) $mat_f = mat^{n-1}$

(2) $mat_f \times mat = mat_f$

This corollary suggests a useful way to compute the FSRM.

2.5 SLN Normalization Theory

2.5.1 *The normal forms of an SLN*

SLN normal forms are used to ensure the correctness and effectiveness of an SLN's semantics and operations. The following definitions help in removing redundancy and inconsistency.

Definition 2.5.1 If there are no semantically equivalent nodes in an SLN, then we say that the SLN is in first normal form, or 1NF.

Definition 2.5.2 If an SLN is in 1NF and there are no inconsistent, equivalent and implication semantic links between nodes, then we say the SLN is in second normal form, or 2NF.

Definition 2.5.3 If an SLN is in 2NF and there are no isolated nodes or parts, then we say that the SLN is in third normal form, or 3NF.

The 3NF guarantees the completeness of browse operations, that is, we can reach all the nodes in SLN starting from any of its nodes.

Definition 2.5.4 If an SLN is in 3NF and there is no other SLN that is semantically equivalent to it and has fewer links, then we say that the SLN is in fourth normal form, or 4NF.

2.5.2 Operations on SLNs

Applications or user interfaces that manage the resources of, or need services such as browsing for, a large-scale SLN need operations applied to that SLN.

Let $SLN_1 = <V_1, E_1>$ and $SLN_2 = <V_2, E_2>$ where V_1 and V_2 are vertex (node) sets, and E_1 and E_2 are edge (semantic link) sets. The following basic operations can be defined as for graphs.

(1) *Intersection*: $SLN_1 \cap SLN_2 = <V_1 \cap V_2, E_1 \cap E_2>$;
(2) *Union*: $SLN_1 \cup SLN_2 = <V_1 \cup V_2, E_1 \cup E_2>$; and
(3) *Inclusion*: returns *true* if $SLN_1 \subseteq SLN_2$, otherwise returns *false*.

Where $E_1 \cap E_2 = \{n \text{—} \alpha \text{→} n' \mid \alpha = minimum\,(\alpha_1, \alpha_2),\ n \text{—} \alpha_1 \text{→} n' \in SLN_1,$ $n \text{—} \alpha_2 \text{→} n' \in SLN_2\}$, if α_2 is equal to or implies α_1, $min\,(\alpha_1, \alpha_2) = \alpha_1$ else $minimum\,(\alpha_1, \alpha_2) = Null.$
$E_1 \cup E_2 = \{n \text{—} (\alpha_1 + \alpha_2) \text{→} n' \mid n \text{—} \alpha_1 \text{→} n' \in SLN_1,\ n \text{—} \alpha_2 \text{→} n' \in SLN_2\}.$

In the following, we focus on the three operations *join*, *split*, and *view*.

Definition 2.5.5 Two SLNs can be joined in one of the following three ways.
(1) If they have one common node, then the join operation (called *join by node*) merges the common node.

(2) If they have one common semantic chain, then the join operation (called *join by chain*) merges the common chain.

(3) If at least one semantically distinct link can be added between two SLNs, then the join operation (called *join by link addition*) adds such a link.

Lemma 2.5.1 The join operation conserves 1–3NF characteristics.

Proof. The join operation (either *by node* or *by link addition*) does not add any semantically equivalent node or link, so join conserves 1NF and 2NF. For the case of 3NF, we consider the following two aspects:

1) *Join by node or by a chain (of semantic links)*. Let SLN_1 and SLN_2 be two SLNs, and let SLN be the join of SLN_1 and SLN_2 by merging the common node n (or chain C) of SLN_1 and SLN_2. If both SLN_1 and SLN_2 are 3NF, then any node in SLN_1 is accessible from any node in SLN_2 through n (or any node of C or chain C), and vice versa. So SLN is 3NF.

2) *Join by link addition*. Let l be the semantic link added between node n in SLN_1 and node n' in SLN_2. If both SLN_1 and SLN_2 are 3NF, then any node in SLN_1 is accessible from n and any node in SLN_2 is accessible from n', so any node in SLN_1 is accessible from any node in SLN_2 through l, vice versa. Hence SLN is 3NF.

Thus we conclude that the join operation conserves 1–3NF characteristics.

By duplicating nodes or links, or by deleting nodes and links, a single SLN can be split into two SLNs.

The split operation does not increase semantically equivalent nodes and links in either of the split SLNs, so it conserves 1NF and 2NF. The split operation may break accessibility within either of the split SLNs, so it does not necessarily conserve 3NF. But we can add some conditions to enable it to conserve both 3NF and 4NF characteristics. Fig. 2.1 shows the different split operations.

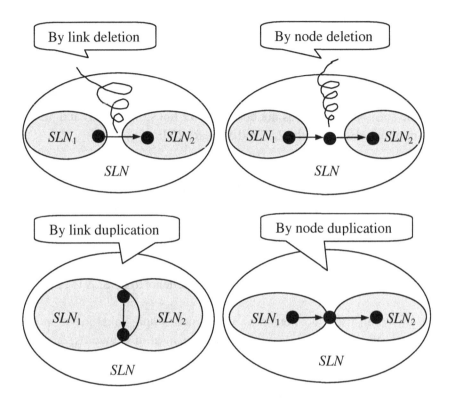

Fig. 2.1 Split operations.

Lemma 2.5.2 The split operation conserves 1NF and 2NF.

Lemma 2.5.3 Let *SLN* be 3NF and let it be split into SLN_1 and SLN_2. If $SLN_1 \cup SLN_2 = SLN$, then both SLN_1 and SLN_2 are 3NF.

Proof. The condition $SLN_1 \cup SLN_2 = SLN$ ensures that the split operation does not remove links or nodes, that is, it allows only splitting by duplication. Hence the connectivity of both SLN_1 and SLN_2 is the same as that of *SLN*. Otherwise, we assume that node *n* in SLN_i ($i = 1, 2$) is not accessible from *p* in *SLN*. Consequently, *n* is also not accessible from *p* because no nodes or links are lost during the split operation. Hence both SLN_1 and SLN_2 are 3NF.

Lemma 2.5.4 Let *SLN* be 4NF and let it be split into SLN_1 and SLN_2. If $SLN_1 \cup SLN_2 = SLN$, then both SLN_1 and SLN_2 are 4NF.

Proof. From the previous lemma, both SLN_1 and SLN_2 are 3NF. Since the split operation does not add nodes or links, both SLN_1 and SLN_2 are minimal. Hence both SLN_1 and SLN_2 are 4NF.

The join and split operations help a user to form a view that reflects the user's interests. The view operation is used to generate a view of an SLN, given the nodes and semantic properties of interest. It enables an SLN to be adapted to the needs of users.

Definition 2.5.6 A view of an SLN is a sub-graph that contains only the node set *N* and the semantic link set *E* denoted by $SLN(V, E)$.

When users do not know which nodes and links are of interest, they can express their interests as a topic, a set of keywords, or a graph consisting of keywords and their relationships, from which existing information retrieval (IR) technology can determine a set of nodes and links of interest. So users can obtain a relevant view by specifying their interests in a simple way. Just as overlays applied to a geographical map can meet a variety of needs, so views of an SLN can help users browse only potentially interesting parts of it and so can make browsing more effective. Since the view operation does not add nodes or links, it conserves 1NF and 2NF characteristics.

Lemma 2.5.5 SLN views conserve 1NF and 2NF characteristics.

Lemma 2.5.6 If two views have the same normal forms, then their join produces a view that conserves these normal forms.

2.6 Criteria, Constraints and Integrity

2.6.1 *Criteria*

The normal forms provide guidance towards precise SLNs. Design criteria can provide guidance towards good SLNs. Criteria 2.6.1–3 are for designing the nodes and links of an SLN.

Criterion 2.6.1 (Semantic completeness). Any node or link of an SLN should have complete semantics described in natural language.

Criterion 2.6.2 (Interconnection). Any operation adding a node to an SLN should be accompanied by an operation adding a link to connect that node to an existing node.

This criterion ensures that no nodes of an SLN are isolated.

Criterion 2.6.3 (Resource usage). Use of the resource represented by any node in an SLN should obey all restrictions and protocols for its use or execution environment laid down when the node was created.

An SLN has three schemas: a *view schema* that enables users to work with an interesting view of the entire SLN, a *universal schema* that provides users with a *single semantic image* of all the SLN's resources, and a *semantic Web schema* that describes the SLN in a semantic Web markup language like XML or RDF (http://www.semanticweb.org). If the three schemas are inconsistent, for example, if a node exists in one schema but is absent from another, then operational errors will occur.

Criterion 2.6.4 (Existence consistency). Any node in an SLN should be present in all the SLN's schemas.

Like a map, an SLN should show the distribution of its entity resources, so we have the following pervasive residence criterion.

Criterion 2.6.5 (Pervasive residence). The entity resource that each node of an SLN represents can be on any Internet application platform.

2.6.2 Constraints and integrity

Traditional hyperlink networks are mainly for human browsing and machine crawling. An SLN can be used for purposes such as browsing, reasoning, reusing and controlling. In some applications, constraints are needed to guarantee the correctness of operations. The SLN maker can apply constraints of the following kinds:

(1) A node constraint, to ensure the integrity and correctness of the content of a node;
(2) A constraint on the relationships between nodes, to ensure coordination between nodes;
(3) A constraint between a node and its links, specifying a relationship between the links (like *and, or, and-split, or-split* in the workflow model) and the conditions on links involved; and
(4) A metaconstraint, that is, a constraint on constraints. The application of a given SLN is a particular form of explanation, reasoning or execution of the network under these constraints.

An SLN has the following three types of integrity with respect to the above constraints:

(1) *Node integrity*: if all of its nodes have coherent content;
(2) *Constraint integrity*: if all of its constraints can be applied in applications; and
(3) *Semantic integrity*: if all of its links are coherently connected.

In applications, constraint integrity can be automatically checked and has the highest priority. Node integrity can only be checked by the content provider. The checking of SLN integrity mostly depends on the SLN maker but software tools can be developed to assist checking of the semantic linking characteristics and rules.

2.6.3 *Browsing, execution and reasoning*

2.6.3.1 *Browsing*

SLN browsing is carried out at the entity resource (document) level or the abstract semantic level, and can shift between these two levels.

An SLN can be very large, but a user is typically only interested in a small portion of the whole SLN. So that users may conveniently and effectively browse an SLN, the browser should support the following modes:

(1) *Browsing*. The browser generates a view of the SLN for browsing of interesting nodes from the semantic values provided by the user. It will also refine a view into a normal form on request. By double clicking on a node, a user can go down a level for browsing, to a view inheriting its parameters from the upper level.

(2) *Wandering*. The browser adds ranks based on the user's input to the display of candidate views. The user will select a view to start browsing on. The browser will display view after view as the user selects interesting semantic links, and rank them. A trace of wandering with possible other paths will be shown to help the user select the next view. A window can display the result of semantic link reasoning at each step of wandering to help the user review possibilities.

2.6.3.2 *Execution and reasoning*

Users can be shown a view of the SLN that reflects the execution relationship between nodes. In this case, the browser acts as execution engine and monitor engine as used in workflow management systems (http://www.wfmc.org). The execution view should show an SLN of at least the 3NF. Constraints can be set from application requirements when establishing the SLN and can be verified during execution.

Unlike traditional logical reasoning, semantic link reasoning is based on large-scale semantic units because semantic links only reflect relationships between such units. Reasoning is usually carried out starting from a user's view of interest, and can be of two kinds:

(1) *View reasoning*: reasoning between views of an SLN is carried out using the transitivity of inclusion ($\subseteq$) and implication ($\rightarrow$) between views. For example:

$view_1 \subseteq view_2, view_2 \subseteq view_3 \Rightarrow view_1 \subseteq view_3$;

$view_1 \rightarrow view_2, view_2 \rightarrow view_3 \Rightarrow view_1 \rightarrow view_3$; and

$view_1 \rightarrow view_2, view_3 \subseteq view_2 \Rightarrow view_1 \rightarrow view_3$.

(2) *Link reasoning* of the following five types:

- *Transitive*: reasoning about transitive semantic links. The general form is: $X_1 \!-\!\alpha\!\rightarrow\! X_2, X_2 \!-\!\alpha\!\rightarrow\! X_3, ..., X_{n-1} \!-\!\alpha\!\rightarrow\! X_n \Rightarrow X_1 \!-\!\alpha\!\rightarrow\! X_n$.

- *Implication*: $\alpha \!\rightarrow\! \beta, X \!-\!\alpha\!\rightarrow\! Y, Y \!-\!\beta\!\rightarrow\! Z \Rightarrow X \!-\!\beta\!\rightarrow\! Z$.

- *Abstraction*: if Z is an abstraction of X, $Z \!-\!\alpha\!\rightarrow\! Y \Rightarrow X \!-\!\alpha\!\rightarrow\! Y$.

- *By analogy*: $X \!-\!\alpha\!\rightarrow\! Y, X \sim X', Y' \sim Y \Rightarrow X' \!-\!\alpha\!\rightarrow\! Y'$, where $\sim$ represents a semantic similarity relationship. The result can be given a certainty degree cd, which can be determined from the similarity degrees of $X \sim X'$ and $Y' \sim Y$.

- *Hybrid*: any combination of the above types.

2.7 SLN Ranking

Nodes in an SLN can be ranked to reflect their semantic importance in the network.

2.7.1 *Hyperlink network ranking*

To rank and refine Web search results, search engines analyze hyperlinks (M.R. Henzinger, "Hyperlink Analysis for the Web", *IEEE Internet Computing*, 2001, Jan/Feb, pp.45-50). The HITS algorithm (J.M. Kleinberg, "Authoritative sources in a hyperlinked environment", *Journal of the ACM*, 1999, 46(5), pp.604-632) and the PageRank algorithm (L. Page, S. Brin, R. Motwani, and T. Winograd, "The pagerank citation ranking: bringing order to the web", *Technical report*, Stanford, Santa Barbara, CA 93106, January, 1998) are typical of the algorithms used to rank Web pages using hyperlink analysis. PageRank is successful in commercial applications.

Both algorithms calculate scores for each page of the entire Web by taking link structure into account. The link relationship among different Web pages is described as a directed graph, called a Web graph, where a hyperlink pointing from page A to page B is treated as an edge from vertex A to vertex B.

The HITS algorithm measures the importance of a single Web page from two aspects: *authority* and *hub*. A page with high authority has many pages pointing to it, which implies its authority; a page with a high hub points to many other pages, which implies its richness in material. The authority of a page is computed by summing up the hub scores of all pages pointing to it, while the hub score is the summation of the authority of all pages pointing to it.

PageRank reduces the importance of a page to a single parameter: "rank". It simply recognizes that a page with many other pages pointing to it is important because it is frequently cited by others. The rank of a page is evenly distributed among all pages it points to. A page gets a small donation from the rank of each page pointing to it. Then its rank is calculated by summing up all the donations it gets.

HITS uses both in-links and out-links of a page, whereas PageRank only uses the in-links. PageRank gives more rational results and has better efficiency and convergence performance than the HITS algorithm.

2.7.2 *SLN ranking*

A semantic link can be assigned a *certainty degree* (denoted by *cd*) to reflect the likelihood of a particular semantic relationship between its components. A component can be an either a simple or complex node (an *SLN*). An inexact link can be shown as $C_1—(l, cd)\rightarrow C_2$, where C_1 and C_2 are components, $l \in \Omega$ and $cd \in (0, 1)$.

The certainty degree is valuable for ranking components according to their semantic importance when using an SLN. Semantic link structure reflects the relationships between components, just as hyperlink structure reflects the relationships between Web pages.

Naturally, we can adopt hyperlink analysis to rank components (nodes) of an SLN, though in the PageRank algorithm every Web page has only one rank. But for an SLN we must take into account different types of semantic links.

For a semantic component C, we can devise an overall rank, called the *T*-rank, and a set of individual *l*-ranks for different *l*-links.

2.7.3 *A ranking algorithm*

Let C and D be components of an SLN, $\Omega = \{e, ce, imp, st, ref, ins, sim, seq, Null, ...\}$, l be a semantic link type ($l \in \Omega$), F_C^l be the set of components of the SLN l-linked from C, and B_C^l be the set of components of the SLN l-linked to C. The sum of the certainty degrees of all l-links from C can be denoted by

$$N_C^l = \sum_{v \in B_C^L} cd_l^{v \rightarrow C},$$

where $cd_l^{v \to C}$ is the certainty degree of an l-link ($l \in \Omega$) from v to C. The rank of a component C can be defined as follows:

$$R_l(C) = \beta_l \times \sum_{D \in B_C^l} \frac{R_l(D) \times R(l)}{N_D^l},$$

where

$$R(l) = w_l \times cd_l^{D \to C}$$

and

$$R(C) = \beta \sum_{l \in \Omega} R_l(C)$$

$R_l(C)$ is the l-rank of C, derived from all the l-links pointing to C. $R(C)$ is the T-rank of C. β_l and β are normalization factors such that the total l-rank (or T-rank) of all components is constant. $R(l)$ is the rank of an l-link, being the product of the weight of the link type (w_l) and the certainty degree of the link ($cd_l^{D \to C}$).

The l-rank of a component is shared among its outward l-links to contribute to the l-ranks of the components pointed to. As far as the inexactness of semantic links is concerned, the certainty degree is attached to the corresponding l-link.

The formulas above show that the rank of a component C depends recursively on the ranks of the semantic links pointing to it. Individual l-ranks $R_l(C)$ can be calculated using an iterative algorithm similar to that of PageRank.

The ranking algorithm

Let A^l be an $n \times n$ matrix with rows and columns corresponding to semantic components, where N is the total number of components of the SLN under consideration.

Assume $A_{i,j}^l = cd_l^{C_i \to C_j} / N_{C_i}^l$ when there is an l-link from C_i to C_j with certainty degree $cd_l^{C_i \to C_j}$, otherwise $A_{i,j}^l = 0$. A^l is called the l-link adjacency matrix.

If we treat R_l as a vector over semantic components, then we have $R_l = \beta_l (A^l)^T R_l$. So R_l is an eigenvector of $(A^l)^T$ with eigenvalue β_l. We want the dominant eigenvector of $(A^l)^T$.

The algorithm for computing T-rank is described as follows:

Function T-rank (S, A^l)

    where A^l is the l-link adjacency matrix and S is an initial vector of l-ranks. S can be almost any vector over the semantic components, so we can simply set S to an n-dimensional vector with every element s_i equal to $1/n$.

{

    For each l in Ω

      {

        $R_l^0 \leftarrow S$

        Do

          $R_l^{i+1} \leftarrow (A^l)^T R_l^i$

          $\delta \leftarrow \left\| R_l^{i+1} - R_l^i \right\|_1$

            // note: $\left\| R \right\|_1$ is the l_1 norm of vector R

        While $\delta > \varepsilon$

      }

      $R \leftarrow O$ // note: O is a zero vector

      For each l in Ω

        $R \leftarrow R + w_l \times R_l$

      Return R

}

Relevant experiments have been described by H. Zhuge and L. Zheng ("Ranking Semantic-linked Network", *Poster Proceedings of WWW2003*, Budapest, May, 2003, available at www2003.org/cdrom /papers/poster/p148/P148-Zhuge/P148-Zhuge.htm).

It is an interesting topic to infer additional semantics from users' behavior when they browse an SLN.

2.8 SLN Operations Implementation

2.8.1 *Matching between SLNs*

The SLNs discussed here contain no isolated nodes. Matching between two SLNs, expressed as graphs $G = (V, E)$ and $G' = (V', E')$, needs to distinguish five types of relationship:

(1) *Intersection.* There exists at least one edge that is contained in both E and E'. An edge expressed as $e = \alpha(x, y)$ comprises two vertices x and y and a semantic property α.
(2) *Null.* The intersection of E and E' is an empty set.
(3) *Equal.* Every edge in E is also in E', and every edge in E' is also in E.
(4) *Inclusion.* Every edge in E is also in E'.
(5) *Inverse inclusion.* Every edge in E' is also in E.

Let G be a 2NF SLN with at least two vertices and one edge, and $mat(G)$ be the SRM of G, with the nodes of rows and columns in the same sequence. Every element of $mat(G)$ is a possibly empty set of semantic properties in $\Omega = \{e, ce, imp, st, sim, ins, seq, ref, \ldots\}$.

Definition 2.8.1 Let SLN $G' = (V', E')$ be a subgraph of $G = (V, E)$. For every edge $e = \alpha(x, y) \in E$, if $x \in V'$ and $y \in V'$, and $e \in E'$, we call $G' = (V', E')$ a *fully induced sub-semantic-graph* of G with vertex set V', denoted by $G_V(V')$.

Definition 2.8.2 (Subtraction of SLN-matrices). For two SLNs $G = (V, E)$ and $G' = (V', E')$, if $V = V'$, let $R(G)$ be the result of a subtraction, $R(G) = mat(G) - mat(G')$.

$$R(G_{ij}) = mat(G_{ij}) - mat(G'_{ij}) = \bigcup_{i=1}^{3} W_i^k, \ k = 0, 1;$$

where $W_i^k = \{0\}$ if $<i=1, k=1>$; $W_i^k = $ null if $<i=1, k=0>$, $<i=2, k=0>$, and $<i=3, k=0>$; $W_i^k = \{+\}$ if $<i=2, k=1>$; and, $W_i^k = \{-\}$ if $<i=3, k=1>$.

$R_{ij}(G) = \{0\}$ means that there is at least one element that is contained in both $mat_{ij}(G)$ and $mat_{ij}(G')$. $R_{ij}(G) = \{+\}$ means that there is at least one element that is contained in $mat_{ij}(G)$ but not in $mat_{ij}(G')$. $R_{ij}(G) = \{-\}$ means that there is at least one element that is contained in $mat_{ij}(G')$ but not in $mat_{ij}(G)$.

The relationship between G and G' can be determined by the following steps.

(1) Let $V_{int} = V \cap V'$, and G_1 and G_2 be their fully induced sub-semantic-graphs with vertex set V_{int}. $G_1 = (V_{int}, E_1) = G_V(V_{int})$ and $G_2 = (V_{int}, E_2) = G'_{V'}(V_{int})$. The relationship between G_1 and G_2 can be determined by the algorithm *Rel_SLN_Vertex* described below, which is also suitable for determining the relationship between any two networks that have the same vertex set.
(2) From the relationship between G_1 and G_2, algorithm *Rel_SLN* determines the relationship between G and G'.

Algorithm 2.8.1 Let $G_1 = (V, E_1)$ and $G_2 = (V, E_2)$ be SLNs, and let $mat(G_1)$ and $mat(G_2)$ be $n \times n$ SLN matrices. The following algorithm sets up a correspondence between the vertices of each SLN and the rows and columns of its matrix, and also a mapping between rows and columns of the two matrices. It is then used to determine the relationship between SLNs.

Rel_SLN_Vertex (SLN G_1, SLN G_2)
{   *Pre_Process* ($mat(G_1)$, $mat(G_2)$); // establishes the node
                                              correspondence between G_1
                                              and G_2.
      Subtract ($mat(G_1)$, $mat(G_2)$, $R(G)$); // $R(G) = mat(G_1) - mat(G_2)$
      RtnStr = Result ($R(G)$);

Return *RtnStr*;

}

The algorithm *Rel_SLN* determines the relationship between any two SLNs $G_1 = (V_1, E_1)$ and $G_2 = (V_2, E_2)$ and returns a value in {"intersection", "empty", "equal", "inclusion", "inverse inclusion"}.

Algorithm 2.8.2

Rel_SLN (SLN G_1, SLN G_2)

{　If ($V_1 == V_2$) Return *Rel_SLN_Vertex* (G_1, G_2);

　If ($V_1 \subset V_2$)

　{　Let $G_3 = (V_1, E_3) = G_2 {}_{V_2} (V_1)$;

　　rtn = *Rel_SLN_Vertex*(G_1, G_3);

　　If (*rtn* == "empty" || *rtn* = "inclusion") Return *rtn*;

　　If(*rtn* == "equal") Return "inclusion";

　　If ((*rtn* == "intersection") || (*rtn* == "inverse inclusion"))

　　　Return "intersection";

　}

　If ($V_1 \supset V_2$)

　{　Let $G_3 = (V_2, E_3) = G_1 {}_{V_1} (V_2)$;

　　rtn = *Rel_SLN_Vertex* (G_2, G_3);

　　If (*rtn* == "empty") Return *rtn*;

　　If ((*rtn* == "inclusion") || (*rtn* == "equal"))

　　　Return "inverse inclusion";

　　If ((*rtn* == "intersection") || (*rtn* == "inverse inclusion"))

　　　Return "intersection";

　}

　Let $V_{int} = V_1 \cap V_2$;　// let V_{int} be the intersection of set V_1 and V_2

　If $V_{int} == \Phi$ Return "empty";

　If ($V_{int} \mathrel{!=} \Phi$)

　{　Let $G_3 = (V_{int}, E_3) = G_1 {}_{V_1} (V_{int})$ and

　　$G_4 = (V_{int}, E_4) = G_2 {}_{V_2} (V_{int})$;

　　rtn = *Rel_SLN_Vertex*(G_3, G_4);

　　If *rtn* == "empty" Return "empty";

　　If (*rtn* != "empty") Return "intersection";

```
    }
}
```

From the relationship returned by algorithm *Rel_SLN*, we can find which SLN contains richer semantics. For example, if the returned value is "inclusion", then G_2 has richer semantics; if the returned value is "inverse inclusion", then G_1 contains richer semantics.

Algorithm *Rel_SLN* can only be applied to a simple SLN — one containing only atomic nodes. A complex SLN is one containing a complex node — a node that is itself an SLN. Algorithms for determining the relationship between complex SLNs can be designed by viewing the complex nodes as atomic nodes, and then determining the relationship between corresponding complex nodes.

2.8.2 The union operation

The union operation is a kind of semantic integration of SLNs, which can combine semantic components. The union operation is useful for forming a complete semantic image (*single semantic image*) during browsing and reasoning.

Definition 2.8.3   The union of two SLNs $G_1 = (V_1, E_1)$ and $G_2 = (V_2, E_2)$, $G_3 = (V_3, E_3) = G_1 \cup G_2$, can be constructed as follows:
(1) View all the nodes in G_1 and G_2 as atomic nodes, $V_3 = V_1 \cup V_2$ and $E_3 = E_1 \cup E_2$.
(2) If a node $V_{1c} \in V_1$ is a complex node, and $V_{1c} \notin V_1 \cap V_2$, then the SLN expanded by V_{1c} yields the SLN expanded by the node V_{3c} (corresponding to V_{1c}) of G_3.
(3) If a node $V_{2c} \in V_2$ is a complex node, and $V_{2c} \notin V_1 \cap V_2$, then the SLN expanded by V_{2c} yields the SLN expanded by the node V_{3c} (corresponding to V_{2c}) of G_3.
(4) If the node $V_c \in V_1 \cap V_2$ is a complex node (let G_{1Vc} and G_{2Vc} be the SLNs expanded by V_c in V_1 and V_2 respectively, $V_{3c} \in V_3$ be the complex node corresponding to V_c, and G_{3V3c} be the SLN expanded by V_{3c}), then we have $G_{3\ V3c} = G_{1Vc} \cup G_{2Vc}$.

Algorithm 2.8.3 The algorithm *Union_SLN* for uniting two SLNs.
Union_SLN (SLN G_1, SLN G_2, SLN G_3)
{ $V_{int} = V_1 \cap V_2$;
    $d = |V_1| + |V_2| - |V_{int}|$;
    $V_3 = V_1 \cup V_2$;
    Let L_1, L_2 and L_3 be arrays with one dimension;
    Set all the nodes in V_1, V_2, and V_3 to arrays L_1, L_2, and L_3
      respectively and ensure each location of L_i only contains one
      node;
   Initialize ($mat(G_3)$);
   // $mat(G_3)$ is a $d \times d$ SLN-matrix, every $mat_{i,j}(G_3)$ is set to *null*
   For every $mat_{i,j}(G_3)$ $(1 \le i \le d, 1 \le j \le d)$
   {   Let $node_i = L_3 [i]$ and $node_j = L_3 [j]$;
     If (both $node_i$ and $node_j$ belong to V_{int})
     {   Let v_{1_i}, v_{1_j}, v_{2_i}, v_{2_j} satisfy the following equations:
         $node_i = L_1 [v_{1\_i}]$, $node_j = L_1 [v_{1\_j}]$,
         $node_i = L_2 [v_{2\_i}]$, $node_j = L_2 [v_{2\_j}]$;
         $mat_{i,j}(G_3) = mat_{v1\_i, v1\_j}(G_1) \cup mat_{v2\_i, v2\_j}(G_2)$;
         // the union of two sets.
     }
     If (only one node belongs to V_{int})
     {   Suppose that another node belongs to V_k;
         // k belongs to {1, 2}
         Let v_{k_i} and v_{k_j} satisfy the following equations:
         $node_i = L_k[v_{k\_i}]$, $node_j = L_k[v_{k\_j}]$;
         $mat_{i,j}(G) = mat_{vk\_i, vk\_j}(G_k)$;
     }
     If (neither $node_i$ nor $node_j$ belongs to V_{int})
     {   if (both $node_i$ and $node_j$ belong to V_k)
         // k belongs to {1, 2}
         {   Let v_{k_i} and v_{k_j} satisfy the following equations:
            $node_i = L_k[v_{k\_i}]$, $node_j = L_k[v_{k\_j}]$;
            $mat_{i,j}(G) = mat_{vk\_i, vk\_j}(G_k)$;
         }

                If (*node$_i$* and *node$_j$* are not in the same SLN)

                mat$_{i,j}$(G$_3$) = *null*;

     }

   }//End for

}

The algorithm *Union_SLN* only applies to simple SLNs. For complex SLNs, the algorithm *Rel_HyperSLN* needs two more steps:

(1) View the complex nodes in two networks as atomic nodes, and then use *Union_SLN* to unite them, and
(2) Use *Rel_HyperSLN* to decide how to unite complex nodes.

2.8.3 *SLN reasoning*

For a given set of SLNs $S = \{G_1, G_2, ..., G_n\}$, the algorithm *Rel_SLN* can yield a set of SLNs that have the relationship *inclusion* or *inverse inclusion*. Suppose that $\{G_{s1}, G_{s2}, ..., G_{sm}\}$ $(1 \leq si \leq n, 1 \leq i \leq m)$ is the result that satisfies $G_{s1} \subseteq G_{s2} \subseteq ... \subseteq G_{sm}$. So when users want to get semantic information from G_{si}, G_{sm} can be used to replace G_{si} (i = 1, 2, ..., m–1) in applications.

The detailed implementation of SLN reasoning and its role in implementing an intelligent browser are described in "Semantic Link Network Builder and Intelligent Semantic Browser" (H. Zhuge and R. Jia, *Concurrency and Computation: Practice and Experience*, 2004, vol.16, no.13).

The SLN inclusion relationship can be extended to an implication-inclusion relationship $\leq$: $G_1 = (V_1, E_1) \leq G_2 = (V_2, E_2)$ if and only if $V_1 \subseteq V_2$ and for any $e \in E_1$, there exists $e' \in E_2$ such that e' is equal to or implies e. Such an implication-inclusion relationship extends SLN reasoning.

To extend SLN applications, the following problems are worth thinking about:

(1) How might the semantic relationship between SLNs be determined? An SLN expresses the semantics of its nodes. There are also semantic relationships between SLNs. Algorithms for finding such semantic relationships would help advance use of the semantics of SLNs.

(2) How might a closely related subset of a large SLN be found that satisfies a user's query?

(3) How might semantic relationships in a given set of resources be automatically found or established? An approach to solving this problem by extending data mining algorithms with analogical and deductive reasoning has been proposed (H. Zhuge, et al., "An Automatic Semantic Relationships Discovery Approach", *Poster Proceedings of the 13th International World Wide Web Conference (WWW2004)*, New York, USA, May 2004,
http://www2004.org/proceedings/docs/2p278.pdf).

2.9 SLN-based Analogical Reasoning

Analogical reasoning is non-deductive, that is, the conclusion does not deductively follow from the premises. Its use can uncover semantic relationships that are not available to simple deduction.

Analogical reasoning has been investigated in the area of AI (R.E. Kling, "A Paradigm for Reasoning by Analogy", *Artificial Intelligence*, vol.10, 1978, pp.147-178). Structural analogical reasoning works by structure mapping between related objects (D. Genter, "Structure Mapping: A Theoretical Framework for Analogy", *Cognitive Science*, 1983, vol.7, pp.155-170). However, research progress has been limited in recent years due to a bottleneck in capturing the structure of objects. By its very nature, an SLN yields structural and semantic data that can be used to support analogical reasoning.

2.9.1 Analogical reasoning modes

A type of simple SLN called a semantic component is a two-tuple: $SC = <C, L>$. C is a set of fine-grained semantic components (nodes). L is the set of semantic links between members of C. $L = \{<c_i, l, cd, c_j> \mid c_i, c_j \in C\}$. $<c_i, l, cd, c_j>$ denotes $c_i \underset{}{\overset{<l, cd>}{\longrightarrow}} c_j$. Let U be the set of all semantic components in an SLN. The following three relations between semantic components in U can be defined:

(1) *Inclusion*. The relationship between a semantic component SC' and its fine-grained components SC. We denote such a relationship by $SC \subseteq SC'$. SC is called a sub-component of SC'. The inclusion degree $IncD\ (SC, SC')$ denotes the proportion of SC' taken up by SC.

(2) *Similarity*. Two semantic components SC and SC' are similar if their graph structures are isomorphic, that is, if there exists a one-to-one correspondence between their nodes and edges. We denote such a relationship by $SC \cong SC'$.

(3) *Partial similarity*. Two semantic components SC and SC' are partially similar if they have similar sub-components. We denote such a relationship as $SC \approx SC'$. $SimD\ (SC, SC')$ denotes the degree of similarity between SC and SC'. The inclusion degree reflects the degree of similarity between a semantic component and its sub-component. If $SC \subseteq SC'$ then $SimD\ (SC, SC') = IncD\ (SC, SC')$.

As the graph structure reflects the semantics of its components, similarity relations reflect the semantic similarity between components.

A structural mapping can be established from the *illustrative problem-solution pair* to the *target problem-solution pair* as shown in Fig. 2.2, where the dashed arrow from the solution S' to the problem P' means that S' is the solution to P' discovered by structural analogy.

The set of SLN analogical rules, *RULES*, is a subset of $U \times U$. A rule $r \in RULES$, denoted by $SC_1 \underset{}{\overset{<l, cd>}{\longrightarrow}} SC_2\ (SC_1, SC_2 \in U)$, means that there is an l-type semantic link with certainty degree cd from SC_1 to SC_2 established manually, or computed by deduction or analogy.

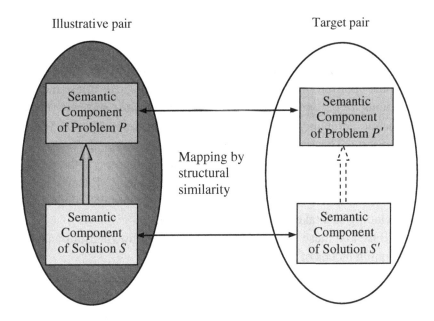

Fig. 2.2 SLN-based reasoning by structural analogy.

Proposition 2.9.1 In solutions to l-type problems, for SC_1, $SC_1 \!\!-\!\!<l, cd> \!\!\rightarrow\!\! SC_2 \Rightarrow SC_2$, means that SC_2 is all resources (components) that have an l-relationship with a resource of SC_1.

SLN analogical rules for two semantic components are stronger than rules for their sub-components. Analogical reasoning should use the strongest rules possible.

For *rule*: $SC_1 \!\!-\!\!<l, cd> \!\!\rightarrow\!\! SC_2$ and *rule'*: $SC_1' \!\!-\!\!<l, cd'> \!\!\rightarrow\!\! SC_2'$, if $SC_1 \subseteq SC_1'$ and $SC_2 \subseteq SC_2'$ then *rule'* is semantically stronger than *rule*, denoted by *rule* < *rule'* or *rule'* > *rule*. The degree to which *rule'* is stronger than *rule* is defined as $PD = 1/(IncD\,(SC_1, SC_1') \times IncD\,(SC_2, SC_2'))$.

Proposition 2.9.2. (1) If SC_1—$<l, cd> \to SC_2$ and $SC_1 \subseteq SC_1'$, then SC_1'—$<l, cd'> \to SC_2$; and, (2) if SC_1—$<l, cd> \to SC_2$ and $SC_2' \subseteq SC_2$, then SC_1—$<l, cd'> \to SC_2'$.

Analogical reasoning goes from premises to conclusion. The premise portion includes existing SLN analogical rules and some relations (e.g., *inclusion, similarity* and *partial similarity*) between semantic components. The conclusion is the rule reasoned from the premises. The certainty degree of the conclusion depends on the various degrees in the premises, the certainty degrees of the rules, the inclusion degrees, and the similarity degrees. Because of the uncertainty inherent in analogical reasoning, the certainty degree of the concluding rule takes the uncertain type $\sim cd$.

Based on these propositions, we offer the following four analogical reasoning modes of SLN:

(1) *Fidelity enforcement mode*

$$\frac{\text{Premises:} \quad SC_1 \text{—} <l, cd> \to SC_2, \ SC_1' \cong SC_1, \ SC_2' \cong SC_2}{\text{Conclusion: } SC_1' \text{—} <l, \sim cd> \to SC_2'}$$

Since a semantic component could be a hierarchy, in some cases it is difficult to determine if $SC_1' \cong SC_1$. Sometimes a transformation function φ (for example, semantic reconstruction by adding, deleting, splitting and merging sub-components) can help. So we have:

$$\frac{\text{Premises:} \quad SC_1 \text{—} <l, cd> \to SC_2,}{\text{Conclusion: } SC_1' \text{—} <l, \sim cd> \to SC_2'}$$
$$\varphi(SC_1') \cong SC_1, \ SC_2' = \varphi'(SC_2''), \ SC_2'' \cong SC_2$$

where φ and φ' reflect a kind of invariance between components.

(2) *General mode*

$$\frac{\text{Premises:} \quad SC_1 \text{—} <l, cd> \to SC_2, \ SC_1' \approx SC_1, \ SC_2' \approx SC_2}{\text{Conclusion: } \quad SC_1' \text{—} <l, \sim cd'> \to SC_2'}$$

where $\sim cd' = cd \times min\ (SimD\ (SC_1, SC_1'), SimD\ (SC_2, SC_2'))$.

As in fidelity enforcement mode, we have:

Premises: $SC_1 \!\!-\!\!<l,\ cd> \to SC_2,$

$$\varphi(SC_1') \approx SC_1, SC_2' = \varphi'(SC_2''), SC_2'' \approx SC_2$$

Conclusion: $SC_1' \!\!-\!\!<l,\ \sim cd'> \to SC_2'$

where $\sim cd' = cd \times min\ ((SimD\ (SC_1, \varphi(SC_1')),\ SimD\ (SC_2, SC_2'')))$.

(3) *Multiple analogy mode*

For two semantic components $SC = <C, L>$ and $SC' = <C', L>$, the union of SC and SC' is $SC \cup SC' = <C \cup C', L \triangle L'>$, where $L \triangle L'$ is the result of eliminating redundant links from $L \cup L'$.

Given $SC_{1i} \subseteq SC_1$, $SC_{2i} \subseteq SC_2$, $SC_{1i}' \subseteq SC_1'$, and $SC_{2i}' \subseteq SC_2'$, if the following fidelity enforcement reasoning is true for $i = 1, 2, ...,$ and k.

Premise: $SC_{1i} \!\!-\!\!<l, cd> \to SC_{2i},\ SC_{1i}' \cong SC_{1i},\ SC_{2i}' \cong SC_{2i}$

Conclusion: $SC_{1i}' \!\!-\!\!<l, \sim cd> \to SC_{2i}'$

then we have:

Premise: $SC_1 \!\!-\!\!<l, cd> \to SC_2$

Conclusion: $SC_1' \!\!-\!\!<l, \sim cd'> \to SC_2'$

where $\sim cd' = cd \times Min\ (\ (\ |\bigcup_{i=1}^{k} C_{1i}\ |\ /\ |C_1|\ ) \times (\ |\underset{i=1}{\overset{k}{\triangle}} L_{1i}\ |\ /\ |L_1|\ ),\ (\ |\bigcup_{i=1}^{k} C_{2i}\ |$

$/\ |C_2|\ ) \times (\ |\underset{i=1}{\overset{k}{\triangle}} L_{2i}\ |\ /\ |L_2|\ ),\ (\ |\bigcup_{i=1}^{k} C_{1i}'\ |\ /\ |C_1'|\ ) \times (\ |\underset{i=1}{\overset{k}{\triangle}} L_{1i}'\ |\ /\ |L_1'|\ ),\ ($

$|\bigcup_{i=1}^{k} C_{2i}'\ |\ /\ |C_2'|\ ) \times (\ |\underset{i=1}{\overset{k}{\triangle}} L_{2i}'\ |\ /\ |L_2'|\ )\ ).$

Multiple analogy employs inductive reasoning.

(4) *Inexact analogy mode*:

Premise: $SC_1 \!\!-\!\!<l, cd\!\!>\!\!\to\!\!SC_2,$
$$\frac{SC_1' \subseteq SC_1,\ IncD\,(SC_1', SC_1) > \sigma,\ SC_2' \subseteq SC_2}{\text{Conclusion: } SC_1' \!\!-\!\!<l, \sim\!cd'\!\!>\!\!\to\!\!SC_2'}$$

where $\sim\!cd' = cd \times min\,(IncD\,(SC_1', SC_1), IncD\,(SC_2', SC_2))$ and σ is the lower bound of the inclusion degree.

Correspondingly, we have:

Premise: $SC_1 \!\!-\!\!<l, cd\!\!>\!\!\to\!\!SC_2,\ \varphi(SC_1') \subseteq SC_1,\ IncD\,(\varphi\,(SC_1'), SC_1) > \sigma,$
$$\frac{SC_2' = \varphi'\,(SC_2''),\ SC_2'' \subseteq SC_2}{\text{Conclusion：} \quad SC_1' \!\!-\!\!<l, \sim\!cd'\!\!>\!\!\to\!\!SC_2'}$$

where $\sim\!cd' = cd \times min\,(IncD\,(\varphi(SC_1'), SC_1), IncD\,(SC_2'', SC_2)).$

The proposed analogical modes still hold if we replace "semantic component" with "SLN".

2.9.2 Process and algorithm of analogical reasoning

Suppose that developers construct some semantic components and store them in a *semantic components base* (*SCB*). Then they store the (problem-solution) component pairs with an *l*-type relationship in an *l-type illustrative pairs base* (*l_IPB*) in three-tuple form (ID_S, ID_P, cd), where *l* is a semantic relation, ID_S is the solution component, ID_P is the problem component, and *cd* is the certainty degree of the *l*-link from ID_S to ID_P.

The general procedure of the fidelity enforcement analogical mode is as follows.

(1) *Discover similar components in the SLN*. The analogical agent analyses the *SCB* and computes the similarity degree of pairs of components. Pairs (c_i, c_j) with similarity degree greater than a certain lower bound are regarded as similar and are stored in the

similar components base (*simB*) in a form such as (*IDc_i*, *IDc_j*, *SimD* (*c_i*, *c_j*)).

(2) *Prepare a new problem.* When a user presents a new problem *r* with the *l*-type relationship, a human or virtual agent checks if it matches an existing component *p* in the *SCB*. If it does not exist, an attempt is made to derive a semantic component *p* from *r*. If *p* exists, it is added to the *SCB* and step (3) is skipped. Otherwise, if there are items like (*ID_S*, *ID_P*, *cd*) in the *l_IPB*, the best of these is used to select *s_{best}* from the *SCB*, *s_{best}* is returned to the user as the best solution to *r*, and the process ends.

(3) *Find components similar to the new problem.* The analogical agent computes the degree of similarity between the new *p* and other components in the *SCB*. Any similar component pairs are stored in the *simB* as (*ID_P*, *ID_{Psim}*, *SimD* (*p_{sim}*, *p*)). If no similar pairs are discovered, the process ends without a result.

(4) *Analogy by similarity.* The matching agent selects the component *p_{max}* with the highest degree of similarity to *p* from all components in the *simB*. If there are solutions to *p_{max}* in the *l_IPB* then the agent finds the best solution *s_{best}'* as in step (3), selects the component *s_{max}* with the highest degree of similarity to *s_{best}'* from the *simB*, adds it to the *l_IPB* as a newly discovered problem-solution pair (*IDs_{max}*, *ID_p*, $\sim$($cd_{s_{best}'-<l,cd>\to p_{max}}$ × *min* (*SimD* (*IDs_{best}'*, *IDs_{max}*), *SimD* (*p*, *p_{max}*)))), and returns *s_{max}* from the *SCB* to the user as the solution to *r*. If there is no *s_{max}*, then the pair (*ID_p*, *ID_{pmax}*, *SimD*(*p_{max}*, *p*)) is taken from the *simB* and step (4) is repeated until all *p_{sim}* have been considered. If there is no *s_{max}* for any *p_{sim}*, the process ends without a result.

The processes for other analogical modes can be obtained by appropriately modifying the process for the fidelity enforcement mode. To ensure the reliability of conclusions, the validity of any computed solution should be verified manually, so that only valid solutions are added to the *l_IPB*.

2.9.3 *Comparing reasoning and rank*

Useful conclusions can be drawn when we look into the relationship between reasoning and rank. Reasoning can affect a semantic component's rank since semantic links added by reasoning will change components' ranks. In reasoning on an SLN, the rank of its components can be different before and after the computation.

The effects of rank on reasoning spring from the following aspects:

(1) *Screening out the best solution.* Problem-solving applications usually work on multiple candidate semantic components. So the candidate solution (semantic component) link with $<l_{strongest},$ $cd_{greatest}>$ for the problem (semantic component) should be taken as the best solution. Here $l_{strongest}$ is the strongest link type from the candidate solutions in semantic priority order; and $cd_{greatest}$ is the highest certainty degree among all the $l_{strongest}$ links from the candidates. Now we take the component's rank into account. The component's rank provides an overall view of the SLN to help in choosing the best candidate solution, especially in analogical reasoning. Since analogical reasoning is uncertain in nature, semantic link deduction is in general more reliable than analogical reasoning. In analogical reasoning, using rank to select the best solutions is more rational than using semantic priority or certainty degree. The candidate solution component with the highest T-rank or with the highest $l_{strongest}$-rank should be selected as the best solution. Thus we need to introduce component rank to modify the definitions of inclusion and similarity degrees.

(2) *Definitions of inclusion and similarity degrees.*

For $SC \subseteq SC'$, the inclusion degree can be redefined as follows:

$$IncD_r(SC, SC') = \left(\frac{\sum_{sc \in \{C\}} R(sc)}{\sum_{sc \in \{C'\}} R(sc)} \right) \times \left(\frac{\sum_{l \in \{L\}} w_l}{\sum_{l \in \{L'\}} w_l} \right)$$

Characteristic 2.9.1 Let $SC_1 = <C_1, L_1>$ and $SC_2 = <C_2, L_2>$ be two semantic components. The symbol $\propto$ denotes: >, = or <. If $SC_1 \subseteq SC$, $SC_2 \subseteq SC$, $SC_1' \subseteq SC'$, $SC_2' \subseteq SC'$, $SC_1 \cong SC_1'$, $SC_2 \cong SC_2'$, and $IncD_r(SC_1, SC) \propto IncD_r(SC_2, SC)$, we do not always have $IncD_r(SC_1, SC) \propto IncD_r(SC_2, SC)$.

The definition of the similarity degree is based on that of the inclusion degree, as follows:

$$SimD_r(SC, SC') = IncD_r(SC_k, SC) \times IncD_r(SC_k', SC'),$$

where $1 \leq k \leq n$ and $IncD_r(SC_k, SC) \times IncD_r(SC_k', SC') = max(IncD_r(SC_1, SC) \times IncD_r(SC_1', SC'), IncD_r(SC_2, SC) \times IncD_r(SC_2', SC'), ..., IncD_r(SC_n, SC) \times IncD_r(SC_n', SC'))$.

2.10 Dynamic SLNs

A dynamic SLN reflects dynamic semantic relationships between its resources. Here we present the notion and principles of dynamic SLNs, and describe a definition tool and a browser.

The Web browser retrieves Web pages from their Web locations as provided by the user or by hyperlinks. The browser displays Web pages only in human readable not in "machine" (software mechanism) understandable forms. On the other hand, the contents of Web pages and their hyperlinks are not easily adapted to new content or new uses.

In a dynamic SLN the semantic relationships between resources can be changed at any time. A semantic link can carry a temporal relationship between its nodes, nodes that can be either a document or another dynamic SLN.

Such a dynamic semantic link can change its nature under different conditions and at different times. The condition can be given by an event name or a Boolean expression. The time duration can be in one of three forms: [-, t] (effective up to time t), [t, $t+\Delta t$] (effective between time t and $t+\Delta t$) or [t, -] (effective from time t on). If there is no condition then the link is static during the given time duration. If there is no time duration then the link depends only on its condition.

2.10.1 *Representation of a dynamic semantic link*

A single dynamic semantic link consists of the link definition and a dynamic semantic description.

$$r_A \rightarrow r_B <dynamic\ semantic\ description>$$

The dynamic semantic description part specifies link types and the condition and duration of each.

$$<dynamic\ semantic\ description> = [l_1\ (condition_1, duration_1), \ldots,$$
$$l_n\ (condition_n, duration_n)]$$

A semantic link l_A implies another semantic link l_B if the semantics of l_A is equal to or implies l_B. Redundant semantic links may exist between a pair of resources with coinciding implication links or conditions. There would be redundancy if (1) $r_A \rightarrow r_B [l_1\ (condition_1, duration_1)]$ and $r_A \rightarrow r_B [l_2\ (condition_2, duration_2)]$, (2) the semantics of l_1 implies l_2, (3) *condition*$_1$ implies *condition*$_2$, and (4) *duration*$_1$ overlaps *duration*$_2$. Each semantic link can be assigned a factor to reflect a known certainty degree. The certainty factor maintenance mechanism will maintain the properties according to the semantic relationship between links.

2.10.2 *Advantages of the dynamic semantic link*

By changing the conditions and durations in a dynamic semantic description, we can dynamically adapt the content of a link to reflect content change in its nodes.

We do not need to re-design an SLN to adapt it to changed circumstances; we just need to change the parameters in the dynamic semantic descriptions.

A dynamic SLN can be given a life cycle, during which its content can be changed by dynamic semantic links or by adding new content.

By using a dynamic SLN to organize the resources of the future Web, we may obtain different content when browsing the same view of the dynamic SLN at different times. This would enable people to get up-to-date content and to put the content to new uses.

2.10.3 *Constraints on semantic link change*

Semantic relationships between links may impose semantic constraints on dynamic change if a change of one link would create incompatibility with another link, and so affect the whole or a portion of an SLN. If a change does not conflict with the transitive and implicative relationships between existing links, then it is a compatible change.

Fig. 2.3 shows an example of semantic link change. The change of the semantic link between A and C does not conflict with the semantic relationship between B and C. We can still derive B—$ce{\rightarrow}C$ from B—$ce{\rightarrow}A$ and A—$st{\rightarrow}C$. So the change is compatible.

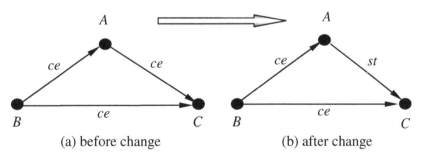

(a) before change   (b) after change

ce: cause-effect; *st*: subtype

Fig. 2.3 Compatible semantic change.

The following measures ensure the compatibility of semantic link change:

(1) Limit change within the semantic scope determined by the transitive and implicative relationships between all types of semantic links. Change can also be carried out smoothly by adjusting the certainty factors of links.

(2) Limit link change according to the link semantics defined in the SLN at the next higher level.

(3) Limit the condition and duration change of a link according to the conditions and durations of its neighbors and of the SLN at the next higher level.

(4) Change all affected semantic links to maintain overall semantic compatibility when incompatible change is otherwise inevitable.

2.10.4 *Dynamic semantic link reasoning*

A dynamic SLN can use the following reasoning paradigms.

Forward dynamic semantic link chaining under a single condition:

$$r_A \rightarrow r_B \ [l_{11} \ (condition_{11}, duration_{11})]$$
$$r_B \rightarrow r_C \ [l_{21} \ (condition_{21}, duration_{21})]$$

$r_A \rightarrow r_C \ [l_{31} \ (condition_{31}, duration_{31})]$, $l_{11} \geq l_{21} \geq l_{31}$, and $duration_{31} = duration_{11} \cap duration_{21}$, where $\geq$ means implies or equal to.

Analogical reasoning:

$$r_A \rightarrow r_B \ [l_1 \ (condition_1, duration_1), \ldots, l_n \ (condition_n, duration_n)]$$
$$r_A \sim r_{A'}, \ r_B \sim r_{B'}$$

$r_{A'} \rightarrow r_{B'} \ [l_1 \ (condition_1, duration_1), \ldots, l_n \ (condition_n, duration_n)], \ CF$

where ~ denotes the similarity relationship between nodes, and the similarity degrees determine the certainty factor *CF* of the result.

2.10.5 *Connectivity*

In a connected SLN any node is accessible from any other node via semantic links. A connected SLN is said to be semantically interconnected if there is no conflict between the semantics of its links. A semantic link will disappear when its conditions and timings do not satisfy its dynamic description. Disappearance of semantic links may destroy the connectivity.

Dynamic change of semantic links may cause an SLN to be continually changing between connected and disconnected states. A connected network may even break into several isolated semantic fragments, some of which may reconnect after semantic changes to their links.

Two criteria — *disruption* and *focus* — can be used to measure the connectivity of an SLN. Computation of these involves the number of fragments, the number of nodes, and the topic. The smaller the degree of disruption and the larger the degree of focus the better the connectivity.

The *degree of disruption* of an SLN depends on the number of fragments and the number of nodes. The degree of disruption for a particular topic depends only on the number of fragments and nodes relevant to the topic.

The *degree of focus* for a topic depends only on the number of fragments relevant to the topic. The degree of focus of the overall network depends on the sum of the degrees of focus of all topics and the total number of topics. The minimum number of fragments is one, so the degree of focus on a topic is equal to or less than one.

disruption (time) = fragments (time) / nodes (time)
disruption (time, topic) = fragments (time, topic) / nodes (time, topic)
focus (time, topic) = 1 / fragments (time, topic)

$$focus\ (time) = \sum_{topic} Focus(time, topic)\ /\ topics$$

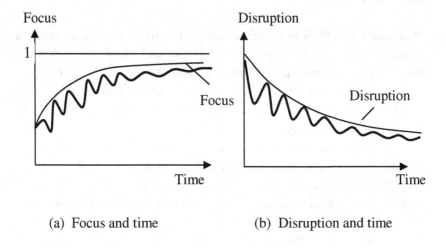

(a) Focus and time   (b) Disruption and time

Fig. 2.4 Evolution of connectivity.

A well-behaved dynamic SLN should evolve by increasing the focus, and decreasing the disruption, of its topics. Fig. 2.4 shows an example of this, where the degree of focus tends to increase and then become stable, and the degree of disruption tends to decrease and then become stable.

2.10.6 *A dynamic semantic browser*

Unlike the Web browser, the dynamic semantic browser is a retrieval mechanism that can generate and display a view of a complete SLN. The view can be displayed either as a network or as a page of text. The browser has the following key features.

(1) *Real-time update.* While they are being browsed, semantic relationships may change as events happen or as conditions are satisfied. The browser updates the view on display in real-time.

(2) *Change tracing.* Each node (or link) will record semantic link (or node) changes so that the nature of the evolution of the SLN can be studied.

(3) *Dynamic semantic link reasoning.* Semantic link reasoning is carried out to provide hints to help users anticipate results. The hints may vary as the semantic links vary.

(4) *Explanation.* The browser can explain a result, and any changes in it, from the reasoning rules and the record of changes.

(5) *Accessibility checking.* Since semantic links between resources change dynamically, accessible resources may become inaccessible. The browser will check the accessibility of the views on display whenever its links change. A resource becoming inaccessible may fragment the view of a topic. The browser will retrieve and display the fragments.

(6) *Evaluation.* The browser will evaluate the degrees of focus and disruption of the SLN for the topic of interest and display these with the content being browsed.

The dynamic SLN is a resource organization and interconnection model that can display semantic relationships between a variety of resources as a *dynamic single semantic image* (DSSeI), that is, mapping everything dynamically onto a common semantic level. This enables users to browse up-to-date content and to easily put that content to new uses.

Definition tools can help people to easily build a dynamic SLN. The dynamic semantic browser can intelligently steer the browsing of any view of the network using various semantic link reasoning paradigms, trace content change and evaluate degrees of focus and disruption.

2.11 SLN Abstraction

Abstraction plays an important role in the transition from the perceptual image of objects to rational thinking about them. Different individuals may come to different conclusions when abstracting from the same perceptions and experiences. Such differences can produce diversity of knowledge, and promote healthy evolution from the viewpoint of ecology. But ontology does not reflect such diversity.

2.11.1 *Concept and operation*

Abstraction simplifies and generalizes an *SLN*.

Definition 2.11.1. Let $SLN = <N, L>$ and $SLN' = <N', L'>$ be two SLNs. *SLN'* is called an abstraction of *SLN* if and only if there exists a onto mapping $A: <N, L> \rightarrow <N', L'>$ such that for any semantic link $n_i—l \rightarrow n_i$ of *SLN*, there exists a corresponding link $A(n_i)—A(l) \rightarrow A(n_i)$ of *SLN'*, $A(n_i)$ is an abstraction of n_i, $A(n_i)$ is the abstraction of n_i, and $A(l)$ is the same as or semantically implies l.

The abstraction of $A(n)$ from n can be seen in the following three cases:

(1) Both n and $A(n)$ are atomic concepts. In this case, node $A(n)$ is the abstraction of n if and only if $A(n)$ is a concept abstracted from n, that is, if $A(n)$ is the father of n in a conceptual abstraction tree.
(2) Node n is an SLN and $A(n)$ is an atomic concept. In this case, node $A(n)$ is the abstraction of n if and only if $A(n)$ represents the semantics of n.
(3) Both n and $A(n)$ are SLNs. In this case, the abstraction between the nodes becomes the abstraction between SLNs (definition 2.11.1).

From the definition above, we can define an abstraction operation $\cap_A$ that generates an abstract SLN from n SLNs: $\cap_A (SLN_1, SLN_2, ...,$

$SLN_n) = SLN$, where A stands for the topic area of the abstraction. The algorithm for realizing this operation is based on the intersection operation of SLNs but using abstraction as outlined above to replace equivalence.

For a given set of SLNs as the original source of abstraction, repeating the following steps can generate an abstraction tree as shown in Fig.2.5:

(1) Generate a set of abstract SLNs by abstracting any combination of source SLNs;
(2) Generate the source set of a new level by clustering the abstract SLNs that are semantically similar; and,
(3) If the result has more than one abstract SLN, repeat from step 2.

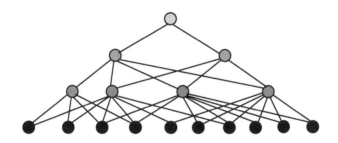

Fig. 2.5 An abstraction tree.

Abstraction usually works by analogy (H. Zhuge et al, "Analogy and Abstract in Cognitive Space: A Software Process Model", *Information and Software Technology*, 1997, vol.39, pp.463-468). Fig. 2.6 shows the relationship between analogy and abstraction. While abstractions are carried out on sets of objective existence, analogy can provides links and references between abstractions.

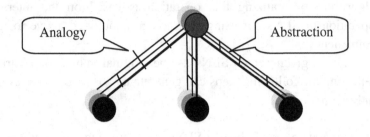

Fig. 2.6 Abstraction with analogy.

2.11.2 *Abstraction, epistemology and ontology*

The abstraction process is a process of semantic selection. The abstraction tree reflects the epistemology of the topic area.

If the abstraction tree is derived from many diverse SLNs, and adding new SLN abstractions doesn't change the tree, then the epistemology of the topic area is completed. Once completed, the abstraction tree can be independent of the SLNs and evolve during use.

A semantic selection is of the form $\alpha \leq_C \beta$, which means that the topic area selects β from candidate set C as more abstract than α. A set of semantic selection results is generated as the epistemology is formed.

Given an SLN and an epistemology, an abstraction of the SLN can be automatically generated from the epistemology. The abstraction tree and the selection set constitute the epistemology of the topic area.

An epistemology can guide the computation of the abstract SLN of a given SLN. The formation of a community's epistemologies from their common SLNs reflects a kind of social selection process based on shared values.

A society consisting of resources and resource producers and consumers can build a mutual understanding between individuals from knowledge of each others' epistemologies. And if the epistemologies can be processed by machine, then mutual understanding will thereby be easier to attain.

Now we can visualize an application scenario for the future interconnection environment: the resources' generators (machine or human) each attach their epistemologies to the resources. The resource consumer can understand the semantics of resources by using the attached epistemologies.

Fig. 2.7 shows the relationship between people, resources and epistemology. Features can be extracted from entities such as texts and images. Hyperlinks and semantic links establish the relevancy among entities. Low-level knowledge comes from crude semantics, which are usually represented by keywords and their relationships. High-level knowledge comes from rules, axioms and methods.

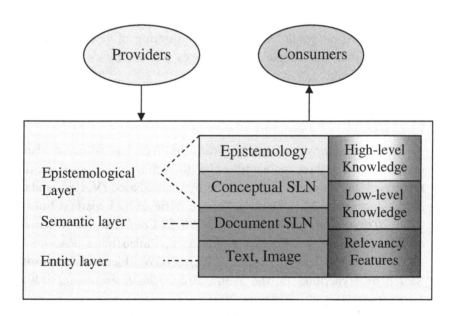

Fig. 2.7 Multiple layers of resources and epistemology.

Current research into ontology seeks to establish consensus between different understandings in domains. The effectiveness of this effort is questionable if we look at the nature of the World Wide Web and the background of evolution of culture and emerging new domains.

Epistemology as described here respects differences between individuals in a social context. All participants construct their own epistemology. This is in line with the diversity of the World Wide Web. Since the epistemologies are constructed using very few semantic primitives, understanding any epistemology should be feasible, if not easy. Epistemology will soon have an important part to play in establishing the future Web.

2.12 Application 1: SLN-based Image Retrieval

Semantic-based image retrieval has the following advantages:

(1) The retrieval result is a semantic clustering of relevant images rather than the simple list of images put out by current search engines; and
(2) Users can browse images by wandering along semantic hints with supporting semantic reasoning and explanation.

Effective retrieval of images from the Web has attracted many researchers. The three main approaches to Web image retrieval are the text-based, the content-based, and the hyperlink-based (V. Harmandas, M. Sanderson and M.D. Dunlop, "Image retrieval by hypertext links", *Proc. 20'th Annual International ACM SIGIR Conference on Research and Development in Information Retrieval*, Philadelphia, PA, USA, 1997; R. Lempel and A. Soffer, "PicASHOW: Pictorial Authority Search by Hyperlinks on the Web", *Proc. 10th International WWW Conference*, Hong Kong, China, 2001).

The text-based approach applies text-based Information Retrieval (IR) algorithms to keywords in annotations of images, captions of images, text near images, the entire text of pages containing an image, and filenames. These approaches support a specific natural language for queries.

The content-based approach applies image analysis techniques to extract visual features from images. The features are extracted in a preprocessing stage and stored in the retrieval system's database. The extracted features are usually of high dimensionality, and need fewer dimensions to allow scalability.

The hyperlink-based approach makes use of the link structure to retrieve relevant images. Their common basic premise is that a page displays or links to an image when its author considers the image to be of value to the viewers (H.Zhuge, "Retrieve Images by Understanding Semantic Links and Clustering Image Fragments", *Journal of Systems and Software*, 2004; vol. 73, no.3, pp.455-466).

These approaches are almost independent of the semantics of the image itself. The main obstacle to semantic-based image retrieval is that it's hard to describe an image semantically. But the semantics of an image can be implied by related images and their semantic relationships. Thus semantic links can help realize semantic-based image retrieval.

The following three sets of semantic links list position relationships:

(1) *X is-above Y*; *X is-below Y*; *X is-left-of Y*; and, *X is-right-of Y*
(2) *X is-north-of Y*; *X is-south-of Y*; *X is-east-of Y*; and, *X is-west-of Y*.
(3) *X is-ahead-of Y*; and, *X is-behind Y*.

The positional links can be abstracted as *X is-β-of Y*, where *β∈ {above, below, left, right, north, south, east, west, ahead, behind}* is called a semantic property. The pairs *above/below*, *left/right*, *south/north*, *east/west*, *ahead/behind* are each symmetric.

Other positional links can be composed from two different semantic properties, depending on their meaning. For example, *X is-north-west-of Y*; *X is-south-east-of Y*; *X is-south-west-of Y*; and, *X is-north-east-of Y* are meaningful semantic links, but *X is-north-south-of*

Y isn't. In general, the composite links can be represented as: *X is-α-β-of Y.*

Table 2.2 Rules for positional links.

No	Rule	Category
1	*X is-above Y ⇒ Y is-below X*	*X is-α-of Y ⇒ Y is-β-of X*
2	*X is-below Y ⇒ Y is-above X*	ditto
3	*X is-left-of Y ⇒ Y is-right-of X*	ditto
4	*X is-right-of Y ⇒ Y is-left-of X*	ditto
5	*X is-north-of Y ⇒ Y is-south-of X*	ditto
6	*X is-south-of Y ⇒ Y is-north-of X*	ditto
7	*X is-east-of Y ⇒ Y is-west-of X*	ditto
8	*X is-west-of Y ⇒ Y is-east-of X*	ditto
9	*X is-ahead-of Y ⇒ Y is-behind X*	ditto
10	*X is-behind Y ⇒ Y is-ahead-of X*	ditto
11	*X is-north-west-of Y ⇒ Y is-south-east-of X*	$X\ is\text{-}\alpha_1\text{-}\alpha_2\text{-}of\ Y \Rightarrow Y\ is\text{-}\beta_1\text{-}\beta_2\text{-}of\ X$
12	*X is-south-east-of Y ⇒ Y is-north-west-of X*	ditto
13	*X is-south-west-of Y ⇒ Y is-north-east-of X*	ditto
14	*X is-north-east-of Y ⇒ Y is-south-west-of X*	ditto

Rules can be derived from the positional links as shown in Table 2.2. From the rules in the table, we can derive two generalization rules and a transitivity rule.

Generalization Rule 1. $X\ is\text{-}\alpha_1\text{-}\alpha_2\text{-}of\ Y \Rightarrow Y\ is\text{-}\beta_1\text{-}\beta_2\text{-}of\ X$ if and only if (1) $is\text{-}\alpha_1\text{-}\alpha_2\text{-}of$ and $is\text{-}\beta_1\text{-}\beta_2\text{-}of$ are both meaningful, (2) $X\ is\text{-}\alpha_1\text{-}of\ Y \Rightarrow Y\ is\text{-}\beta_1\text{-}of\ X$, and (3) $X\ is\text{-}\alpha_2\text{-}of\ Y \Rightarrow Y\ is\text{-}\beta_2\text{-}of\ X$.

Generalization Rule 2. If α and β are mutually symmetric, then *X is-α-of Y ⇒ Y is-β-of X.*

Transitive Rule. *X is-α-of Y* and *Y is-α-of Z* $\Rightarrow$ *X is-α-of Z*.

Orthogonal semantics exists between positional properties. We use $\alpha_1 \perp \alpha_2$ to denote that α_1 is orthogonal to α_2. Such orthogonal relationships provide knowledge that helps image retrieval and assists high-level applications on images. The following are six sets of orthogonal relationships:

(1) *below $\perp$ left, below $\perp$ right, above $\perp$ left*, and *above $\perp$ right*;
(2) *south $\perp$ west, south $\perp$ east, north $\perp$ west*, and *north $\perp$ east*;
(3) *behind $\perp$ left, behind $\perp$ right, behind $\perp$ above, behind $\perp$ below*;
(4) *behind $\perp$ south, behind $\perp$ east, behind $\perp$ west, behind $\perp$ north*;
(5) *ahead $\perp$ south, ahead $\perp$ east, ahead $\perp$ west, ahead $\perp$ north*;
(6) *ahead $\perp$ left, ahead $\perp$ right, ahead $\perp$ above, ahead $\perp$ below*.

Two more rules follow from these orthogonalities.

Symmetry Rule. If $\alpha_1 \perp \alpha_2$, then we have $\alpha_2 \perp \alpha_1$.

Orthogonal Rule. If $\alpha_1 \perp \alpha_2$, $\alpha_3 \perp \alpha_1$ and $\alpha_4 \perp \alpha_2$ in a two-dimensional space, then $\alpha_3 \perp \alpha_4$.

The position of an image can be determined using the following rule.

Position Determination Rule. *The position of image* X *can be determined by two positional links* X *is-α_1-of* A *and* X *is-α_2-of* B *if and only if* α_1 *and* α_2 *are positionally orthogonal.*

Besides the semantic and positional links discussed so far, the following *existence semantic* relationships also help to cluster images.

(1) *X is-coincident-with Y*;
(2) *X is-not-coincident-with Y*;

(3) *X is-compatible-with Y*;

(4) *X is-not-compatible-with Y*; and

(5) *X is-complementary-to Y.*

Further, experience with layout, hierarchy, importance and relevance also help image retrieval. Capturing such experience for computation is a challenge.

Actually, semantic information was often lost, distorted, or hidden in Web pages when they were made. So discovering hidden semantics, correcting distortion, and inferring semantics is also a challenge.

2.13 Application 2: Active Document Framework (ADF)

Current e-documents are as passive as hardcopy documents. People need to use a search engine to retrieve documents of possible interest and to browse the content manually. Passive documents have two shortcomings: first, the user will feel it is difficult to get information when browsing a large document; second, the search engine does not have any supplementary data about the document's content, so it cannot provide an ideal information service.

What is an Active Document Framework?

An ADF *is a self-representable, self-explainable and self-executable document mechanism. A document's content can be reflected in four aspects: scale hierarchy, template hierarchy, background knowledge, and semantic links between its parts. An active document* (AD) *has a set of built-in engines for browsing, retrieving, and reasoning, which can work in the manner that is best suited to the document's content.*

Besides browsing and retrieval services, the AD supports information services like complex question answering, online teaching, and problem solving assistance. The client-side service provider is only responsible for the retrieval of the required AD. The information services are provided by the AD's own engine. This improves on the current Web IR approaches by raising the effectiveness of IR, enhancing the preciseness and mobility of information services, and enabling intelligent information services.

An AD encapsulates the textual document, its content, and the operations on it. Such an AD can work like a teacher with a textbook. The user need not have much background knowledge of the document or have much reading skill but can learn from the document like a student. This feature can enhance the quality of information services for a large-scale document or a large collection of interrelated documents.

An AD is a function of the input requirement, denoted by I. The output, denoted by O and caused by the input, depends on the content of the document (denoted by C) and a set of engines (denoted by E). So an AD can be described as a function:

$$O = AD\ (I, C, E).$$

The document content consists of the structural knowledge (SK), the background knowledge (BK), and the SLN, represented as $C = <SK, BK, SLN>$. $SLN = <FS, Link>$, where FS is a set of document fragments, and $Link$ is a set of semantic links between the fragments.

The user working with SLN can be in a kind of workflow, where the user or users can be at one place or geographically distributed. The difference here is that the flows are along various types of semantic link, so we call flow in the network *textflow* to differentiate it from workflow. SLN can provide different views for simplifying its use. A view of SLN shows only one type of link between fragments.

An AD has three engines:

(1) The *execution engine*, responsible for providing the textflow according to the ordered view of its SLN, like the workflow engine;

(2) The *search engine*, responsible for searching the fragment that matches the input requirement according to the SLN and the reasoning rules behind the search result; and
(3) The *reasoning engine*, responsible for reasoning by rule about the SLN.

Any user can use a search engine to retrieve an AD, and then asking the AD for a service whose operations are done by its reasoning engine.

An *AD* category is a set of documents that share the same background knowledge. To avoid redundancy, an *AD* only contains the structural knowledge and the SLN. The background knowledge is shared by all the *AD*s in its category. The category *ADC* can be represented as follows:

$ADC = <\{AD_1, ..., AD_n\}, BK>$, where the output of AD_i is defined as $O_i = AD_i (I_i, C_i, E_i)$ and $C_i = <SK_i, SLN_i>$.

Detailed discussion of the ADF is available in "Active e-Document Framework ADF: Model and Platform" (H. Zhuge, *Information and Management*, 2003, vol.41, no.1, pp.87-97).

2.14 Discussion

There is great scope for the SLN to develop.

When the nodes and links only represent concepts and cause-effect relations respectively, then the SLN model is very similar to Cognitive Maps and Fuzzy Cognitive Maps (Z.Q. Liu and R. Satur, "Contextual Fuzzy Cognitive Maps for Decision Support in Geographic Information Systems", *IEEE Transactions on Fuzzy Systems*, 1999, vol.7, no.10, pp.495-502; Y. Miao, et al., "Dynamic Cognitive Network", *IEEE Transactions on Fuzzy System*, 2001, vol.9, no.5, pp.760-770; H. Zhuge and X. Luo, "Automatic Generation of

Document Semantics in Knowledge Grid", *Proceedings of the 2nd International Workshop on Knowledge Grid and Grid Intelligence*, Beijing, Sept. 20, 2004, pp.1-18). So the Cognitive Map approach can be used with SLNs for high-level fuzzy knowledge representation and computation. Mapping from text space to concept space is a crucial problem in combining them.

The normalization theory of SLNs can help the normalization of Cognitive Maps. Forming a uniform model for the two is also an interesting challenge.

The SLN is an attempt to realize a semantically rich Web. It is significant in method and theory, but its real application relies on the transition to SLNs from current standards (http://www.w3c.org) as well as on industry efforts to establish standards for semantic link primitives.

Two more applications of SLNs are worth mentioning:

(1) Use of SLNs to organize teaching materials and support cooperative research and adaptive e-learning (H. Zhuge and Y. Li, "Semantic Profile-based Document Logistics for Cooperative Research", *Future Generation Computer Systems*, 2004, vol.20, pp.47-60; H. Zhuge and Y. Li, "Learning with Active E-Course in Knowledge Grid Environment", *Concurrency and Computation: Practice and Experience*, in print, Wiley). Applications in this area have shown that it is feasible to use SLNs to organize teaching materials locally.

(2) Use of SLNs to organize data sources in a semantic network to realize semantic-based peer-to-peer data management (H. Zhuge, et al., "Semantic-Based Query Routing and Heterogeneous Data Integration in Peer-to-Peer Semantic Link Network", *Proceedings of IC-SNW, SIGMOD Workshop*, Paris, France, 2004, pp.90-107).

Other relevant work includes the Topic Map (P. Auillans, et al., "A Formal Model for Topic Maps", *Proc. 1st International Semantic Web Conference*, June, Sardinia, Italia, LNCS 2002, vol.2342, pp.69-83), standardized in 1999, which organizes information by using the concepts of *topics*, *occurrence* and *association* (http://www.topicmaps.net/pmtm4.htm). The semantic network of traditional AI is a well-known knowledge representation approach for expressing the relationships between concepts. It was proposed as a human associative memory model in the late 1960s and applied to natural language processing in the early 1970s.

An SLN is a kind of semantically relational space. The following chapter will introduce an orthogonal classification semantic space: the Resource Space Model (RSM), in which coordinates of axes play roles like those of latitudes and longitudes in geographical maps as outlined at the beginning of this chapter.

Chapter 3

A Resource Space Model

Systematic organization is the basis for using resources effectively. The Resource Space Model described here uses orthogonal classification semantics to organize resources.

3.1 The Virtual Grid

The *Virtual Grid* is a platform independent interconnection environment, based on a resource organization model, that can effectively specify, share, use and manage a variety of resources (H. Zhuge, "Semantics, Resource and Grid", *Future Generation Computer Systems*, 2004, vol.20, no.1, pp.1-5). It has two key parts:

(1) The *Resource Space Model* (RSM) — a semantic space for accurately locating resources.
(2) The *Resource Using Mechanism* (RUM) — a *resource browser*, a *resource management engine*, a *Resource Operation Language* (ROL), an *ROL interpreter* and an *application development environment*.

The resource browser provides an easy-to-use interface that helps end-users select resources and operations, specify parameters, and then have operations carried out. The resource management engine accepts instructions and then has them carried out according to the types of the resources to be operated on.

The ROL enables end-users to carry out simple operations, and application developers to compose a program to apply complex operations to resources.

The ROL interpreter supports not only complex applications in their use of resources, but also the resource browser in its use of resources. End-users can either run an application system to carry out operations of a specific kind or use the resource browser to operate directly on resources.

Developers build programs with the support of the development environment, which is in turn supported partly by the Virtual Grid and partly by application development tools.

A resource space has three views as discussed in "Resource Space Grid: model, method and platform" (H. Zhuge, *Concurrency and Computation: Practice and Experience*, 2004, vol. 16, no. 3):

(1) The *user* view, a two- or three-dimensional resource space, is used by the resource browser to make it easy for end-users to locate and use resources. It is hard for end-users to deal with multi-dimensional spaces without such help.
(2) The *universal* view, the entire *n*-dimensional resource space. A user view is a slice (or a subspace) of the universal view.
(3) The *semantic* view, a semantically rich representation of a variety of resources based on markup languages like RDF (http://www.w3.org/rdf), ontological mechanisms, and semantic link networks.

3.2 The Resource Space Model (RSM)

3.2.1 *Resource spaces*

The external semantics of a resource can be represented by:

(1) *Name* — the identifier differentiating one resource from another.

(2) *Author* — the name(s) of the creator(s).

(3) *Abstract* — a brief description of the content of an information or knowledge resource, or of the function or purpose of a service resource. It could be simply a set of keywords, natural language description, formal description, semantic link network, or template.

(4) *Version* — the number that identifies different versions of the same resource.

(5) *Location* — the Internet and logical addresses in the virtual environment.

(6) *Privilege* — it has three possible values: a) *public*, any user can access the resource; b) *group*, only group members can access the resource; and, c) *private*, only the author(s) can access the resource.

(7) *Access-approach* — the valid operations on the resource.

(8) *Duration* — the life span of the resource.

In the following, we assume that an ontology service mechanism *Output = Ontology-Service (Input, k)* is available. The *Input* parameter is a word or phrase. The second parameter is a numeric variable used for controlling the output. If $k = 0$, the service puts out sets of words related to *Input* of the following kinds: synonym, abstract concept, specific concept, and instance. If $k = 1$, the ontology service puts out one more element— a quasi-synonym of the input word or phrase, if one exists.

Coordinates are commonly used to locate objects in a space efficiently. By establishing a good coordinate system for a resource space, we can precisely store and retrieve its resources by their coordinates. To distinguish resources of the same name in different resource spaces, the space name can be used with the resource name, thus: *Resource-name. Space-name*.

Definition 3.2.1 A resource space is an n-dimensional space in which every point uniquely locates a (possibly null) set of related resources. A resource space has a name, a type, a logical location, and an access privilege.

The uniqueness dictates that the coordinates of each dimension be defined independently. In the discussion below, we use the following notations:

(1) A resource space is represented by $RS(X_1, X_2, ..., X_n)$, or RS for short, where RS is the name of the space and X_i is the name of an axis. $|RS|$ denotes the number of dimensions of RS.

(2) $X_i = \{C_{i1}, C_{i2}, ..., C_{im}\}$ represents an axis with its coordinates. Each element denotes a coordinate name in the form of a noun or a noun phrase. Any coordinate name must be defined formally or informally in its domain ontology, as in the Word Net

(http://www.cogsci.princeton.edu/~wn/).

Definition 3.2.2 Two axes are deemed the same if their names are the same and the names of the corresponding coordinates are the same. If two axes $X_1 = \{C_{11}, C_{12}, ..., C_{1n}\}$ and $X_2 = \{C_{21}, C_{22}, ..., C_{2m}\}$ have the same axis name but have different coordinates, they can be joined into one: $X = X_1 \cup X_2$, denoted by $X_1 \cup X_2 \Rightarrow X$.

Characteristic 3.2.1 An axis X can be split into two axes X' and X'' by dividing the coordinate set of X into two: the coordinate set of X' and that of X'', such that $X = X' \cup X''$.

A coordinate can be a hierarchy, with lower-level coordinates as subclasses of their common ancestor. We use $Sup(C)$ to denote the direct ancestor or immediate superior of C in a coordinate hierarchy. The name of each coordinate of a hierarchy can be differentiated from others of the same name by giving its name together with the names of all of its ancestors. The nature of coordinates in a hierarchy can be defined as follows:

Definition 3.2.3 A coordinate C selects a class of resources (denoted by $R(C)$) such that if $C = Sup(C')$ then $R(C') \subseteq R(C)$.

From this definition, if $C = Sup(C')$ and $C' = Sup(C'')$ then $R(C'') \subseteq R(C)$.

An axis with hierarchical coordinates can be mapped onto an axis with flat coordinates by projecting its leaves onto the axis. The following discussion considers only the flat case.

Good resource space design should ensure correct resource sharing and management. Synonyms like "teacher", "instructor" and "tutor" should not be used together as flat coordinates, because that could lead to resource operations making mistakes.

Definition 3.2.4 A coordinate C is dependent on coordinate C' if $C \in Output = Ontology\text{-}Service\,(C', 1)$.

Definition 3.2.5 If $X = (C_1, C_2, ..., C_n)$ is an axis and C_i' is a coordinate of another axis X', we say that X finely classifies C_i' (denoted by C_i'/X) if and only if:

(1) $(R(C_k) \cap R(C_i')) \cap (R(C_p) \cap R(C_i')) = \phi$ $(k \neq p,$ and $k, p \in [1, n])$; and

(2) $(R(C_1) \cap R(C_i')) \cup (R(C_2) \cap R(C_i')) \cup ... \cup (R(C_n) \cap R(C_i')) = R(C_i')$.

As the result of the fine classification, $R(C')$ is classified into n categories: $R(C_i'/X) = \{R(C_1) \cap R(C_i'), R(C_2) \cap R(C_i'), ..., R(C_n) \cap R(C_i')\}$.

Definition 3.2.6 For two axes $X = \{C_1, C_2, ..., C_n\}$ and $X' = \{C_1', C_2', ..., C_m'\}$, we say that X finely classifies X' (denoted by X'/X) if and only if X finely classifies $C_1', C_2', ..., C_m'$.

Characteristic 3.2.2 Fine classification is transitive, that is, if X''/X' and X'/X, then X''/X.

Definition 3.2.7 Two axes X and X' are said to be orthogonal to each other (denoted by $X \perp X'$) if X finely classifies X' and vice versa, that is, both X'/X and X/X'.

For example, *KnowledgeLevel* = *<Concept, Axiom, Rule, Method>* $\perp$ *Discipline* = *<Computer, Communication, Ecology, Physics>* because *<Concept, Axiom, Rule, Method>* is a fine classification of every coordinate of the *Discipline* axis and the *<Computer, Communication, Ecology, Physics>* is a fine classification of every coordinate of the *KnowledgeLevel* axis. Because fine classification is transitive, we can assert the following.

Characteristic 3.2.3 Orthogonality between axes is transitive, that is, if $X \perp X'$ and $X' \perp X''$, then $X \perp X''$.

3.2.2 *Normal forms*

To answer the question of what is good design of a resource space, we need to define the following normal forms for the space.

Definition 3.2.8
(1) A resource space is in first normal form (1NF) if no coordinate names are duplicated within any axes.
(2) A space in 1NF is also in second normal form (2NF) if no two coordinates are dependent on each other.
(3) A space in 2NF is also in third normal form (3NF) if any two axes are orthogonal.

These normal forms provide designers with guidelines for designing a good resource space. The 1NF avoids explicit coordinate duplication. The 2NF avoids implicit coordinate duplication, and prevents one coordinate from semantically depending on another. The 3NF ensures that resources are properly used. The choice of coordinates for a resource space should respect the type of the resources being classified.

Characteristic 3.2.4 If two spaces RS_1 and RS_2 hold the same type of resources and they have n (≥ 1) axes in common, then they can be joined as one RS such that RS_1 and RS_2 share these n common axes and

$|RS| = |RS_1| + |RS_2| - n$. RS is called the join of RS_1 and RS_2 and is denoted by $RS_1 \cdot RS_2 \Rightarrow RS$.

Characteristic 3.2.5 A space RS can be separated into two spaces RS_1 and RS_2 (denoted by $RS \Rightarrow RS_1 \cdot RS_2$) such that they have n ($1 \leq n \leq minimum\,(|RS_1|, |RS_2|)$) axes in common, $|RS| - n$ different axes, and $|RS_1| + |RS_2| = |RS| + n$.

Characteristic 3.2.6 If two spaces RS_1 and RS_2 hold the same type of resources and satisfy: (1) $|RS_1| = |RS_2| = n$, (2) they have $n - 1$ common axes, and (3) the distinct axes X_1 and X_2 satisfy the merge condition, then they can be merged into one RS by retaining the $n - 1$ common axes and adding a new axis $X = X_1 \cup X_2$. RS is called the merge of RS_1 and RS_2, denoted by $RS_1 \cup RS_2 \Rightarrow RS$, and $|RS| = n$.

Characteristic 3.2.7 A resource space RS can be split into two spaces RS_1 and RS_2 that hold the same type of resources as that of RS and have $|RS| - 1$ common axes, by splitting an axis X into two axes X' and X'' such that $X = X' \cup X''$. This split operation is denoted by $RS \Rightarrow RS_1 \cup RS_2$.

Using these definitions and characteristics, we can prove the following three lemmas.

Lemma 3.2.1 Let $RS_1 \cdot RS_2 \Rightarrow RS$.
(1) RS is in 1NF if and only if both RS_1 and RS_2 are in 1NF.
(2) RS is in 2NF if and only if both RS_1 and RS_2 are in 2NF.
(3) RS is in 3NF if and only if both RS_1 and RS_2 are in 3NF.

Lemma 3.2.2 (1) $RS \Rightarrow RS_1 \cdot RS_2$ if and only if $RS_1 \cdot RS_2 \Rightarrow RS$; and, (2) $RS \Rightarrow RS_1 \cup RS_2$ if and only if $RS_1 \cup RS_2 \Rightarrow RS$.

The following lemma ensures that a resource space of many dimensions can be separated into several spaces of fewer dimensions that keep the same normal form as the original space. For instance, a five-dimensional space can be separated into two three-dimensional spaces that have an axis in common.

Lemma 3.2.3 If $RS \Rightarrow RS_1 \cdot RS_2$, we have:
RS is in 1/2/3NF if and only if both RS_1 and RS_2 are in that form.

From the definition of the normal forms, we have the following two lemmas about the merge and split operations.

Lemma 3.2.4 If $RS \Rightarrow RS_1 \cup RS_2$, and if RS is in 1/2/3NF, then RS_1 and RS_2 are in that form.

Lemma 3.2.5 If $RS_1 \cup RS_2 \Rightarrow RS$ and if RS_1 and RS_2 are in 3NF and RS is in 2NF, then RS is in 3NF.

Semantic overlaps may exist between resource definitions in some applications. In this case, the space designer must use quasi-synonyms as coordinates on an axis.

Lemma 3.2.6 Resources in a 3NF resource space can be accessed from any axis.

Proof. Let $X_i = \{C_{i1}, C_{i2}, ..., C_{ip}\}$, $1 \leq i \leq n$. If the RS is in 3NF, then for any two axes $X_k = \{C_{k1}, C_{k2}, ..., C_{kl}\}$ and $X_j = \{C_{j1}, C_{j2}, ..., C_{jm}\}$ $(1 \leq k \neq j \leq n)$, $X_k \perp X_j$. We have C_{kq} / X_j for every C_{kq} $(1 \leq q \leq l)$. From the definition of fine classification, we have:
$R(C_{kq}) = (R(C_{kq}) \cap R(C_{j1})) \cup (R(C_{kq}) \cap R(C_{j2})) \cup \cdots$
$\cup (R(C_{kq}) \cap R(C_{jm}))$
$\quad = R(C_{kq}) \cap (R(C_{j1}) \cup R(C_{j2}) \cup \cdots \cup R(C_{jm}))$.
Then $R(C_{kq}) \subseteq (R(C_{j1}) \cup R(C_{j2}) \cup \cdots \cup R(C_{jm}))$ for $1 \leq q \leq l$.
Hence, we have $(R(C_{k1}) \cup R(C_{k2}) \cup \cdots \cup R(C_{kl})) \subseteq (R(C_{j1}) \cup R(C_{j2}) \cup \cdots \cup R(C_{jm}))$ for $1 \leq k \neq j \leq n$.

Similarly, we have:
$(R(C_{j1}) \cup R(C_{j2}) \cup \cdots \cup R(C_{jm})) \subseteq (R(C_{k1}) \cup R(C_{k2}) \cup \cdots \cup R(C_{kl}))$
for $1 \leq k \neq j \leq n$.
And then we have: $(R(C_{j1}) \cup R(C_{j2}) \cup \cdots \cup R(C_{jm})) = (R(C_{k1}) \cup R(C_{k2}) \cup \cdots \cup R(C_{kl}))$ for $1 \leq k \neq j \leq n$.
So if $R = (R(C_{j1}) \cup R(C_{j2}) \cup \cdots \cup R(C_{jm}))$, then for every axis $X_i = \{C_{i1}, C_{i2}, ..., C_{ip}\}$, $1 \leq i \leq n$, $R = R(C_{i1}) \cup R(C_{i2}) \cup \cdots \cup R(C_{ip})$. This means that the resources that are accessible from any axis are the same. Hence a resource retrieval algorithm does not need to depend on the order of the axes.

Definition 3.2.9. A coordinate C is called weakly independent on another coordinate C' if $C \notin Output = Ontology\text{-}Service\,(C', 0)$.

The second normal form has a weak analog.

Definition 3.2.10 The weak 2NF of a space is a 1NF, but in addition, for every one of its axes, any pair of coordinates are weakly independent on each other.

The third normal form also has a weak analog that can be useful in some applications.

Definition 3.2.11 The weak 3NF of a resource space is a weak 2NF, but in addition, all pairs of axes are orthogonal.

A 3NF resource space may contain points without resources, which lower the efficiency of resource management. We can further normalize a resource space by ruling out such empty points.

Definition 3.2.12 Let $X = (C_1, C_2, ..., C_n)$ be an axis and C_i' be a coordinate on another axis X'. We say that X regularly and finely classifies C_i' (denoted by C_i'/X) if and only if
(1) $R(C_1) \cap R(C_i') = \phi$, $R(C_2) \cap R(C_i') \neq \phi$, ..., and $R(C_n)) \cap R(C_i') \neq \phi$,
(2) $(R(C_k) \cap R(C_i')) \cap (R(C_p) \cap R(C_i')) = \phi$ $(k \neq p$ and $k, p \in [1, n])$, and

$$(R(C_1) \cap R(C_i')) \cup (R(C_2) \cap R(C_i')) \cup \dots \cup (R(C_n) \cap R(C_i')) = R(C_i').$$

Definition 3.2.13 For two axes $X = \{C_1, C_2, \dots, C_n\}$ and $X' = \{C_1', C_2', \dots, C_m'\}$, we say that X regularly and finely classifies X' if and only if X regularly and finely classifies $C_1', C_2', \dots, C_m'$.

Definition 3.2.14 If two axes regularly and finely classify each other, then the two axes are called regularly orthogonal.

Definition 3.2.15 The fourth normal form (4NF) of a resource space is a 3NF, but in addition, all pairs of axes are regularly orthogonal.

A generic *reference resource space* is a three-dimensional resource space: $RS = (category, level, location)$. The category dimension is a classification of resources. Each coordinate on this axis represents a distinct category. A category coordinate can hold subcategories, and each subcategory can hold subcategories, and so on. A category together with all its lower subcategories forms a category hierarchy. Coordinates on the category axis are scalable because people usually consider resources across different levels. Except for certain basic subcategories, each coordinate of the category axis can be spread down onto a set of lower level coordinates, which can then be spread down again or collected back up to its higher level coordinates. Name duplication can be avoided by denoting a subcategory as: *category · subcategory*.

A resource can be located by its category and level parameters. The generic reference resource space can have different specializations depending on the types of resource that it contains.

3.3 Criteria for Designing Resource Spaces

The normal forms defined above can now be used to consider in what ways a resource space may be good or bad. The following are criteria for a resource in a good resource space.

(1) The *semantic completeness* criterion. Any resource in a resource space should have complete semantics expressed in natural language. That is, a resource space should not be given a resource that cannot be described or has not been described.

(2) The *resource positioning* criterion. Any resource in a resource space should belong to a set of resources that corresponds to a point in the resource space. Such a resource is said to be "well positioned" in the resource space.

(3) The *resource use* criterion. The use of any resource in a resource space should obey all restrictions on its usage that were defined when it was created.

A resource space has a logical representation layer and a physical storage layer. If the two layers are not consistent, for example, if a resource exists in one layer but not in the other, then the RUM will be unable to operate on it properly. To ensure consistency, we set the following criteria.

(1) The *existence consistency* criterion. Any resource in a resource space should ensure the consistency of its existence in schemas of different level. In other words, if a resource is in one schema it must be in another schema. Resource operations should maintain this consistency.

(2) The *pervasive residence* criterion. The resources of a resource space should be allowed to reside on various hardware and software platforms.

(3) The *operability* criterion. An RUM should support at least three basic resource operations: get a resource from a resource space, put a resource into a space, and remove a resource from a space. These operations must also be available for managing through any view of a resource space.

3.4 Designing Resource Spaces

Logical level application design has the following steps:

(1) *Resource analysis.* Resource analysis determines the application scope, surveys possible resources, and then specifies all the relevant resources by using a *Resource Dictionary* (RD), which records them as a local resource space for the application. These resources can be described in XML, and the RD can be managed using the ROL or any other XML query language.

(2) *Top-down resource partitioning.* Different designers may partition resources differently, so a uniform approach to partitioning is needed. The first step is to unify the highest-level partition. Humans, information, and natural or artificial objects are three key factors in human society, and the resources of human society may be cleanly partitioned in this way. The top-level partitioning of a domain can be regarded as a special case of this partitioning of human society. For example, an institute's resources can be classified at the highest level within three exclusive categories: human resources, information resources, and service resources. This step, and the preceding one, are carried out on each category and its subcategories and so on until the resources in the lowest level category are few enough for the application being designed.

(3) *Design bidimensional resource spaces.* People can manage bidimensional spaces better than higher dimensional spaces. So we can first design a set of bidimensional resource spaces, and then consider joining them to form higher dimensional spaces. This design process has the following steps.

- *Name the axes.* Each axis name should reflect one category of the top-level partition of resources.
- *Name the top-level coordinates.* Each coordinate should reflect one subcategory of the category of its axis.
- *Name the coordinate within each hierarchy.* For each top-level coordinate, name its lower level coordinates until all the coordinates at all levels have been named.

- *Remove any dependence between coordinates.* Look for dependence between coordinates at all levels. Where it occurs, redesign the partitioning at that level and then name any new coordinates.
- *Make all axes orthogonal.* If any pair of axes is not orthogonal, redesign and rename their coordinates.

(4) *Join spaces.* Look at the join characteristics (3.2.4) of the bidimensional spaces to determine whether these spaces can be joined ultimately to form a single resource space.

Making use of abstraction, and analogy between the existing (or reference) resource spaces and the new resource space, are important techniques for designing a good resource space (H. Zhuge, "Resource Space Model, Its Design Method and Applications", *Journal of Systems and Software*, 2004, vol.72, no.1, pp. 71-81).

3.5 Representation of Resource Semantics

The semantics of a resource could be seen as a black box if the semantics come from those of related resources, or as a glass box if they come from the features and functions of the resource itself. Combining the two ways could be more effective than either alone.

A resource template represents the common features of a class of resources of the same type. Resources defined in a space need a set of templates, organized as a hierarchy, where the lower level templates are expansions of higher level ones. The root template takes the following form:

ResourceTemplate{
    Resource-name: *<string>* (*domain name*);
    Description: **;
    Related-materials: [
        Relationships: [*LinkTo:<SemanticLinkType$_1$, Resource$_1$>*,
            ·······,

$$LinkTo:<SemanticLinkType_m,$$
$$Resource_m>];$$
$$References: [material\text{-}name_1: <address_1>,$$
$$\cdots\cdots,$$
$$material\text{-}name_n:<address_n>]$$
$$Others] \}.$$

where an "address" can be a URL or a book or paper citation. A book citation takes the form: <BookName: *String*; Author: *String*; Publisher: *String*; PublisherAddress: *String* or URL>. A paper citation takes the form: (JournalName: *String*; Volume: *Number*; Issue: *Number*; PaperTitle: *String*; AuthorName: *String*; Publisher: *String*; PublisherAddress: *String* or URL).

"Related-materials" specifies relationships between resources and the references of the related resources. The relationship is a kind of semantic link that describes the relationship between resources.

"Others" can be relationships such as "Peer-resources: <name-list>" and "Meta-resources: <name-list>".

To satisfy the pervasive residence criterion, the XML (http://www.w3.org/XML) or XML-based markup languages can be adopted to encode the worldwide resource space and local resource spaces. An example of representing a worldwide and a local knowledge space in XML is given in (H. Zhuge, "Resource Space Grid: Model, Method and Platform", *Concurrency and Computation: Practice and Experience*, 2004, vol.16, no.13).

3.6 The Resource Using Mechanism (RUM)

An RSM has two types of users: the end-users who use resources directly through an enabling interface or indirectly through an application system, and the application developers who build complex application systems for end-users with the support of the RUM.

The ROL defines a set of basic operations for creating resource spaces and for sharing and managing resources. Some of these operations allow the user to create a local space and to get resources for that space from the universal view of all the local resource spaces. Others allow the user to put a set of resources into a local space, to remove those resources if privileged to do so, to browse resources, to join a local space to the universal view or to separate it from that view, to open a local space to a specific set of users, and to join several spaces into one.

Thus the ROL includes operations called Create, Get, Place, Remove, Browse, Log, Open, Join, Separate, Merge and Split. These can be supplied with a list of resources and their locations, but at least one resource must be listed. Resources can be retrieved by specifying constraints in the condition portion of an ROL statement (discussed in detail in Chapter 4).

A resource browser has the ROL interpreter carry out ROL statements, but also helps users to locate resources they need and display the content of those resources in a template form. A resource browser has the following main functions.

(1) Provide an easy-to-use interface for users to specify what they want done.
(2) Provide either a local view or the universal view of all resources.
(3) Check the format and grammar of the ROL statements.
(4) Deliver operations to the ROL interpreter, and take results back.
(5) Show the results of those operations.

The browser allows a user to:

(1) choose an operation by clicking a button,
(2) choose the resources to be operated on by specifying their coordinates in a resource space (for example, by clicking the left resource tree then clicking the rectangle standing for the desired point of the resource space), and
(3) put in or select parameters to refine the operation.

Information is the basis for knowledge, and knowledge in turn supports the understanding of information. A resource space may hold information, knowledge or services. An information space provides support for both knowledge and service spaces. A knowledge space supports both service and information resources. A service resource can get information from an information space or knowledge from a knowledge space for processing, then put the results back into the information or knowledge space.

The RUM is responsible for carrying out the operations fed to it by the browser and feeding back the content of resources according to their type. Different types of resource need different RUM operations. An implementation of the RUM must

(1) ensure an appropriate granularity of resource during operation (for instance, rules should be used together because a single rule may not be meaningful and the deletion of a single rule may cause incompleteness of the component it belongs to),

(2) feed the resources back in a meaningful way, because the end-user may not be able to understand their formal expression, and

(3) obtain any needed support from types of resource other than that of the resource being operated on.

The RUM can provide the following functions for experienced users:

(1) Apply reasoning, and supply explanation, based on knowledge in the resource space used when extracting answers to users' queries.

(2) Acquire knowledge resources from information resources automatically.

(3) Convert raw resources into finely classified resources, and eliminate inconsistency and redundancy.

3.7 Comparisons

There are two commonalities between the RSM described here and the RDBM (R. Bocy, et al., "Specifying Queries as Relational Expressions", *Communications of the ACM*, 1975, vol.18, no.11, pp.621-628; E.F. Codd, "A Relational Model of Data for Large Shared Data Banks", *Communications of the ACM*, 1970, vol.13, no.6, pp.377-387). The first is that the operations are separated from the objects to be managed. The second is the form of the operational languages: both SQL-like (ANSI, The Database Language SQL, Document ANSI X3.315, 1986; A.Eisenberg, and J.Melton, Sql:1999, Formerly Known as Sql3, *SIGMOD Record*, 1999, vol.28, no.1, pp.131-138). This enables RDB users to easily understand the syntax and semantics of the ROL.

The six major points of difference between the RSM and the RDBM are the following:

(1)   The RSM is based on resource ontology, the RDBM on relational algebra.

(2)   The objects managed by the RSM are structured or semi-structured information, knowledge, and resources, while the objects managed by the RDBM are atomic data.

(3)   The data model of the RSM is a uniform coordinate system, while that of the RDBM is the relational table.

(4)   The RSM is normally independent and orthogonal, while the functions of the RDBM are normally dependent.
      The differences so far mean that the RSM is concerned with the contents and classification (semantics) of its resources so that it can carry out content-based operations and locate resources, but the RDBM is concerned with the attributes of the managed objects so that it can support attribute-based operation.

(5)   The RSM supports a uniform classification-based semantic view when using resources, while the RDBM essentially supports the viewing of attributes. This feature enables the RSM to uniformly share and manage Internet resources.

(6)   The RSM is based on the Semantic Web for exchange of data, as it provides a machine understandable semantic basis for resources, while the RDBM is not concerned with exchange. The ODBC standard is used for exchange of data between different commercial RDBMs.

Differences between OLTP and OLAP were compared in J. Han, and M. Kambr, *Data Mining: Concepts and Techniques* (Morgan Kaufmann Publishers, 2000). The multidimensional data model used for data warehousing and OLAP differs from the RSM in its foundation, its managed objects, its normalization, its operational features, and the basis for its exchange of data.

The object-oriented methodology (G. Booch, J. Rumbaugh, and I. Jacobson, *The Unified Modeling Language: User Guide.* Reading, Mass.: Addison-Wesley, 1999) provides a method and mechanism for uniform domain modeling and system implementation. It reduces the complexity of systems of objects by using notions such as class and object to abstract a variety of entities, by encapsulating operations into each class, and by an inheritance mechanism. It supports reuse during software development.

Object-relational databases (ORDBs) combine object-oriented and relational data base technologies (M. Stonebraker, P. Brown, and D. Moore, *Object-Relational DBMs: Tracking the Next Great Wave*, second ed., San Francisco: Morgan Kaufmann Publishers, 1999). In an ORDB, a table need not be in the first normal form of the relational data base model, and tables can be nested.

Various nested normal forms have been studied as extensions of traditional flat normal forms in RDBMs (W.Y. Mok, "A Comparative Study of Various Nested Normal Forms", *IEEE Trans. on Knowledge and Data Engineering*, vol.14, no.2, 2002; Z.M. Ozsoyoglu, and L.Y. Yuan, "A New Normal Form for Nested Relations", *ACM Trans. Database Systems*, vol.12, no.1, pp.111-136, 1987; Z. Tari, J. Stokes, and S. Spaccapietra, "Object Normal Forms and Dependency Constraints for Object-Oriented Schemata", *ACM Trans. Database Systems*, vol.22, no.4, pp.513-569, 1997), but these extensions are based on relational algebra and a relational data model. The RSM differs from the ORDB in its foundation, its managed objects, its data model, its normalization, its operational features, and its basis for data exchange.

The resource browser helps users work on resources. Major differences between the resource browser and the typical current Web browser are as follows:

(1) the objects used by the resource browser are various Internet resources, while the Web browser uses Web pages;

(2) the resource browser locates resources by coordinates, a kind of classification semantics, while the Web browser locates Web pages by URL;

(3) the resource browser can locate resources and then operate on them by setting appropriate parameters, but the Web browser can only search Web pages using keywords;

(4) the resource browser supports a uniform semantic view of resources, while the Web browser only supports the viewing of a single Web page at a time; and

(5) the resource browser is supported by the RSM, while the current Web browser lacks the support of a coherent data model.

The design method for the RSM does not include a conceptual model, so a designer's experience and the reference model play key roles in designing a good resource space. The hierarchical resource organization approach is in line with top-down resource partitioning as described above, and with the "from general to specific" style of thought. The RSM is based on the Semantic Web, so it does not need a physical level schema as does the RDBM.

For application development, the ROL is not only an SQL-like language but also it uses XML syntax to support programming based on a semi-structured data model. The XML query language XQL is a concise language and is developed as an extension of the XSL pattern language. It builds upon the capability of identifying classes of nodes by applying Boolean logic, filters, and indexing to collections of nodes.

LOREL (http://www.db.stanford.edu/lore) is a simple language in SQL style.

The ROL borrows its syntax and semantics from standard SQL. The statements of the ROL are SQL-like and have the SQL SELECT-FROM-WHERE pattern. The ROL can perform operations like those of the classical relational database, such as nested queries, aggregates, set operations, join and result ordering.

The ROL also borrows the following features from XML query languages:

(1)   management of structured and semi-structured data,
(2)   abstract data types,
(3)   the XML-based data format and the result semantics,
(4)   the skelom functions to associate a unique ID with a given resource space Grid,
(5)   document selection, and
(6)   partial path specification.

A distinctive feature of the ROL is that it can use various types of resource with hierarchical structure including information, knowledge, service resources and even Virtual Grids, with a universal semantic view supported by the RSM. But standard SQL only works on flat relational tables, and the XML query languages only work on XML documents. A detailed comparison is given in "Resource Space Grid: Model, Method and Platform" (H.Zhuge, *Concurrency and Computation*: *Practice and Experience*, 2004, vol.16, no.13).

Exponential growth of resources is an obstacle to their effective management. When this kind of growth happens, a resource space with a fixed number of dimensions cannot avoid exponential expansion of its resources at some points at least. This problem can be solved in theory by increasing the number of dimensions. If resources expand at rate e^n, we could for example use a resource space of n-dimensions with each dimension having n coordinates to manage the resource explosion since $n^n > e^n$ when $n > e$.

In practice, resources are usually first classified by communities, and then classified by resource spaces on different topics. More importantly, resources in the future interconnection environment should have finite life spans, which could reduce expansion of resources to a certain extent.

A unified resource model called the *soft-device* has been proposed for modeling resources in the future interconnection environment (H.Zhuge, "Clustering Soft-Devices in Semantic Grid", *Computing in Science and Engineering*, 2002, vol.4, no.6, pp.60-62).

The orthogonal resource space only solves the normal organization problem. The ideal resource management approach still needs mobility. For example, an ideal approach would be able to locate a resource even if it is has been misplaced.

3.8 Extension of the Resource Space Model

3.8.1 *Formalizing resource space*

Let O be a domain terminology set, with a mapping from O onto the domain ontology that explains the domain's semantics. The resource space can be formalized as follows.

Definition 3.8.1 Let $S = 2^O$ be the power set of O. The resource space defined on O can be represented as $RS(X_1, X_2, ..., X_n)$, where RS is the name of the space and $X_i = \{C_{i1}, C_{i2}, ..., C_{ip}\}$ is an axis, $1 \le i \le n$, C_{ij} is the root of the hierarchical structure of coordinates on X_i, $C_{ij} = \{<V_{ij}, E_{ij}> \mid V_{ij} \in S, E_{ij} = \{<v_t, v_s> \mid v_t, v_s \in V_{ij}, R(v_t) \supseteq R(v_s)\}\}$, $1 \le j \le p$, where $R(v)$ is a class of resources represented by v. Every point in RS is an element of the Cartesian product $X_1 \times X_2 \times ... \times X_n$, represented as $p(x_1, x_2, ..., x_n)$.

Tuples of relational data models reflect the attributes of entities, not the semantics. In the RSM, x_i in a point $p(x_1, x_2, ..., x_n)$ reflects the semantic partitioning. Resources represented by a point $p(x_1, x_2, ..., x_n)$

$\in RS$ can be represented as $R(p(x_1, x_2, ..., x_n)) = R(x_1) \cap R(x_2) \cap ... \cap R(x_n)$, where $R(x_i)$ is a class of resources represented by x_i, $1 \leq i \leq n$.

3.8.2 *Resource space schemas and normal forms*

A resource space schema formally describes a resource space. The major task in the logical design of a space is to specify its schema, and to define the axes and coordinates.

Application domains require that resources in a space schema satisfy certain integrity constraints. The schema should satisfy all these constraints, so it is defined as follows:

Definition 3.8.2 A resource space schema is a 5-tuple: $RS < A, C, S, dom>$, where:

(1) RS is the space name;
(2) $A = \{X_i \mid 1 \leq i \leq n\}$ is the set of axes;
(3) $C = \{C_{ij} \mid C_{ij} \in X_i, 1 \leq i \leq n\}$ is the set of coordinates;
(4) S is the power set of the domain ontology O;
(5) *dom* is the mapping from the axes A and coordinates C to S, *dom*: $A \times C \rightarrow S$, for any axis $X_i = \{C_{i1}, C_{i2}, ..., C_{ip}\}$, $dom(X_i, C_{ij}) = V_{ij}$, $V_{ij} \in S$, where $1 \leq i \leq n$ and $1 \leq j \leq p$.

In applications, (4) and (5) should be determined before the schema is designed, so that the schema can be simplified as a 3-tuple: $RS < A, C>$.

The schema is static and stable, but the space can be dynamic due to the resource operations on the space. The design of a resource space is the design of its schema.

An axis with hierarchical coordinates can be transformed into an axis with flat coordinates if only the leaf nodes of each hierarchy are considered. Here we discuss only the flat case, and assume that an RS is always in 2NF. We give the equivalent definitions of the normal forms.

For the space $RS(X_1, X_2, ..., X_n)$, we use $R(X_i)$ to denote resources represented by axis X_i, where $X_i = \{C_{i1}, C_{i2}, ..., C_{ip}\}$, $1 \leq i \leq n$. $R(X_i) = R(C_{i1}) \cup R(C_{i2}) \cup ... \cup R(C_{ip})$. First we define fine classification.

Lemma 3.8.1 For two axes $X_i = \{C_{i1}, C_{i2}, \ldots, C_{ip}\}$ and $X_j = \{C_{j1}, C_{j2}, \ldots, C_{jq}\}$ of the space RS, $X_j/X_i \Leftrightarrow R(X_j) \subseteq R(X_i)$.

Definition 3.8.3 For two axes $X_i = \{C_{i1}, C_{i2}, \ldots, C_{ip}\}$ and $X_j = \{C_{j1}, C_{j2}, \ldots, C_{jq}\}$ of the space RS, we say X_j/X_i if $R(X_j) \subseteq R(X_i)$.

From this we can get the following definition of orthogonality.

Lemma 3.8.2 For two axes $X_i = \{C_{i1}, C_{i2}, \ldots, C_{ip}\}$ and $X_j = \{C_{j1}, C_{j2}, \ldots, C_{jq}\}$ in the space RS, $X_j \perp X_i \Leftrightarrow R(X_j) = R(X_i)$.

Proof: (1) If $X_j \perp X_i$, then we have X_j/X_i and X_i/X_j from the definition of orthogonality. From lemma 3.8.1 we have $R(X_j) \subseteq R(X_i)$ and $R(X_i) \subseteq R(X_j)$. So $R(X_j) = R(X_i)$.
(2) If $R(X_j) = R(X_i)$, then $R(X_j) \subseteq R(X_i)$ and $R(X_i) \subseteq R(X_j)$. From lemma 3.8.1, we have X_j/X_i and X_i/X_j. That means $X_j \perp X_i$. From (1) and (2), we have $X_j \perp X_i \Leftrightarrow R(X_j) = R(X_i)$. $\square$

Definition 3.8.4 For two axes $X_i = \{C_{i1}, C_{i2}, \ldots, C_{ip}\}$ and $X_j = \{C_{j1}, C_{j2}, \ldots, C_{jq}\}$ in the space RS, we say $X_j \perp X_i$ if $R(X_j) = R(X_i)$.

Clearly $X_i \perp X_j \Leftrightarrow X_j \perp X_i$, which means the orthogonal operation $\perp$ is symmetrical. From all this follows a new proof of the transitivity of *fine classification* and the *orthogonal* operation.

Theorem 3.8.1 The fine classification and orthogonal operations are transitive.

Proof: From Lemma 3.8.1 and Lemma 3.8.2, we can get $X_j/X_i \Leftrightarrow R(X_j) \subseteq R(X_i)$ and $X_j \perp X_i \Leftrightarrow R(X_j) = R(X_i)$. Because the set operations $\subseteq$ and $=$ are transitive, fine classification and the orthogonal operation is transitive. $\square$

From this follows the definition of third normal form.

Theorem 3.8.2 For space $RS(X_1, X_2, ..., X_n)$, RS is in 3NF $\Leftrightarrow R(X_1) = R(X_2) = ... = R(X_n)$, that is, every axis X_i can retrieve all the resources in RS.

Proof: (1) If RS is in 3NF, then $X_1 \perp X_2 \perp ... \perp X_n$. From Lemma 3.8.2, $R(X_1) = R(X_2) = ... = R(X_n)$. (2) Similarly if $R(X_1) = R(X_2) = ... = R(X_n)$, we get $X_1 \perp X_2 \perp ... \perp X_n$, and because $\perp$ is both transitive and symmetrical, then for any two axes X_i and X_j in RS, $X_i \perp X_j$. That means RS is in 3NF. From (1) and (2), it follows that RS is in 3NF $\Leftrightarrow R(X_1) = R(X_2) = ... = R(X_n)$. $\square$

Theorem 3.8.2 can be restated as a definition of the 3NF.

Definition 3.8.5 For the space $RS(X_1, X_2, ..., X_n)$, we say RS is in 3NF if $R(X_1) = R(X_2) = ... = R(X_n)$, that is, if every axis X_i can retrieve all the resources in RS.

Beyond the three normal forms, we can define other normal forms of the resource space schema for the convenience of partitioning and other operations.

Definition 3.8.6 (2^+NF) A space $RS(X_1, X_2, ..., X_n)$ is in 2^+NF, if it is in 2NF and $X_2/X_1, X_3/X_2, ..., X_n/X_{n-1}$.

The above definition means $R(X_1) \supseteq R(X_2) \supseteq ... \supseteq R(X_n)$ from Lemma 3.8.1. If RS is in 2^+NF, then, because fine classification $/$ is transitive, we have: for every two axes X_i and X_j, $1 \le i \ne j \le n$, either X_i/X_j or X_j/X_i. So $/$ is a full ordering on the set $\{X_1, X_2, ..., X_n\}$. On the other hand, it is obvious that if $/$ constitutes a full ordering on the axes of RS, then RS is in 2^+NF. In the following, we discuss the properties of the 2^+NF under the operations on resource spaces.

Corollary 3.8.1 For two spaces RS_1 and RS_2, let $RS_1 \cdot RS_2 \Rightarrow RS$. Then although both RS_1 and RS_2 are 2^+NF, RS needs not be in 2^+NF.

Proof: Suppose $RS_1 = \{X_1, X_2\}$ and $RS_2 = \{Y_1, Y_2\}$, where X_i and Y_i are axes and satisfy X_2/X_1, Y_2/Y_1 and $X_2 = Y_2$. Then we can join RS_1 and RS_2. Let $RS_1 \cdot RS_2 \Rightarrow RS$, so that $RS = \{X_1, X_2, Y_1\}$.

    (1)   If either $R(X_1) \subseteq R(Y_1)$ or $R(Y_1) \subseteq R(X_1)$, either $R(X_2) \subseteq R(X_1) \subseteq R(Y_1)$ or $R(X_2) \subseteq R(Y_1) \subseteq R(X_1)$. From Definition 3.8.6, RS is in 2^+NF.

    (2)   Otherwise if both $R(X_1) \subseteq R(Y_1)$ and $R(Y_1) \subseteq R(X_1)$ are false, then neither Y_1/X_1 nor X_1/Y_1. Since $/$ is a full order on the axes of RS, if RS is in 2^+NF then RS is not in 2^+NF, a contradiction.

    Therefore from (1) and (2), RS is in 2^+NF. $\square$

Corollary 3.8.1 tells us that 2^+NF does not persist under the Join operation. But if we add some conditions, 2^+NF will persist.

Corollary 3.8.2 (Join) Let $RS_1 = \{X_1, X_2, ..., X_n\}$ and $RS_2 = \{Y_1, Y_2, ..., Y_m\}$ be two 2^+NF resource spaces, and $RS_1 \cdot RS_2 \Rightarrow RS$. If $Y_1 = X_n$ or $X_1 = Y_m$, then RS is in 2^+NF.

Proof: (1) If $X_1 = Y_m$, then from $RS_1 \cdot RS_2 \Rightarrow RS$, we have $RS_2 = \{Y_1, Y_2, ..., Y_{m-1}, X_1, X_2, ..., X_n\}$. Since RS_1 and RS_2 are in 2^+NF, we have $X_n/X_{n-1}/.../X_2/X_1$ and $Y_m/Y_{m-1}/.../Y_2/Y_1$, then, from the transitivity of $/$ we have: $X_n/X_{n-1}/.../X_2/X_1 = Y_m/Y_{m-1}/.../Y_2/Y_1$. From definition 3.8.6, RS is in 2^+NF. (2) Also, if $Y_1 = X_n$, RS is in 2^+NF for the same reason as (1). $\square$

Corollary 3.8.3 If $RS \Rightarrow RS_1 \cdot RS_2$, and RS is in 2^+NF, then RS_1 and RS_2 are also in 2^+NF.

Proof: Suppose $RS = \{X_1, X_2, ..., X_n\}$. Because RS is in 2^+NF, and $/$ is a full ordering on RS, and $RS \Rightarrow RS_1 \cdot RS_2$, then the axes of RS_1 are a subset of the axes RS, so $/$ is also a full ordering on the axes of RS_1, and RS_1 is in 2^+NF. For the same reason, RS_2 is also in 2^+NF. $\square$

Corollary 3.8.3 tells that 2^+NF persists under the operation Separate. From the definitions of Join and Separate, we can get $RS_1 \cdot RS_2 \Rightarrow RS$ if and only if $RS \Rightarrow RS_1 \cdot RS_2$. Then from corollary 3.8.3 we have the following corollary.

Corollary 3.8.4 For resource spaces RS_1 and RS_2, let $RS_1 \cdot RS_2 \Rightarrow RS$. If either RS_1 or RS_2 is not in 2^+NF, then RS is not in 2^+NF.

From the above corollaries, we can get the following:

Corollary 3.8.5 If $RS \Rightarrow RS_1 \cdot RS_2$, and RS is not in 2^+NF, then either RS_1 or RS_2 or both could be in 2^+NF.

Corollary 3.8.6 For resource spaces RS_1 and RS_2, let $RS_1 \cup RS_2 \Rightarrow RS$. Then if RS_1 and RS_2 are in 2^+NF, RS is in 2^+NF.

Proof: Suppose $RS_1 = \{X_1, X_2, ..., X_n\}$ satisfies $X_n/X_{n-1}/.../X_2/X_1$, and $RS_2 = \{Y_1, Y_2, ..., Y_n\}$ satisfies $Y_n/Y_{n-1}/.../Y_2/Y_1$. Since $RS_1 \cup RS_2 \Rightarrow RS$, RS_1 and RS_2 have n-1 common axes and one different axis. Suppose that $X_i = Y_i$, $1 \le i \ne k \le n$, and $X_k \ne Y_k$. Then $RS = \{X_1, ..., (X_k \cup Y_k), ..., X_n\}$. Because $X_{k+1}/X_k/X_{k-1}$ and $X_{k+1} = Y_{k+1}/Y_k/Y_{k-1} = X_{k-1}$, from Lemma 3.8.1, we have: $R(X_{k-1}) \supseteq R(X_k) \supseteq R(X_{k+1})$ and $R(X_{k-1}) \supseteq R(Y_k) \supseteq R(X_{k+1})$.
So $R(X_{k-1}) \supseteq (R(X_k) \cup R(Y_k)) \supseteq R(X_{k+1})$, which means $R(X_{k-1}) \supseteq R(X_k \cup Y_k) \supseteq R(X_{k+1})$. From Lemma 3.8.1 $X_{k+1}/(X_k \cup Y_k)/X_{k-1}$, so $X_n/ ... /X_{k+1}/(X_k \cup Y_k)/X_{k-1}/ ... /X_1$, hence RS is in 2^+NF. $\square$

This corollary tells us that 2^+NF persists under the Merge operation.

Corollary 3.8.7 Let $RS \Rightarrow RS_1 \cup RS_2$. Although RS is in 2^+NF, neither RS_1 nor RS_2 need be in 2^+NF.

Proof: Suppose $RS = \{X_1, X_2, X_3\}$, $X_3/X_2/X_1$ and $X_2 = X_2' \cup X_2''$. Then $RS_1 = \{X_1, X_2', X_3\}$ and $RS_2 = \{X_1, X_2'', X_3\}$.
(1) If either $R(X_3) \subseteq R(X_2')$ or $R(X_2') \subseteq R(X_3)$, then we have: either $R(X_3) \subseteq R(X_2') \subseteq R(X_1)$ or $R(X_2') \subseteq R(X_3) \subseteq R(X_1)$ respectively. From Definition 3.8.6, we have: RS_1 is in 2^+NF.

(2) Otherwise if neither $R(X_3) \subseteq R(X_2')$ nor $R(X_2') \subseteq R(X_3)$, then neither X_2'/X_3 nor X_3/X_2'. Since / is a full ordering on the axes of RS_1, if RS_1 is 2^+NF then RS_1 is not in 2^+NF.

According to (1) and (2), RS_1 need not be in 2^+NF. For the same reason, RS_2 need not be in 2^+NF. □

Corollary 3.8.7 tells us that the 2^+NF does not persist under the Split operation. From Corollary 3.8.7 we have the next corollary.

Corollary 3.8.8 Let $RS \Rightarrow RS_1 \cup RS_2$, let RS be in 2^+NF, and let $RS = \{X_1, ..., X_{k-1}, X_k, X_{k+1}, ..., X_n\}$, $X_n/X_{n-1}/.../X_2/X_1$, $X_k = X_k' \cup X_k''$, $RS_1 = \{X_1, ..., X_{k-1}, X_k', X_{k+1}, ..., X_n\}$, and $RS_2 = \{X_1, ..., X_{k-1}, X_k'', X_{k+1}, ..., X_n\}$, if $X_{k+1}/X_k'/X_{k-1}$, then RS_1 is in 2^+NF, and if $X_{k+1}/X_k''/X_{k-1}$, then RS_2 is in 2^+NF.

From these three corollaries, we have the following:

Corollary 3.8.9 For two spaces RS_1 and RS_2, let $RS_1 \cup RS_2 \Rightarrow RS$. Although neither RS_1 nor RS_2 is in 2^+NF, RS could be.

Corollary 3.8.10 Let $RS \Rightarrow RS_1 \cup RS_2$. Although RS is not in 2^+NF, either RS_1 or RS_2 or both could be.

The 2^+NF is the weakened form of the 3NF. We can also define a strengthened form of the 3NF as follows:

Definition 3.8.7 A space $RS(X_1, X_2, ..., X_n)$ is 4NF if it is a 3NF, and for any point $p(x_1, x_2, ..., x_n) \in RS$, $R(p(x_1, x_2, ..., x_n)) = R(x_1) \cap R(x_2) \cap ... \cap R(x_n) \neq \Phi$.

Because a 4NF space is also in a space 3NF, it has the same properties as 3NF in a space under resource space operations.

3.8.3 *Topological properties of resource spaces*

If we define a distance between two points in an n dimensional space $RS(X_1, X_2, ..., X_n)$, then the distance can be used to define a topological space. We focus on the 2NF space, and first define a distance d on axis X_i, $1 \le i \le n$, then construct from d a distance D on the whole space RS.

For a given set G, if there exists a function $d: G \times G \rightarrow \Re^+$, where $\Re^+$ represents the set of non-negative real numbers, then d is called a distance on G if it satisfies the following three axioms:

Axiom 1. $d(g_1, g_2) = 0 \Leftrightarrow g_1 = g_2$.
Axiom 2. $d(g_1, g_2) = d(g_2, g_1)$.
Axiom 3. $d(g_1, g_2) \le d(g_1, g_3) + d(g_3, g_2)$, for any g_1, g_2 and $g_3 \in G$.

For an axis $X = \{C_1, C_2, ..., C_n\}$, where coordinate $C_i = <V_i, E_i>$, we define the function d on X as follows.

Definition 3.8.8 For points x_1 and x_2 on axis X,
$d(x_1, x_2) =$

$$
\begin{cases}
0, & \text{if } x_1 = x_2. \\
\infty, & \text{if } x_1 \in V_i, x_2 \in V_j \text{ and } i \ne j. \\
\min\{length(\Gamma) \mid \Gamma = (x_1, x_1', \cdots, x_m', x_2)\} & \text{if } x_1 \text{ and } x_2 \in V_i, \text{ and } x_1 \ne x_2.
\end{cases}
$$

where $<x_1, x_1'>, <x_j', x_{j+1}'>, <x_m', x_2> \in E_i, 1 \le j \le m-1$, $length(\Gamma)$ is the length of the path Γ with a weight on each link. And we make a reasonable assumption: if x_1 and $x_2 \in V_i$ and $x_1 \ne x_2$, there is a path $\Gamma = (x_1, x_1', ..., x_k', x_2)$ from x_1 to x_2. So $d(x_1, x_2) < length(\Gamma) < \infty$.

Theorem 3.8.3 d is a distance on axis X.

In the following, we first give the definition of function D on RS, and then prove that it is a distance on RS.

Definition 3.8.9 For any two points $p_1(x_1, x_2, ..., x_n)$ and $p_2(y_1, y_2, ..., y_n)$ in the space $RS(X_1, X_2, ..., X_n)$, we define

$D(p_1, p_2) = (\sum_{i=1}^{n} d^2(x_i, y_i))^{\frac{1}{2}}$, where d is the distance on axis X_i, $1 \le i \le n$.

Theorem 3.8.4 D is a distance on RS.

So the space $RS(X_1, X_2, ..., X_n)$ is a metric space (RS, D) with distance D. The distance D in RS defines a discrete topological space (RS, ρ). The following section discusses the properties of the topological space (RS, ρ).

According to the definition of distance d, we have $d(x_1, x_2) < \infty \Leftrightarrow x_1$ and x_2 belong to the same coordinate hierarchy.

Definition 3.8.10 For two points $p_1(x_1, x_2, ..., x_n)$ and $p_2(y_1, y_2, ..., y_n)$ in the resource space RS, p_1 is said to be linked to p_2 if $D(p_1, p_2) < \infty$. For a set of points P in RS, P is called a linked branch if for any two points p_i and p_j in P $(i \ne j)$, p_i is linked to p_j.

From Definition 3.8.10 comes the following corollary.

Corollary 3.8.11 In a space $RS(X_1, X_2, ..., X_n)$, if a set of points P constitutes a linked branch, then for any two points $p_1(x_1, x_2, ..., x_n)$ and $p_2(y_1, y_2, ..., y_n)$ in P, x_i and y_i $(1 \le i \le n)$ belong to the same coordinate hierarchy.

Proof: If P is a linked branch, then for any two points $p_1(x_1, x_2, ..., x_n)$ and $p_2(y_1, y_2, ..., y_n)$ in P, $D(p_1, p_2) < \infty$. Since

$$D(p_1, p_2) = (\sum_{i=1}^{n} d^2(x_i, y_i))^{\frac{1}{2}},$$

we can get $d(x_i, y_i) < \infty$, $1 \le i \le n$. Hence, x_i and y_i belong to the same coordinate hierarchy. $\square$

Corollary 3.8.11 tells us that if two points in a space are linked to each other, then their corresponding coordinates belong to the same coordinate hierarchy.

It is obvious that the connective relation (denoted by ~) is an equivalent relation on the topological space *RS*. So *RS/~* is a quotient space of *RS*. The next corollary describes the structure of the quotient space *RS/~*.

Corollary 3.8.12 The quotient space $RS/\sim = \{\; p^{'}(C_{i1}^{1}, C_{i2}^{2}, \cdots, C_{in}^{n}) \mid C_{ik}^{k}$ is a root coordinate on axis X_k in $RS(X_1, X_2, ..., X_n)$, $1 \le k \le n\}$, where $p'(x_1, x_2, ..., x_n)$ in *RS/~* is the linked branch including point $p(x_1, x_2, ..., x_n)$ in *RS*.

Proof: (1) It is clear that any point $p^{'}(C_{i1}^{1}, C_{i2}^{2}, \cdots, C_{in}^{n})$ is in *RS/~*. So $RS/\sim \supseteq \{\; p^{'}(C_{i1}^{1}, C_{i2}^{2}, \cdots, C_{in}^{n}) \mid C_{ik}^{k}$ is a root coordinate on axis X_k in $RS\}$.

(2) For any point $p(x_1, x_2, ..., x_n)$ in $RS(X_1, X_2, ..., X_n)$, from Corollary 3.8.11, we get that there exists a root coordinate C_{i1}^{1} on axis $X_1, ...,$ and C_{in}^{n} on axis X_n, such that x_1 is in $C_{i1}^{1}, ...,$ and x_n is in C_{in}^{n}. So $p(x_1, x_2, ..., x_n)$ is in the linked branch of $p^{'}(C_{i1}^{1}, C_{i2}^{2}, \cdots, C_{in}^{n})$, which means $p^{'}(x_1, x_2, \cdots, x_n) = p^{'}(C_{i1}^{1}, C_{i2}^{2}, \cdots, C_{in}^{n})$. Then we have $RS/\sim \subseteq \{\; p^{'}(C_{i1}^{1}, C_{i2}^{2}, \cdots, C_{in}^{n}) \mid C_{ik}^{k}$ is a root coordinate on axis X_k in $RS\}$.

From (1) and (2), $RS/\sim = \{\; p^{'}(C_{i1}^{1}, C_{i2}^{2}, \cdots, C_{in}^{n}) \mid C_{ik}^{k}$ is a root coordinate on axis X_k in $RS(X_1, X_2, ..., X_n)$, $1 \le k \le n\}$. $\square$

In the quotient space *RS/~*, we can define a distance $D_\sim$ on *RS/~* as induced from the distance D on *RS*. $D_\sim(p_1', p_2') = min \{D(p_1, p_2) \mid p_1 \in p_1'$ and $p_2 \in p_2'\}$, where p_1' and p_2' represent the linked branches including p_1 and p_2 respectively. Then for any $p_1', p_2' \in RS/\sim$, $p_1' \ne p_2'$, $D_\sim(p_1', p_2') = \infty$, $D_\sim(p_1', p_1') = 0$, which means that *RS/~* is a discrete topological space with the distance $D_\sim$ on it.

The resource space *RS* enables us to locate resources by coordinates. The quotient space *RS/~* enables us to search in a more abstract space.

Theorem 3.8.5 A point exists in *RS* if and only if it belongs to a point of *RS/~*.

Proof: (1) For a $p(x_1, x_2, \ldots, x_n)$ in *RS*, from Corollary 3.8.12, there exists $p'(C_{i1}^1, C_{i2}^2, \cdots, C_{in}^n)$ in *RS/~* such that $p(x_1, x_2, \ldots, x_n)$ is in the linked branch of $p'(C_{i1}^1, C_{i2}^2, \cdots, C_{in}^n)$. So $p(x_1, x_2, \ldots, x_n)$ belongs to a point of *RS/~*.

(2) Suppose $p(x_1, x_2, \ldots, x_n)$ belongs to a point $p'(x_1, x_2, \ldots, x_n)$ in *RS/~*. From Corollary 3.8.12, all the points in the linked branch $p'(x_1, x_2, \ldots, x_n)$ are in *RS*, so $p(x_1, x_2, \ldots, x_n)$ exists in *RS*.

From (1) and (2), we can infer that a point is in *RS* if and only if it also belongs to a point in *RS/~*. □

This theorem provides a top-down refinement search strategy for a large-scale space: from the quotient space down to the resource space. It also ensures that all resources in space *RS* can be found through *RS/~*.

3.9 Integrity Constraints for the Resource Space Model

The integrity constraints for the RSM are of four kinds: *entity*, *membership*, *referential* and *user-defined*. These work together so that the RSM can correctly and efficiently specify and manage resources.

3.9.1 Entity integrity constraints

In relational databases, keys play a fundamental role in the data model and in conceptual design. They enable tuples to refer to one another and ensure that operations can accurately locate tuples.

As a coordinate system, naturally the RSM supports precise resource location. However, it is not always necessary to have the user painstakingly specify all the coordinates of a point, especially when a axis is added. The RSM needs better resource location.

Definition 3.9.1. Let $p \cdot X_i$ be the coordinate of p at axis X_i in $RS(X_1, X_2, \ldots, X_n)$, that is, the projection of p on X_i. If $p_1 \cdot X_i = p_2 \cdot X_i$ for $1 \leq i \leq n$, then we say that p_1 is equal to p_2, denoted by $p_1 =_p p_2$.

Using this definition, a *candidate key* of the RSM can be defined as follows.

Definition 3.9.2. Let CK be a subset of $(X_1, X_2, ..., X_n)$, and let p_1 and p_2 be two non-null points in $RS(X_1, X_2, ..., X_n)$. CK is called a candidate key of RS if we can derive $p_1 =_p p_2$ from $p_1 \cdot X_i = p_2 \cdot X_i$, $X_i \in CK$.

A candidate key is specific enough to identify non-null points of a given space.

The *primary key* is a candidate key specified by the designer of the space. The axes of the primary key are called *primary axes*.

Point constraint. If axis X is a primary axis of the space RS, then no X coordinate of any point in RS should be null.

This constraint is used to ensure that primary keys can distinguish non-null points in a given space. One type of null value is "at present unknown".

In the RSM one can infer some keys from the presence of others. This is of great importance in query optimization, especially when creating new spaces. Inference rules for candidate keys come from the following four theorems.

Theorem 3.9.1. If a set of axes CK is a candidate key of the space RS, then any axis set that includes CK is also a candidate key of RS.

From the definition of Join we have the following theorem.

Theorem 3.9.2. Let RS_1 and RS_2 be two spaces which can be joined to produce a new space RS. If CK_1 and CK_2 are candidate keys of RS_1 and RS_2 respectively. then $CK = CK_1 \cup CK_2$ is a candidate key of RS.

From the definition of Merge we have the following theorem.

Theorem 3.9.3. Let RS_1 and RS_2 be two spaces that can be merged into one space RS. Let X_1 and X_2 be two different axes of RS_1 and RS_2 respectively, and let $X_c = X_1 \cup X_2$. If CK_1 and CK_2 are candidate keys of RS_1 and RS_2 respectively, then $CK = (CK_1 - \{X_1\}) \cup (CK_2 - \{X_2\}) \cup \{X_c\}$ is a candidate key of RS.

From the definition of Split we have the following theorem.

Theorem 3.9.4. Let RS_1 and RS_2 be two spaces created by splitting the space RS. Suppose that the axis X_c of RS is split into X_1 and X_2 belonging to RS_1 and RS_2 respectively. Let CK be a candidate key of RS. If $X_c \notin CK$, let $CK_1 = CK_2 = CK$, otherwise let $CK_1 = CK - \{X_c\} \cup \{X_1\}$ and $CK_2 = CK - \{X_c\} \cup \{X_2\}$. Then CK_1 and CK_2 are candidate keys of RS_1 and RS_2 respectively.

Proof. Let A be the set of all axes of RS and A_1 be the set of all axes of RS_1. Assuming that CK_1 is not a candidate key of RS_1, there must be two non-null points p_1 and p_2 in RS_1 which satisfy both $(\forall X \in CK_1) (p_1 \cdot X = p_2 \cdot X)$ and $(\exists X^* \in A_1) (p_1 \cdot X^* \neq p_2 \cdot X^*)$. Let p_1' and p_2' in RS have the same coordinate values as p_1 and p_2 respectively. Clearly $(\forall X \in CK)$ $(p_1' \cdot X = p_2' \cdot X)$ if $CK_1 = CK$ or $CK_1 = CK - \{X_c\} \cup \{X_1\}$.
(1) When $CK_1 = CK$, if $X^* \neq X_1$, then $p_1' \cdot X^* \neq p_2' \cdot X^*$, otherwise $p_1' \cdot X_c \neq p_2' \cdot X_c$;
(2) When $CK_1 = CK - \{X_c\} \cup \{X_1\}$, then $X^* \neq X_1$. So $p_1' \cdot X^* \neq p_2' \cdot X^*$.
From (1) and (2), $p_1' \neq_p p_2'$. Clearly this conclusion contradicts the assumption that CK is a candidate key of RS. So CK_1 is a candidate key of RS_1. Similarly, we can prove that CK_2 is a candidate key of RS_2.

In resource space systems, there are often spaces created by join, merge and split operations. Theorems 3.9.2, 3.9.3 and 3.9.4 provide an efficient means of deriving candidate keys of these spaces.

In the RSM, a resource entry denoted by a 3-tuple *Resource-Entry <ID, Index, Semantic-Description>* is used to index into a resource representation layer. The *ID* field is used to specify the entries at a given point. Two entries at different points could have the same *ID*. The *Index* field is the index data linked to the representation layer. To facilitate semantic operations, the *Semantic-Description* uses a set of attributes to reflect the simple semantics of the resource in the given space. The resource representation layer describes the detailed semantics of all resources. In the following discussion, $re \cdot ID$, $re \cdot index$ and $re \cdot SD$ denote the *ID*, *index* and *Semantic-Description* of entry *re* respectively.

Resource entry constraint 1. No ID should be null, and for any two entries re_1 and re_2 at the same non-null point, $re_1 \cdot ID \neq re_2 \cdot ID$.

This constraint requires that all entries in a given non-null point should have distinct *ID*s. This ensures that any operation can precisely locate its target entry.

Resource entry constraint 2. No index of an entry should be null, and for any two entries re_1 and re_2 at the same non-null point, $re_1 \cdot index \neq re_2 \cdot index$.

This constraint requires that:
(1) every entry should include index data linking to the representation layer, and
(2) no two entries at the same non-null point should have the same index data.

Otherwise, it will lead to information redundancy and unnecessary maintenance of consistency between resource entries at the same point.

The syntactic structure of the index data of entries depends on the implementation of the representation layer. For instance, an XML-based implementation of a representation layer commonly uses XPath expressions, whereas filenames are often used for file-based implementations.

To analyze the index of a resource entry, not only the syntactic structure but also the semantics should be considered. For example, an absolute path differs from a relative path syntactically. However, these two types of paths may indicate the same data.

Resource entry constraint 3. The semantic description *SD* of any entry should not be null, and no two entries re_1 and re_2 at the same non-null point should be the same or imply each other, that is, neither $re_1 \cdot SD \Rightarrow re_2 \cdot SD$ nor $re_2 \cdot SD \Rightarrow re_1 \cdot SD$.

This is the entity integrity constraint for the *Semantic-Description* of an entry. It is optional but stricter than constraint 2. Since an $re \cdot SD$ embodies the semantic existence of an entry in a resource space, clearly $re \cdot SD$ should not be null. Furthermore, entries at a given non-null point should neither be the same nor imply each other in semantics. For example, a resource and its copies are allowed to coexist at a non-null point by constraint 2, but not by constraint 3.

3.9.2 The membership integrity constraint

In relational databases, a tuple can be inserted into a table only if all fields of the tuple satisfy the domain constraints of the table. So the relationship between the tuple and the table should be checked before insertion. In the RSM, a resource space holds the semantic classification of its resources. The existence of entry *re* at point *p* means that the resource indexed by *re* belongs to the type represented by *p*. An entry can be placed at a point by the following operation:

PLACE *re* <*ID, Index, Semantic-Description*> **AT** *p* ($C_{1,i1}, C_{2,i2}, ..., C_{n,in}$).

If there were no restrictions, an entry could be placed at any point of the space. So, checking the memberships of resource entries plays an important role in the RSM.

$R_\Delta(RS)$, $R_\Delta(C)$ and $R_\Delta(p)$ denote the sets of resources currently stored by space RS, coordinate C and point p respectively. For any entry re, if re has been placed at the point p, then $re \in R_\Delta(p)$.

Membership constraint. Let $re <ID, Index, Semantic\text{-}Description>$ be a resource entry. For any point $p(C_{1,i1}, C_{2,i2}, ..., C_{n,in})$ in a given space, $re \in R_\Delta(p) \rightarrow re \in R(p)$.

An entry re can be placed at point p only if re belongs to the type that p represents. Constraining membership in this way can ensure correct resource classification. When a place or update operation is applied to an entry, this constraint should be checked.

3.9.3 Referential integrity constraints

In relational databases, it is often required that a value that appears in one relation for one set of attributes should also appear for another set of attributes in another relation. This condition is called a referential integrity constraint.

In the following discussion, three types of referential integrity constraints for the RSM are considered.

In the RSM, the basic function of an entry is to index a resource in the representation layer. For any entry $re <ID, index, Semantic\text{-}Description>$, $re \cdot index$ is the index of the resource. Resource entry constraint 2 ensures that $re \cdot index$ is non-null. But it cannot ensure that $re \cdot index$ makes sense. This is mainly because modifications to entries or representation layers may cause the indices of entries to become dead links. The first referential integrity constraint is intended to eliminate dead links

Referential constraint 1. For every entry re in a resource space system, there exists a resource in the representation layer which is referred to by its index ($re \cdot index$).

The resource space layer refers to the representation layer. The above constraint ensures that $re \cdot index$ makes sense for any entry re. This constraint should be checked when an re is placed or an $re \cdot index$ updated.

When changes take place in a representation layer, this integrity should also be satisfied. The layer can be viewed as a Semantic Link Network (SLN). An SLN consists of semantic nodes and semantic links. A semantic node can be an atomic node (a piece of text or image) or complex node (another SLN). For most applications, the domain is a subset of the whole resource representation layer. This subset SLN is denoted by SLN^*.

In the resource representation layer, any resource denoted by a 3-tuple *Resource* (*ID, Semantic-Description, Resource-Entry-List*) can be regarded as a semantic node. The *ID* is the identifier of a resource in a given SLN^*. It is helpful for locating the target resource. The *Semantic-Description* is the detailed semantic description of a resource, used to facilitate semantic operations. The *Semantic-Description* of a resource can be represented by an SLN. There may exist many indices (resource entries) in the resource space layer to a resource in the representation layer. The *Resource-Entry-List* of a resource is used to record all entries indexing this resource.

For any entry, an item of the *Resource-Entry-List* should include the name of its space, the coordinate of its point, and its *ID*. So, from the *Resource-Entry-List*, all corresponding entries can be obtained. In the following $res \cdot ID$, $res \cdot SD$ and $res \cdot REL$ denote the *ID, Semantic-Description* and *Resource-Entry-List* of resource *res* respectively.

There exists a variety of relations between resources. The following discussion is about the relations of similarity and inclusion. Two functions, *Similarity* and *Inclusion,* are introduced to evaluate the similarity and inclusion between resources. *Similarity* (res_1, res_2) returns a real number between 0 and 1 giving the similarity between resources res_1 and res_2. *Inclusion* (res_1, res_2) returns a real number between 0 and 1 giving the degree of inclusion of resource res_2 in resource res_1.

For a given threshold value δ, if *Similarity* (res_1, res_2) $\geq \delta$, then resources res_1 and res_2 are regarded as equal. And, if *Inclusion* (res_1, res_2) $\geq \delta$, then res_2 is viewed as a subset of res_1. Both equality and inclusion between resources lead to semantic redundancy and unnecessary maintenance of consistency between resources in a given SLN*. To eliminate this redundancy, the following constraint is introduced.

Resource redundancy constraint. Let res_1 and res_2 be two resources in the SLN*. For a given threshold value δ, both *Similarity* $(res_1, res_2) < \delta$ and *Inclusion* $(res_1, res_2) < \delta$.

Before placing a resource in the SLN* or after updating a resource, this constraint should be checked. In case of placement, if the above constraint has been violated, the operation will be canceled. But suppose resource res_1 is to be updated to res_1'. If there already exists a resource res_2 such that either *Similarity* $(res_1', res_2) \geq \delta$ or *Inclusion* $(res_1', res_2) \geq \delta$, the alternative actions are:

(1) the update operation is canceled, or
(2) after the update of res_1, resource res_2 is deleted.

If the second action is taken, the alternative actions are:

(1) all resource entries indicated by $res_2 \cdot REL$ are deleted, or
(2) all resource entries indicated by $res_2 \cdot REL$ are redirected to res_1'.

Thus, dead links in the space layer will be avoided after the changes take place in the representation layer.

The first referential integrity constraint specifically between resource spaces relates to the join operation.

Referential constraint 2. If RS_1, RS_2 and RS are three spaces that satisfy $RS_1 \cdot RS_2 \Rightarrow RS$, then $R_\Delta(RS) \subseteq R_\Delta(RS_1) \cup R_\Delta(RS_2)$.

RS is derived from RS_1 and RS_2, and this referential constraint maintains the dependency of RS on RS_1 and RS_2. Thus, when an entry is placed in RS or removed from RS_1 or RS_2, this constraint should be checked.

The second type of referential integrity constraint applies to 3NF spaces. We first define the *foreign* key of the RSM.

Definition 3.9.3. Let S be a subset of axes of the space RS_1, but not the primary key of RS_1. If there exists another space RS_2 such that $R(RS_1) = R(RS_2)$ and S is the primary key of RS_2, then S is called the foreign key of RS_1, RS_1 is called the referencing space of RS_2 and RS_2 is called the referenced space of RS_1.

From this definition, we have the following theorem.

Theorem 3.9.5. Let $S = \{X_1, X_2, ..., X_m\}$ be the foreign key of the referencing space $RS_1(X_1, X_2, ..., X_m, X_{m+1}, ..., X_n)$, and $RS_2(X_1, X_2, ..., X_m, Y_{m+1}, ..., Y_t)$ be the corresponding referenced space. For two non-null points $p(C_1, C_2, ..., C_m, C_{m+1}, ..., C_n)$ and $p'(C_1, C_2, ..., C_m, C'_{m+1}, ..., C'_t)$ in RS_1 and RS_2 respectively, $R(p) \subseteq R(p')$.

This theorem indicates the inclusion relationship between points in the referencing space and their counterparts in the referenced space. The next constraint aims to maintain the legal referential relationship between the referencing space and its referenced space.

Referential constraint 3. Let $S = \{X_1, X_2, ..., X_m\}$ be the foreign key of the referencing space $RS_1(X_1, X_2, ..., X_m, X_{m+1}, ..., X_n)$, and $RS_2(X_1, X_2, ..., X_m, Y_{m+1}, ..., Y_t)$ be the corresponding referenced space. For two non-null points $p(C_1, C_2, ..., C_m, C_{m+1}, ..., C_n)$ and $p'(C_1, C_2, ..., C_m, C'_{m+1}, ..., C'_t)$ in RS_1 and RS_2 respectively, $R_\Delta(p) \subseteq R_\Delta(p')$.

This constraint ensures that if an entry *re* appears at a certain point p in the referencing space, then *re* must exist as the counterpart of p in the referenced space.

3.9.4 User-defined integrity constraints

Any resource space system should conform to the entity, membership and referential integrity constraints. In specific applications, different space systems should obey certain context-relevant constraints. These constraints are called user-defined integrity constraints. This section introduces three frequently used types of user-defined constraints. Two spaces shown in Fig. 3.1 are used to illustrate these constraints.

In Fig. 3.1 (a), the resource space *Salary-Post* is used to hold data about employees. Every point classifies these employees by their salary and post. In Fig. 3.1 (b), *Keeper-Warehouse* is used to hold data about goods. Each point of *Keeper-Warehouse* classifies these goods by their keeper and warehouse.

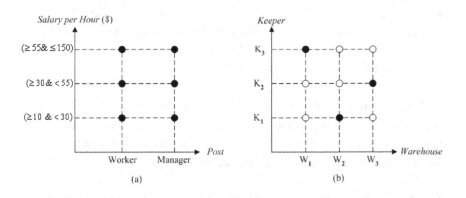

Fig. 3.1 Examples of bidimensional resource spaces.

User-defined constraints require the attribute values in the resource description to satisfy some rules. The function *GetAttribute* (*re, attr*) returns the value of attribute *attr* specified in the *Semantic-Description* of the entry *re*. The Boolean function *JudgeRelation* (*operand$_1$, operand$_2$, relational-operator*) judges whether *operand$_1$* and *operand$_2$* satisfy the relation specified by *relational-operator*. This constraint can be described as follows:

<Constraint expression> ::=
   JudgeRelation(*GetAttribute*(*re, attr*), user-defined-constant-value,
   <Relational-Op>) |
   <Constraint expression> ∨ <Constraint expression> |
   <Constraint expression> ∧ <Constraint expression> |
   ¬<Constraint expression>;
   <Relational-Op> ::= < | > | = | ≤ | ≥ |≠.

Take Fig.3.1(a) for example. If the resource space designer requires of *Salary-Post* that the salary per hour of any worker should not be lower than \$12 and that the salary per hour of any manager should not be lower than \$50, then this user-defined constraint for entry *re* is:

(*JudgeRelation* (*GetAttribute* (*re, post*), "worker", =)
   ∧ *JudgeRelation* (*GetAttribute* (*re, salary per hour*), 12, ≥)) ∨ (
   JudgeRelation (*GetAttribute* (*re, post*), "manager", =)
   ∧*JudgeRelation* (*GetAttribute* (*re, salary per hour*), 50, ≥)).

Before the entry *re* can be placed in *Salary-Post* or updated, the system should check whether the above constraint has been violated.

In some applications, rich semantic relations among entries should be taken into consideration. Operations on an entry may require other operations on semantically relevant entries. This type of user-defined constraint is called a resource-entry-based constraint. For example, suppose *RS* is a space holding all the registration data about students of a school and *RS'* is another holding all the health data of the same students. Let *re* be the entry holding a particular student's registration data and *re'* be the entry holding his/her health data. The health data depend on the validity of the registration data, that is, $re' \in R_\Delta(RS') \rightarrow re \in R_\Delta(RS)$. So this constraint should be checked before *re'* is placed or after *re* is deleted.

As resource sets, points are often required to satisfy some application relevant rules from the viewpoint of set theory. Take Fig. 3.1 (b) for example. Suppose that a warehouse could have only one keeper in *Keeper-Warehouse* and that each keeper is in charge of only one warehouse.

For any K_i, there exists at most one W_j such that $R_\Delta(p(K_i, W_j)) \neq \varnothing$, and for any W_m there exists at most one K_n such that $R_\Delta(p(K_n, W_m)) \neq \varnothing$. We define the following function:

$$NotNull(p) = \begin{cases} 1, & R_\Delta(p) \neq \varnothing \\ 0, & R_\Delta(p) = \varnothing \end{cases}$$

And, use p_{ij} to denote the point $p(K_i, W_j)$. Then, the formal description of this constraint is:

$$\forall i (\sum_{j=1}^{3} NotNull(p_{ij}) \leq 1) \ \wedge \ \forall j (\sum_{i=1}^{3} NotNull(p_{ij}) \leq 1).$$

Thus, before any goods can be placed in *Keeper-Warehouse*, the system must check whether the above constraint is violated or not.

The effectiveness of resource use also depends on the users' beliefs about resource classification and the semantic relationships between resources. Further discussion can be found in "Fuzzy Resource Space Model and Platform" (H. Zhuge, *Journal of Systems and Software*, vol.73, no.3, pp.389-396).

Chapter 4

The Single Semantic Image

A major goal for the future interconnection environment is to use semantics to accurately obtain and effectively share and manage resources. The *single semantic image* (SSeI) is a crucial step towards this goal, in describing and using various resources as being in a single semantic space. People can access resources on-demand only through a single semantic entry point. This chapter introduces the SSeI approach, the *SSeI query language,* SSeIQL (pronounced *say-quill*), the semantic browser and the semantic view, and shows how they can be used to effectively organize, share, and manage globally distributed resources at the semantic level in a peer-to-peer environment.

4.1 Combining the SLN and the Resource Space Model

A Resource Space Model (RSM) organizes versatile Web resources according to orthogonal classification semantics and relevant normal forms. A set of coordinates of the space can uniquely determine one or a set of resources. The SLN model organizes Web resources by using semantic links and relevant normal forms. The semantic relationship between resources can be derived from the semantic links between the resources.

The combination of RSM and SLN forms a rich semantic layer for the future Web, which has the advantage of both classification and reasoning. A solution is to map resources in the RSM to resources in the SLN. Users can first limit the scope of interest by locating a category in the RSM and then browsing the SLN within the scope of the category.

The integration of RSM and SLN establishes a kind of map of the future Web, a Knowledge Web as shown in Fig. 4.1. Its purpose is different from knowledge portals that only provide knowledge services.

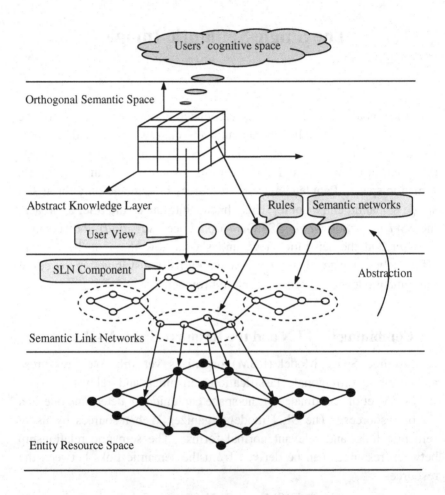

Fig. 4.1 Semantic spaces of multiple layers.

Users make and use the orthogonal semantic space and the semantic link network according to their cognitive spaces. The orthogonal semantic space can help users focus their intention. The SLN reflects the explicit and tacit semantic relationships between a variety of resources.

The normalization theories of RSM and SLN support a single semantic point for accessing relevant semantic content. Ordinary knowledge portals cannot easily do this.

Abstract knowledge like a traditional semantic network and its rule base can be derived from the SLN by generalization, can be organized according to the orthogonal semantics in the top level space, and can thus enable the future Web to support intelligent services.

4.2 The SSeI Mechanism

The notion of the *single semantic image* is best understood in the light of related concepts in database systems. At the heart of a database system is a collection of tables. Views of those tables are "virtual relations" defined by query expressions (J.D. Ullman, "Principles of Database and Knowledge-Base Systems", *Computer Science Press, Inc.*, 1988). The viewing mechanism has the following advantages.

(1)   Only relevant data are collected from different tables.
(2)   Interaction between users and database systems is simplified.
(3)   Different users of a database can get different views of it.
(4)   Data independence is supported.
(5)   Security can be more easily enforced.

However, this viewing mechanism can only be applied to formal relational tables, and is not suitable for unstructured or semi-structured Web resources. Also, only someone who knows the structure of a database can create a new view of it. This limits the scope of the viewing mechanism.

The SSeI mechanism combines orthogonal semantic classification and semantic linking by mapping between resources. *An SSeI is dynamically formed according to users' requirements.* Fig.4.2 shows the mechanism's general architecture. The entity resources are various kinds of data files with names in the name space. The representation layer is the description of the structure of the entity resources.

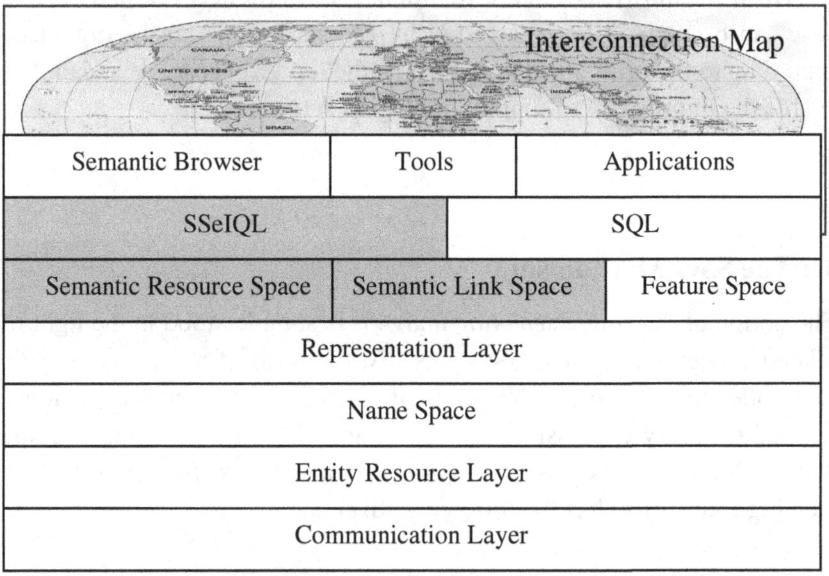

Interconnection Map		
Semantic Browser	Tools	Applications
SSeIQL		SQL
Semantic Resource Space	Semantic Link Space	Feature Space
Representation Layer		
Name Space		
Entity Resource Layer		
Communication Layer		

Fig. 4.2 General architecture of the SSeI mechanism.

Resources can be operated on uniformly at the SSeI level. We can use the following form to express the semantics of both the orthogonal classification and the semantic linkage:

$$P(C_1, C_2, C_3) \overset{\alpha_1}{\longrightarrow} Q(C_1', C_2', C_3')$$

where (C_1, C_2, C_3) and (C_1', C_2', C_3') are coordinates that accurately locate P and Q in a three-dimensional orthogonal semantic space, and α_1 denotes the semantic relationship linking P and Q.

Formally, the SSeI mechanism under the Resource Space Model and the Semantic Link Network is an algebra system: $<SSeI, RSM, SLN>$. For any two resources r_1 and r_2 in SSeI, if $<r_1, r_2> \in RSM$, then $<r_1, r_2> \in SSeI$; and if $<r_1, r_2> \in SLN$, then $<r_1, r_2> \in SSeI$.

An SSeI mechanism supports multiple SSeIs, which can be reorganized by operations like Join, Merge and Split. The formation of the classification semantic space and the formation of the semantic linkage space are two aspects or phases of constructing the unified semantic space. Operaitons on the resource space and the semantic linkage space can be defined and used separately.

4.3 The Single Semantic Image Query Language

The SSeI query language (SSeIQL) is a language in which a user describes which data are to be retrieved from where. SSeIQL can select one or more resource spaces, semantic link spaces, and entity spaces, and can define and modify the structure of the resource spaces.

SSeIQL includes the following components and capabilities:

(1) *Resource Space Definition Language.* The RSDL provides commands for defining and modifying the structure of resource spaces, and for deleting resource spaces.
(2) *Resource Space Manipulation Language.* The RSML provides commands for combining and separating resource spaces.
(3) *Resource Manipulation Language.* The RML provides commands for adding resources to, and removing them from, resource spaces, and for modifying mapping within resource spaces.
(4) *Semantic Link Space Definition Language.* The SLSDL provides commands for defining the semantic relationships between resources in a resource space or between resource spaces.
(5) *View Definition.* SSeIQL includes commands for defining views to map resources in resource or semantic link spaces into resources in entity spaces.
(6) *Authorization.* SSeIQL includes controls for specifying privileges

for access to resources and views.

(7) *Integrity Constraints.* SSeIQL includes controls for specifying constraints to preserve the integrity of resources in resource spaces, semantic link spaces and entity spaces. Updates that violate such integrity constraints will be blocked.

The syntax and semantics of SSeIQL are like those of SQL. A SSeIQL *query* has three clauses:

(1) The **SELECT** clause lists the resource attributes required in the answer.
(2) The **FROM** <*RS* (X_1, X_2, ..., X_m)> clause specifies the orthogonal semantic resource spaces to be used in the selection, where X_i is an axis of the space *RS*.
(3) The **WHERE** <*conditional expression*> clause conditions the answer in terms of coordinates of resources and semantic relationships required between the coordinates.

A typical SSeIQL query has the following form:

> **SELECT** $A_1, A_2, ..., A_n$
> **FROM** $R_1, R_2, ... , R_m$
> **WHERE** <*conditional expression*>

Each A_i names an attribute, and each R_i names a resource space. A **SELECT** * clause specifies that all attributes of all resources appearing in the **FROM** clause are to be selected. SSeIQL uses the compound name *resource_space . attribute* to avoid ambiguity when an attribute appears in more than one resource space. However if an attribute appears in only one of the resource spaces in the **FROM** clause, the *resource_space* qualifier can be omitted. The result of a SSeIQL query is called a *resource result set*.

The *ACM Computing Classification System* can be construed as a normalized three-dimensional information space: *ACM–CCS (Category, Publication, Letter)*. Consider the query "Find all journal papers in the resource space ACM–CCS which relate to *Semantic Web*". This query can be written in SSeIQL as follows:

SELECT * **FROM** *ACM–CCS*
WHERE *Category* = "Semantic Web" **&** *Publication* = "Journal"

The result is a resource set consisting of all journal papers satisfying the condition.

SSeIQL provides for the nesting of subqueries. A subquery is a **SELECT/FROM/WHERE** expression that is nested within another query.

A SSeIQL program is a composition of SSeIQL statements. Execution sequence within a SSeIQL program is specified as follows:

Sequential process:
    <SSeIQL statement>; {*<SSeIQL statement>*;}
Branch-statement:
    IF *<conditional expression>*
    THEN *<SSeIQL statement>*
    ELSE *<SSeIQL statement>*
    END IF;
Loop-statement:
    DO *<SSeIQL statement>*
    WHILE *<conditional expression>*;
Begin-End-statement:
    {*Sequential-process*}

4.4 SSeIQL Syntax Specification

4.4.1 *Syntax for resource space definition*

SSeIQL's RSDL provides commands to specify and modify resource spaces, in particular the schema and axes for each resource space, the coordinates associated with each axis, and the integrity constraints.

We define a resource space using the following **CREATE** command:

> **CREATE RSPACE** $RS (X_1, X_2, ..., X_n)$ [**AT** *URSL*]
> **WHERE** $X_1 = \{C_{11}, ..., C_{1u}\}, ..., X_n = \{C_{n1}, ..., C_{nv}\}$
>   *<integrity constraint$_1$>*
> ......
>   *<integrity constraint$_m$>*

where RS is the name of the resource space, each X_i is the name of an axis of RS, C_{ij} is the coordinate or coordinate hierarchy of axis X_i, and *URSL* is the location of the resource space. The integrity constraints are applied to the new resource space RS.

The **DROP** command deletes all data about its resource spaces. Not only is all resource mapping in RS deleted, but also the schemas for RS.

> **DROP RSPACE** RS

The **MODIFY** command is used on an existing resource space to add or drop axes or coordinates. In the case of adding, all resource mapping in the resource space assigns *null* as the value for the new axes or coordinates.

An axis can be added to a resource space by using the following command:

MODIFY RSPACE *RS*
ADD AXIS $axis_i <C_{i1}, ..., C_{ij}>$

where *RS* is the name of an existing resource space, $axis_i$ is the name of the axis to be added, and $<C_{i1}, ..., C_{ij}>$ is the coordinate list of the additional axis.

Coordinates can be added to an axis of a resource space by using the following command.

MODIFY RSPACE *RS*
ADD COORD $<C_u, ..., C_v>$ **TO** $axis_i$ [$<sup\_C_u,..., sup\_C_v>$]

where *RS* is the name of an existing resource space, $<C_u, ..., C_v>$ is the coordinate hierarchy to be added, $axis_i$ is the name of the axis it is to be added to, and $<sup\_C_u, ..., sup\_C_v>$ specifies the direct ancestor of each of $<C_u, ..., C_v>$. If $<sup\_C_u, ..., sup\_C_v>$ is omitted, then $<C_u, ..., C_v>$ will be appended to $axis_i$.

An axis can be dropped from a resource space by using the following command:

MODIFY RSPACE *RS*
DROP AXIS $axis_i$

where *RS* is the name of an existing resource space, $axis_i$ is the name of an axis of the resource space.

Coordinates can be dropped from an axis of a resource space by using the following command.

MODIFY RSPACE *RS*
DROP COORD $<C_u, ..., C_v>$
FROM $axis_i$ [$<sup\_C_u, ..., sup\_C_v>$]

where *RS* is the name of an existing resource space, $<C_u, ..., C_v>$ is the coordinate hierarchy to be dropped, $axis_i$ is the name of an axis of the resource space, and $<sup\_C_u, ..., sup\_C_v>$ is the direct ancestor of $<C_u, ..., C_v>$.

The axes of a resource space can be listed using the following command:

USING *RS* LIST AXES

where *RS* is the name of an existing resource space.

The coordinates of a given axis in a resource space can be listed using the following command:

USING *RS* LIST COORD OF *axis_i*

where *RS* is the name of an existing resource space, and $axis_i$ is an axis in *RS*.

4.4.2 *Multiple resource space manipulation*

Multiple semantic resource spaces can be manipulated using the following operations:

(1) The Merge operation

If two axes $X_1 = <C_{11}, C_{12}, ..., C_{1n}>$ and $X_2 = <C_{21}, C_{22}, ..., C_{2m}>$ have the same axis name but different coordinates, then they can be merged into one: $X = X_1 \cup X_2 = <C_{11}, C_{12}, ..., C_{1n}, C_{21}, C_{22}, ..., C_{2m}>$

The **MERGE** operation makes resource spaces $RS_1, ..., RS_n$ at $URSL_1, ..., URSL_n$ respectively into a single resource space *RS* and places the new resource space at *URSL* subject to any specified conditions. It can be written in SSeIQL as follows:

MERGE $RS_1, ..., RS_n$ [**AT** $URSL_1, ..., URSL_n$]
INTO RS [**AT** $URSL$]
WHERE $new\_axis\ (RS) = X_{1\mu}\ (RS_1)\ \&...\&\ X_{nv}\ (RS_n)$
CONSTRAINT $axis\_number$
    CHECK $|RS_1| = ... = |RS_n| = |RS|$
CONSTRAINT $common\_axis\_number$
    CHECK $number\ (common\_axes) = |RS| - 1$

where $|RS_i|$ is the number of axes of resource space RS_i and $X_i\ (RS_j)$ indicates axis X_i of resource space RS_j is to be merged. The **CONSTRAINT** clause specifies $common\_axis\_number$ as the constraint name. The predicate of the **CHECK** clause must be satisfied for the resource spaces to be merged.

(2) The Split operation

A resource space RS can be split into two resource spaces RS_1 and RS_2 that store the same type of resource as RS and have $|RS| - 1$ common axes by splitting an axis X into two: X' and X'', such that $X = X' \cup X''$.

The **SPLIT** operation splits a resource space RS at $URSL$ into each RS_i at each $URSL_i$. The axis X of RS will be split into $X_{1\alpha}\ (RS_1)$, ..., $X_{n\beta}(RS_n)$. We can write the SSeIQL **SPLIT** expression as follows:

SPLIT RS [**AT** $URSL$]
INTO $RS_1, ..., RS_n$ [**AT** $URSL_1, ..., URSL_n$]
WHERE $X\ (RS)$ **JOIN-INTO** $X_{1\alpha}\ (RS_1) = <coordinate\_set_1> \&\ ...$
    $\&\ X_{n\beta}\ (RS_n) = <coordinate\_set_n>$
CONSTRAINT $axis\_split$
CHECK $X\ (RS) = X_{1\alpha}\ (RS_1) \cup ... \cup X_{n\beta}\ (RS_n)$

The **CHECK** clause requires that no coordinate or axis be removed in the split operation.

(3) The Join operation

If two resource spaces RS_1 and RS_2 store the same type of resources and they have k ($k \in$ [1, minimum($|RS_1|$, $|RS_2|$))) common axes, then they can be joined together as one RS such that RS_1 and RS_2 share these k common axes and $|RS| = |RS_1| + |RS_2| - k$. RS is called the join of RS_1 and RS_2.

The **JOIN** operation can be written in SSeIQL as follows:

> **JOIN** $RS_1, ..., RS_n$ [**AT** $URSL_1, ..., URSL_n$]
> **INTO** RS [**AT** $URSL$]
> **WHERE COMMON AXES** $(axis_1, ..., axis_\mu)$
> **CONSTRAINT** common_axis_number
> **CHECK** number (common_axes) $\leq |RS| - 1$

(4) The Separate operation

A resource space RS can be separate into two resource spaces RS_1 and RS_2 that store the same type of resource as that of RS such that they have n ($1 \leq n \leq$ min ($|RS_1|$, $|RS_2|$)) common axes and $|RS| - n$ different axes, and $|RS| = |RS_1| + |RS_2| - n$.

The **SEPARATE** operation separates the resource space RS at $URSL$ into $RS_1, ..., RS_m$ at $URSL_1, ..., URSL_m$ respectively, subject to specified conditions. It can be written in SSeIQL as follows:

> **SEPARATE** RS [**AT** $URSL$]
> **INTO** RS_1 $(X_{11}, ..., X_{1\mu}), ..., RS_m$ $(X_{m1}, ..., X_{mv})$
> [**AT** $URSL_1, ..., URSL_m$]
> **WHERE COMMON AXES** $(axis_1, ..., axis_k)$
> **CONSTRAINT** axis_disjoin
> **CHECK** $X(RS) = X_{1\alpha}(RS_1) \cup ... \cup X_{m\beta}(RS_m)$

The constraint *axis_disjoin* requires that the operation should not remove any axis of the original resource space.

(5) The Union operation

If two resource spaces RS_1 and RS_2 store the same type of resources and have n ($n = |RS_1| = |RS_2|$) common axes, they can be united into one resource space RS by eliminating duplicates. RS is called the union of RS_1 and RS_2, and $|RS| = n$. The Union operation can be written in SSeIQL as follows:

> **UNION** $RS_1, ..., RS_n$ [**AT** $URSL_1, ..., URSL_n$] **INTO** RS
> **CONSTRAINT** *axis_number*
>   **CHECK** $|RS_1| = ... = |RS_n| = |RS|$
> **CONSTRAINT** *common_axis_number*
>   **CHECK** *number* (*common_axes*) = $|RS|$

The Union operation requires that the resource spaces to be united have the same number of axes and the same axis names.

4.4.3 *Resource modification*

The SSeIQL RML is used to modify resource mapping in a resource space. Resource mapping can be inserted, removed, or changed.

(1) Insertion

A newly created resource space is empty. We can use the **INSERT** command to insert resources in the entity space into the resource space.

> **INSERT** $R_1..., R_m$ **INTO** $RS_1..., RS_m$ [**AT** $URSL_1, ..., URSL_m$]
>   [**WHERE** <*conditional expression*>];

To insert resources into a resource space, we either directly specify a resource set to be inserted or write a query that gives the set of resources to be inserted. The simplest **INSERT** statement is for a single resource set. Suppose that we wish to insert a resource set {*ResourceID*} into resource space RS <*axis$_1$*, *axis$_2$*, *axis$_3$*> at <*coord$_1$*, *coord$_2$*, *coord$_3$*>. We write the statement as follows:

> **INSERT** {*ResourceID*} **INTO** RS <*axis$_1$*, *axis$_2$*, *axis$_3$*>
> **COORD** <*coord$_1$*, *coord$_2$*, *coord$_3$*>

Instead of specifying a resource set directly, we can use a **SELECT** statement to extract a set of resources.

> **INSERT INTO** RS <*axis$_1$*, *axis$_2$*, *axis$_3$*>
> **COORD** <*coord$_1$*, *coord$_2$*, *coord$_3$*>
> **BY SELECT** $A_1, A_2, ..., A_n$
> **FROM** $RS_1, RS_2, ... , RS_m$
> [**WHERE** <*conditional expression*>]

(2) Deletion

In SSeIQL, a deletion is expressed by the following statement:

> **DELETE** R **FROM** $RS_1,..., RS_m$ [**AT** $URSL_1,..., URSL_m$]
> [**WHERE** <*conditional expression*>]

The deletion statement means that if the specified resource exists at the specified point of the given resource space and the user has the authority to delete it, then it will be deleted.

(3) Update

In SSeIQL, the following **UPDATE** statement is used to change a resource index in a given resource space.

> **UPDATE** *RS*
> **REPLACE** R_1 **WITH** R_2
> [**WHERE** *<conditional expression>*]

The **WHERE** clause of the **UPDATE** statement means the same as the **WHERE** clause of the **SELECT** statement.

4.4.4 *Semantic link space*

In SSeIQL, the semantic relationship between resources can be specified by the following command:

> **CREATE SLINK** α
> **WHERE PRIOR** $RSP <P_u, ..., P_v>$
> **AND NEXT** $RSS < R_u, ..., R_v>$

where α denotes the semantic relationship between two resources, $RSP <P_u, ..., P_v>$ and $RSS <R_u, ..., R_v>$ denote the coordinates of the predecessor and the successor.

4.4.5 *View definition*

A view in SSeIQL can be defined by using the **CREATE VIEW** command. To define a view, the name of the view as well as the query that computes the view is required. The form of the **CREATE VIEW** command is as follows:

> **CREATE VIEW** *v* **AS** *<query expression>*

where *<query expression>* is any valid query expression. The view name is represented by *v*.

As a simple example, consider the view consisting of *m* axes of a resource space. Assume that the view name is *RS–view*. We define this view as follows:

CREATE VIEW *RS–view* (*axis*₁, ..., *axis*ₘ) **AS**
SELECT $X_1 = <c_{11},...,c_{1,k_1}>,..., X_m = <c_{m,1},...,c_{m,k_m}>$
FROM *RS*

The list of axis names can be omitted. We define a view over two resource spaces by using the **MERGE** operation as follows:

CREATE VIEW *RS–view* (*axis*₁, ..., *axis*ₘ) **AS**
SELECT $X_1, X_2,..., X_m < C_{X_m,1}, C_{X_m,2},..., C_{X_m,i} >$ **FROM** *RS*₁
MERGE
SELECT $Y_1, Y_2,..., Y_m < C_{Y_m,1}, C_{Y_m,2},..., C_{Y_m,j} >$ **FROM** *RS*₂
WHERE $X_1 = Y_1, ..., X_{m-1}=Y_{m-1}$
AND $X_m.axis\_name = Y_m.axis\_name$

The new axis *axis*ₘ is formed by
$$X_m \bigcup Y_m = <C_{X_m,1},...,C_{X_m,i}, C_{Y_m,1},...,C_{Y_m,j}>.$$

We define a view combining two resource spaces by using **JOIN** operation as follows:

CREATE VIEW *RS–view* (*axis*₁, ..., *axis*ₘ) **AS**
SELECT $X_1, X_2,..., X_m < C_{X_m,1}, C_{X_m,2},..., C_{X_m,i} >$ **FROM** *RS*₁
JOIN
SELECT $Y_1, Y_2,..., Y_n < C_{Y_n,1}, C_{Y_n,2},..., C_{Y_n,j} >$ **FROM** *RS*₂
WHERE $X_1 = Y_1, ..., X_i = Y_i$ (*i*<=minimum (*m,n*))

Once a view has been defined, we can use the view name to refer to the virtual resource space that the view represents. View names may appear in any place where a resource space name may appear. A **CREATE VIEW** clause creates a view definition in the resource dictionary, and the view definition stays in the resource dictionary until a **DROP VIEW** command removes it.

If there is any modification to resources in a resource space, the set of resources in the view changes as well. Views are typically implemented as follows: When a view is defined, the resource dictionary stores the definition of the view, rather than the result of the command that defines the view. Whenever a viewed resource space is used in a query, it is replaced by the stored view expression. Thus, whenever the query is evaluated, the viewed resource space is recomputed.

4.5 The Programming Environment

The general architecture of the SSeIQL programming environment is shown in Fig. 4.3. The SSeIQL program or statement is carried out by parsing, interpreting, executing, and generating a source tree.

The parser analyzes the SSeIQL code syntactically and generates a source tree. The interpreter extracts the sequence of operations and their parameters. The execution engine takes the operations and parameters and carries them out in three steps:

(1) Resource Space locating;

(2) Resource Space loading; and,

(3) API invoking.

The result generator applies XSL (Extensible Stylesheet Language, http://www.w3.org/Style/XSL) to match nodes in the output instance generated by the execution engine. It can generate complex data and multiple types of XML outputs. The result is in the form of either a complete XML document or a set of XML fragments representing the sub-results.

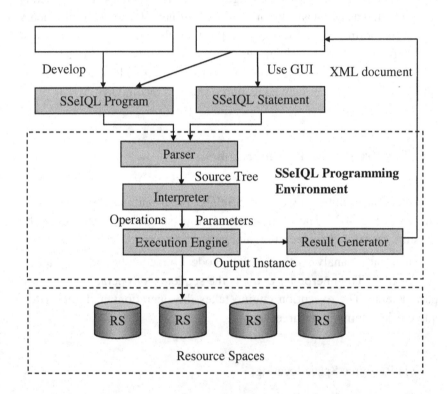

Fig. 4.3 The SSeIQL programming environment.

4.6 Comparison

SSeIQL is not only an SQL-like language but also a programming environment based on a resource space model and a semantic link model. Much as A. Bonifati and S. Ceri compared LOREL, XML-QL, XML-GL, XSL and XQL ("Comparative Analysis of Five XML Query Languages". *ACM SIGMOD Record*, 29 (1) (2000) 68-79), we compare SSeIQL to XQL, LOREL and SQL in Table 4.1, where an asterisk denotes a feature distinct to SSeIQL.

Table 4.1 Comparison of SSeIQL, XQL, LOREL and SQL.

Feature Items	SSeIQL	XQL	LOREL	SQL
Data format	XML	XML	XML	Table
Operating object*	Resources	XML	XML	Table
Operation result	XML	XML	Set of OIDs	Table
Abstract data types	Yes	No	Yes	No
SQL-like	Yes	No	Yes	Yes
Specific data model	Yes	No	Yes	Yes
Partial specified path expression	Yes	Yes	Yes	No
Nested queries*	Yes	No	Yes	Yes
Update language*	Yes	No	Yes	Yes
Loop statement*	Yes	No	No	No
Branch statement*	Yes	No	No	No
Set operations	Partially	Yes	Yes	Yes
Aggregates	Partially	Partially	Yes	Yes
Join operation*	Yes	No	Yes	Yes
Support of view*	Yes	No	No	Yes
Query structure	Yes	No	No	No
Query content	Yes	Yes	Yes	Yes
Support of RDF	No	No	No	No
Support of typed links*	Yes	No	No	No
Universal resource view*	Yes	No	No	No

The table shows that SSeIQL borrows its syntax and semantics from the SQL language. The statements of SSeIQL are SQL-like and have the SQL **SELECT/FROM/WHERE** pattern. SSeIQL can perform operations like those of the classical relational database, such as query nesting, aggregation, set operations, joining and result ordering.

A distinctive feature of SSeIQL is that it can take a universal view of various types of hierarchical resources, including information, knowledge and services. The specific data model of SSeIQL is a three-dimensional resource space. But standard SQL uses only flat relational tables, while the XML query languages manage only XML documents. Another feature of SSeIQL is that it is an update language with control statements.

A set of typed links is established between resources, with types like *abstraction* and *similar*, so that resources can be used more effectively and made more mobile.

SSeIQL also borrows the following features from the XML query languages:

(1)   Management of structured and semi-structured data.
(2)   Abstract data types.
(3)   The XML-based data format and result semantics.
(4)   Document selection.
(5)   Partially specified path expressions.

4.7 The Single Semantic Image Browser

The common function of current Web browsers is to obtain a Web page coded with HTML from a Web location and then to display it for reading. The browsers work only for humans, always in read-only mode, and without regard to the semantics of Web pages. On the other hand, Web pages do not encode machine-understandable semantics. Future browsers will need to help people and virtual roles to describe, obtain and predict the semantics of resources of interest.

The future Web browser will be a semantic browser that enables users to exploit a variety of distributed resources through their semantics rather than their location and medium, and can intelligently assist users to effectively accomplish operations such as the description, publication, capture, visualization and maintenance of semantics. An ideal semantic browser could normally organize, effectively share, dynamically cluster and uniformly manage globally distributed versatile resources.

In the current Web, semantic information is lost and distorted as pages are added or modified because resource providers cannot encode semantic data in Web pages, and the Web browsers and search engines are not able to understand the HTML-based Web pages.

People can understand each other to some extent even if they speak different languages. This phenomenon implies that a primitive common semantic space exists behind versatile communication media such as spoken and sign languages and body language. If resource providers can describe resources in a common semantic space, then a variety of resources can implement semantic interconnection. A common semantic space has several semantic layers as illustrated in Fig. 4.1. If we establish these semantic layers above the entity resources, then the semantic browser can obtain more complete semantic information.

Existing mark-up languages like XML and RDF enable us to establish: a name space where resources are uniquely identified; a structural space where structural information of resources is specified; and a relational space where associations between resources are described. We still need to create new techniques to support semantic description in a logical semantic space where logical relationships are described and reasoning carried out, and in a process semantic space where the processes that integrate multiple active resources are described and carried out.

Users either provide resources or consume resources. Resource providers describe the semantics of the newly added resources and consumers browse in multi-layered semantic spaces. The providers and consumers can be humans, virtual roles and soft-devices. A multi-layered semantic space helps the semantic browser to provide the following distinctive capabilities:

(1) Users can exploit resources according to their privilege and the resource's semantic description;
(2) A variety of resources can be given a single semantic image in which the semantic layers unify and interconnect resources, and eliminate semantic isolation; and,
(3) Resources can be clustered on demand according to the user's needs and the semantics of relevant resources.

Current technologies supporting the definition of process semantics include: Workflow which can further execute and monitor the process; PetriNets which can verify the correctness of concurrent process semantics; and description logic which allows resource providers to specify a terminological hierarchy using a restricted set of first order formulas (http://www.semanticweb.org).

We have developed a semantic browser consisting of a semantic description tool, an intelligent browsing engine, and a browser interface.

The *semantic description tool* allows resource providers to establish a semantic link network or to add new nodes to an existing network. To simplify the use of large-scale semantic networks, we have taken the component-based description approach. Just like software components, semantic components have the characteristics of "encapsulation", which requires the interconnection between components to be realized by its "interface" consisting of an input and an output (a fail exit or a succeed output). The internal nodes and links of a semantic component satisfy process and logical correctness.

Fig. 4.4 shows the process of establishing a semantic link network by top-down component definition. Users can define the network by clicking the buttons arranged at the top of the display, drawing the semantic link network, and defining the features of each node and link as shown in the central portion of the first interface.

Users can define the lower-level component corresponding to C_2 as shown in the second interface by double clicking the corresponding node listed in the left column of the first interface. The third interface is for making the semantic links in the text represented by C_3 in the second interface.

The intelligent semantic browser engine includes an intelligent user profile mechanism that helps the browser understand the user's requirements and automatically traces and analyzes the user's resource handling, and evolves according to the analysis.

The browser engine can carry out semantic-based reasoning and display a hint to help users decide on the next browsing step.

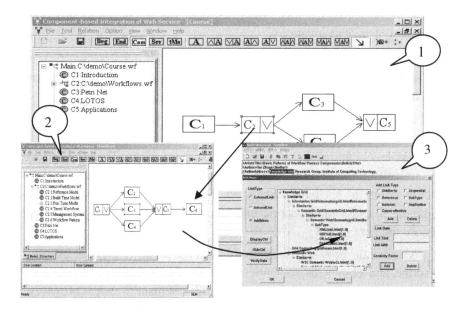

Fig. 4.4 Component-based semantic link network definition tool.

The *browser interface* includes: 1) a depiction of the semantic space that displays an orthogonal semantic space or a componential semantic link network according to internal semantic expressions; and 2) an SQL-like query interface that can express users' operational requirements in a structural way.

Fig. 4.5 illustrates the work process and shows the advantages of the semantic browser. In the first interface, the user can firstly either upload the topic and define the relevant axes of the semantic space or select an entry of interest in the topic list, and then click the "input coordinate" button to select the axes involved. The interface will automatically generate a three-dimensional semantic space. The user can browse in the space by moving the mouse and clicking the button on the top portion. The depicted orthogonal semantic space consists of concept and storage, helps users focus on their interests and can more efficiently and effectively locate destinations.

Double clicking the selected point shifts from the first interface to the second, which enables users to efficiently find the right component and determine the relationship between components.

The user can select any node and double click on it to see its details: a finer granularity component is shown in the third interface of Fig. 4.5 or a text-level interface is shown in the fourth interface. The browser can dynamically form a hierarchical list of relevant semantic links when the mouse points to each link displayed in the semantic-linked text. The reminder displays the semantic-link reasoning results to help the user to choose the next step.

A semantic browser is an interface mechanism that helps users to describe and obtain the semantics of resources of interest. It supports four-layer browsing: high-level orthogonal semantic space browsing, middle-level relational, logical and process semantic space (like the semantic link network) browsing, low-level structure browsing, and deep resource (like text or image) browsing. The intelligent engine enables users to choose the next step during browsing. Users can be people, virtual roles and intelligent soft-devices. People can use the depiction interface while the others can use the XML-based internal description.

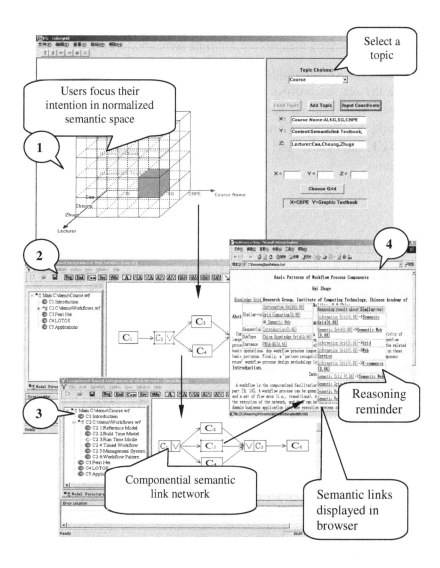

Fig. 4.5 Browsing in three semantic layers.

We have implemented a semantic browser based on the proposed method and used it in two areas:

On-line teaching. The teacher uses the semantic browser to conveniently put teaching materials together, and the students use it to browse the teaching materials at multiple semantic levels;

Web service integration. Users employ the semantic browser to define the service process needed for a business process. The browser retrieves the required services in the UDDI repositories (Universal Description, Discovery and Integration, http:// www.uddi.org), clusters retrieved fragments, and integrates them according to the process definition.

4.8 SSeIQL Grammar

The syntax of SSeIQL is defined in an extended BNF notation, where "[ ]" means optional, *RS* represents a resource space, X_i denotes an axis, and C_{ij} denotes a coordinate. The words in bold capitals are fixed SSeIQL keywords.

(1) CREATE statement
CREATE RSPACE RS $(X_1, X_2, ..., X_n)$ [**AT** *URSL*]
WHERE $X_1 = \{C_{11}, ..., C_{1u}\}, ..., X_n = \{C_{n1}, ..., C_{nv}\}$
<integrity constraint$_1$>
......
<integrity constraint$_m$>

(2) SELECT statement
SELECT $A_1, A_2, ..., A_n$
FROM $R_1, R_2, ..., R_m$

[**WHERE** *<conditional expression>*]

(3) INSERT statement
INSERT *R* **INTO** *RS* [**AT** *URSL*]
WHERE $X_1 = C_{1i}, \ldots, X_n = C_{nj}$

(4) DELETE statement
DELETE *R* **FROM** *RS* [**AT** *URSL*]
WHERE $X_1 = C_{1i}, \ldots, X_n = C_{nj}$

(5) LOG statement is to log a resource space on a community.
LOG *RS* [**AT** *URSL*] **ON/OFF** [*community*]

(6) OPEN statement is to open a resource space to other resource spaces.
OPEN *RS* [**AT** *URSL*]
TO $RS_1, \ldots, RS_m$ [**AT** $URSL_1, URSL_2, \ldots, URSL_m$]

(7) MERGE statement
MERGE $RS_1, \ldots, RS_n$ [**AT** $URSL_1, \ldots, URSL_n$]
INTO *RS* [**AT** *URSL*]
WHERE $new\_axis\ (RS) = X_{1\mu}\ (RS_1)$ **&**$\ldots$**&** $X_{nv}\ (RS_n)$
CONSTRAINT *axis_number*
CHECK $|RS_1| = \ldots = |RS_n| = |RS|$
CONSTRAINT *common_axis_number*
CHECK $number\ (common\_axes) = |RS|{-}1$

(8) SPLIT statement
SPLIT *RS* [**AT** *URSL*]
INTO $RS_1, \ldots, RS_n$ [**AT** $URSL_1, \ldots, URSL_n$]
WHERE $X\ (RS)$ **JOIN-INTO** $X_{1\alpha}\ (RS_1) = $ *<coordinate-set$_1$>* **&** $\ldots$**&** $X_{n\beta}\ (RS_n) = $ *<coordinate_set$_n$>*
CONSTRAINT *axis_split*
CHECK $X\ (RS) = X_{1\alpha}\ (RS_1) \cup \ldots \cup X_{n\beta}\ (RS_n)$

(9) JOIN statement

JOIN RS_1, ..., RS_n [**AT** $URSL_1$, ..., $URSL_n$]
INTO RS [**AT** $URSL$]
WHERE COMMON AXES $(axis_1, \ldots, axis_\mu)$
CONSTRAINT *common_axis_number*
CHECK *number* $(common\_axes) \leq |RS| - 1$

(10) DISJOIN statement
DISJOIN RS [**AT** $URSL$]
INTO RS_1 $(X_{11}, \ldots, X_{1\mu})$, ..., RS_m $(X_{m1}, \ldots, X_{mv})$
[**AT** $URSL_1$, ..., $URSL_m$]
WHERE COMMON AXES $(axis_1, \ldots, axis_k)$
CONSTRAINT *axis_disjoin*
CHECK $X(RS) = X_{1\alpha}(RS_1) \cup \ldots \cup X_{n\beta}(RS_n)$

(11) UNION statement
UNION RS_1, ..., RS_n [**AT** $URSL_1$, ..., $URSL_n$] **INTO** RS
CONSTRAINT *axis_number*
CHECK $|RS_1| = \ldots = |RS_n| = |RS|$
CONSTRAINT *common_axis_number*
CHECK *number* $(common\_axes) = |RS|$

(12) SLINK statement
CREATE SLINK α
WHERE PRIOR $RSP <P_u, \ldots, P_v>$
     AND NEXT $RSS < R_u, \ldots, R_v>$

4.9 The SSeI in a Peer-to-Peer Semantic Link Network

The scalability and autonomy of a Peer-to-Peer (P2P) network make it a promising infrastructure for a scalable Knowledge Grid.

The original motivation for most early P2P systems such as Gnutella (http://www.gnutella.com) and Napster (http://www.napster.com) was only file sharing. Peer Data Management Systems (PDMSs) aim at an adaptable architecture for decentralized data sharing, and usually consist of a set of peers, with each peer having an associated XML schema.

Integrating heterogeneous data in large-scale P2P networks is a challenging problem because the data held in the peers are autonomous, scalable, dynamic and heterogeneous. Heterogeneous data management in a PDMS presents the following three key problems:

(1) Identifying semantically relevant peers autonomously.
(2) Routing a query accurately and efficiently from the originating peer to relevant other peers to reduce network flooding.
(3) Integrating heterogeneous data returned from different peers to provide users and other peers with an SSeI data usage mode (P2P systems do not have a global schema like that of traditional data integration systems).

Previous research on P2P computing systems and PDMSs mainly considered data models for P2P databases, peer clustering, peer searching, query routing algorithms, and peer schema mediation mechanisms (W.S. Ng et al., "PeerDB: A P2P-Based System for Distributed Data Sharing", *Proc. of International Conference on Data Engineering, ICDE*, 2003, Bangalore, India, March 2003; I. Stoica et al., "Chord: A Scalable Peer-to-Peer Lookup Protocol for Internet Applications", *IEEE/ACM Transactions on Networking*, 11 (2003) 17–32).

But the above three key issues remain resolved.

A P2P Semantic Link Network (P2PSLN) is a directed network, where nodes are peers or P2PSLNs, and edges are typed semantic links specifying semantic relationships between peers (H. Zhuge, "Active E-Document Framework ADF: Model and Tool", *Information and Management*, 41 (1) (2003) 87-97). In a P2PSLN, each peer is an active and intelligent soft-device, which can dynamically and intelligently establish semantic connections with others. A *semantic link* between two peers is a pointer with a type (α) directed from one peer (predecessor) to another (successor).

A peer can be a server when providing data, information and services, a mediator when forwarding queries, and a client when receiving data, information and services from other peers.

Each peer in a P2PSLN has two main modules: a *communication* module and a *data management* module. Peers communicate with each other through SOAP (Simple Object Access Protocol) messages. Users can query a peer through a GUI (Graphical User Interface) or by using SSeIQL.

The data management module of each peer is responsible for managing the queries and the answers. Upon receiving a query, the data management module performs the following tasks:

(1) *Query Processing* — Analyze the query and extract its parameters.
(2) *Query Translation* — Match the query to the XML schema of the current peer to check whether it might be able to answer the query. If not, the query will be forwarded to successors that are likely to be able to answer the query or to forward the query suitably.
(3) *Query Evaluation* — Put the query to the current peer for answering.
(4) *Peer Selection* — Select promising successors according to the semantic relationship and similarity between the current peer and possible successors.
(5) *Query Reformulation* — Reformulate a query posed on the current peer over schemas of its immediate successors.
(6) *Query Forwarding* — Autonomously forward the query to selected successors according to the routing policy and a predefined TTL (Time To Live) value.

Upon receiving an answer from a successor, the data management module of the peer initiating the query will analyze the answer to detect inconsistent data. If a successor was sent the query but returned few answers, the current peer will send SOAP messages to it to find out whether it still exists in the current P2PSLN and whether there are any schema changes, and then update the schema mapping, semantic link type and the similarity degree between them. Finally, the data management module will combine the data in the answers and so provide users or peers with data from multiple sources in a single semantic image.

An approach including automatic semantic link discovery, a method for constructing and maintaining P2P semantic link networks, a semantic-based peer similarity measurement approach for efficient query routing, and peer schema mapping algorithms for query reformulation and heterogeneous data integration has been proposed (H. Zhuge, J. Liu, L. Feng and C. He, "Semantic-Based Query Routing and Heterogeneous Data Integration in Peer-to-Peer Semantic Link Network", *Proc. of 1ˢᵗ International Conference on Semantics of a Networked World, in cooperation with ACM SIGMOD*, Paris, France, June 17-19, pp.90-107).

The proposed approach has the following characteristics:

(1) Enriches the relationships between peers' data schemas by using semantic links.
(2) Uses not only nodes, but also XML structure, in measuring the similarity between schemas to efficiently and accurately forward queries to relevant peers.
(3) Deals with semantic and structural heterogeneity and data inconsistency so that peers can exchange and translate heterogeneous information using a single semantic image.

The integration of the P2P semantic link network and the orthogonal semantic space provides a scalable semantic layer in the Knowledge Grid environment. An integrated normalization theory is useful and important to the SSeI.

4.10 SSeI's Hierarchy, Time and Epistemology

The SSeI of resources will be different if it is viewed from different abstraction levels and different semantic levels (for example, process level and logic level). Views of an SSeI can be operated as an SSeI. The SSeI of resources would be also different if it is viewed at different time (fixed time or duration). Considering the *level* and *time* factors, the *SSeI* can be expressed as:

$$SSeI(level, time): P_1(C_1, C_2, ..., C_n) \xrightarrow{\alpha} P_2(C_1', C_2', ..., C_n').$$

A sequence of SSeIs at the same level $<SSeI(level, time_1), SSeI(level, time_2), SSeI(level, time_3), ..., SSeI(level, time_n)>$ can be expressed as $SSeI(level, time=<time_1, time_2, ..., time_n>)$.

Further more, the *SSeI* of resources varies with epistemology, that is, the SSeI of different epistemology would be different. So the *SSeI* can be further expressed as:

$$SSeI(epistemology, level, time): P_1(C_1, C_2, ..., C_n) \xrightarrow{\alpha} P_2(C_1', C_2', ..., C_n').$$

The factors discussed above require operations on the SSeI to impose the following criteria.

Criterion 4.1. Join, Merge and Split operations should be carried out at the same abstraction/semantic level, formally, $Operation(r_1, r_2)$ is at the same abstraction/semantic level as r_1 and r_2.

Criterion 4.2. If SSeIs are bound by durations, then the result of Join, Merge and Split operations are bounded by the overlap of these durations.

Criterion 4.3. Abstraction of one or more SSeIs generates a view at the next higher level of the abstraction hierarchy of SSeI.

Criterion 4.4. Only SSeIs of the same epistemology can be joined or merged.

This section presents the notion and mechanism of an SSeI based on classification semantic space and semantic linkage space. It would be interesting to incorporate more types of semantics into the SSeI.

Chapter 5

Knowledge Flow

Knowledge is power, but knowledge is not just statically stored in a Knowledge Grid. It evolves through being shared and developed by roles, people, and various resources within the Grid.

A *knowledge flow* is a passing of knowledge between people or through machinery. It has three crucial attributes: *direction* (sender and receiver), *carrier* (medium) and *content* (shareable). Good knowledge flow enables intelligent participants (people, roles and soft-devices) to cooperate effectively.

5.1 Definition

Although knowledge flow is intangible, any teamwork relies on it, even if team members are unaware of its happening. They share knowledge using various forms of networking, where the links are knowledge flows working like the conveyor belts in a production line. Any team member can put knowledge onto the appropriate belt to have it automatically conveyed to the team member who needs it. Team members can be helped by knowledge from the "conveyor belts" connected to them when working on a task. The linkages of such "knowledge conveyor belts" together with the team members as nodes make up a knowledge flow network. Designing the network properly, and controlling its operation effectively, will raise the efficiency of knowledge sharing within teams (H. Zhuge, "A Knowledge Flow Model for Peer-to-Peer Team Knowledge Sharing and Management", *Expert Systems with Applications*, 2002, vol.23, no.1, 23-30).

174

Effective knowledge flow will avoid redundant knowledge passing between team members, recognizing that different members may be given different kinds of tasks and need different kinds of knowledge. Members then do not need to spend time and energy in searching for knowledge in a traditional centralized repository.

The carrier can be the Internet, local networks, various wireless networks, and even sensor networks. The content being shareable means that the knowledge can be understood by all team members. A connective network means that the content can be passed from any team member to any other member.

Knowledge content can be specified as being within a knowledge space where each point places knowledge of a specific type and level at a specific location (H. Zhuge, "A Knowledge Grid Model and Platform for Global Knowledge Sharing", *Expert Systems with Applications*, 2002, vol.22, no.4, pp.313-320). Such a specification meets the following needs:

People working in different roles need knowledge at different levels.

People working at different kinds of tasks need different kinds of knowledge.

Thus the knowledge of a flow *KF* has a field (a two-dimensional region in a knowledge space) defined by a type field *TFd* and a level field *LFd*: $Field(KF) = <TFd, LFd>$, where $TFd = <t \mid t$ is a knowledge type> and $LFd = <level \mid level$ is a knowledge level>.

The operation $TFd_1 \cup TFd_2$ is a set union such that the order of the knowledge types of each along the knowledge type axis is maintained. Similarly, the set operations $\cup$, $\cap$, $-$ can be carried out between any two *TFd*s and between any two *LFd*s.

Let $<TFd_1, LFd_1>$ and $<TFd_2, LFd_2>$ be the fields of two knowledge flows KF_1 and KF_2. The following operations hold:

(1) $<TFd_1, LFd_1> \cup <TFd_2, LFd_2> = <TFd_1 \cup TFd_2, LFd_1 \cup LFd_2>$;
(2) $<TFd_1, LFd_1> \cap <TFd_2, LFd_2> = <TFd_1 \cap TFd_2, LFd_1 \cap LFd_2>$;
(3) $<TFd_1, LFd_1> - <TFd_2, LFd_2> = <TFd_1 - TFd_2, LFd_1 - LFd_2>$;

(4) $<TFd_1, LFd_1> \subseteq <TFd_2, LFd_2>$
$\qquad$ if and only if $<TFd_1 \subseteq TFd_2, LFd_1 \subseteq LFd_2>$.

A knowledge node, the sender or receiver of a flow, can also generate and request knowledge. What a node can put out depends on what knowledge it has stored and what it can get in. A node can be an automaton that holds its own store of knowledge and uses an agent to help team members use that knowledge.

When a knowledge node is working it is said to be *active*. Otherwise, it is *inactive*. A node switches between these states.

The following are properties of a good knowledge flow network.

(1) A knowledge flow network is *connective* if there is a flow path between every pair of nodes. A connective knowledge flow network requires a connective actual network, but a connective actual network does not ensure a connective knowledge flow network.

(2) A knowledge flow network is *complete* for a task if it is connective and its nodes correspond to the team members or their roles in the task. A complete network means that no team member is isolated from the knowledge of any other.

(3) A complete knowledge flow network is the *smallest* if it has the fewest possible flows between nodes. A smallest network can not only eliminate isolation but also achieve effective team knowledge sharing.

(4) A smallest complete knowledge flow network has no redundant paths between any two nodes.

5.2 A Knowledge Flow Process Model

Knowledge can flow through any of the following four types of connections:

Sequential connection. Two flows, KF_1 and KF_2 merge into one, KF_1/KF_2, such that a) $Field(KF_1/KF_2) = Field(KF_1) = Field(KF_2)$, or b) $Field(KF_1/KF_2) = Field(KF_2)$ if $Field(KF_1) \subseteq Field(KF_2)$.
Join-connection. Two or more flows converge to form one, denoted by $KF_1 \wedge KF_2 \wedge ... \wedge KF_n \Rightarrow KF$, such that $Field(KF_1 \wedge KF_2 \wedge ... \wedge KF_n \Rightarrow KF) = Field(KF_1) \cup Field(KF_2) \cup ... \cup Field(KF_n) = <LFd_1 \cup LFd_2 \cup ... \cup LFd_n, TFd_1 \cup TFd_2 \cup ... \cup TFd_n>$.

Split-connection. A flow KF can be split into two or more flows, denoted by $KF \Rightarrow KF_1 \vee KF_2 \vee ... \vee KF_n$, such that $Field(KF \Rightarrow KF_1 \vee KF_2 \vee ... \vee KF_n) = Field(KF_1) \cup Field(KF_2) \cup ... \cup Field(KF_n) = <LFd_1 \cup LFd_2 \cup ... \cup LFd_n, TFd_1 \cup TFd_2 \cup ... \cup TFd_n>$.

Broadcast. A flow KF can be broadcast to many flows $KF_1, KF_2, ..., KF_n$ such that $Field(KF = (KF_1, KF_2, ..., KF_n)) = Field(KF_1) = Field(KF_2) = ... = Field(KF_n)$.

The difference between workflow (http://www.wfmc.org) and knowledge flow has the following aspects:

(1) A knowledge flow can take in the knowledge generated at a node as it flows through it. Workflows do not.
(2) Much knowledge flow content comes from team members' experience carrying out a task and cannot be anticipated. Workflow networks reflect existing business domains and can be designed.
(3) Knowledge flow content comes from team members, while workflow content reflects either data or execution dependence between activities (tasks).

For teamwork, the knowledge flow can be made consistent with the workflow by having the same roles in both networks.

5.3 Peer-to-Peer Knowledge Sharing

Team members are called peers if they do the same work for the same type of tasks at the same level of the organizational hierarchy. Knowledge sharing makes use of the knowledge within a team to solve problems more quickly or effectively. Sharing between peers is more effective than that between non-peers for the following reasons.

(1) Peers work on the same types of tasks so their experiences are more relevant for sharing with each other to solve their problems.
(2) Peers have similar knowledge structures so can understand each other more easily when sharing knowledge.
(3) Peers have more interests in common so they can more effectively share knowledge. For example, two programmers can better share programming knowledge than either can with a manager.

Organizational innovation is one of the key issues of knowledge management. A successful large-scale knowledge organization tends to have fewer middle layers than an unsuccessful one. Organizations in some domains, like orchestras, may even have no middle layers at all (P.F. Drucker (ed.), "Harvard Business Review on Knowledge Management", *Boston, MA: Harvard Business School Press*, 1998). So peer-to-peer knowledge sharing is also a useful aim in structuring a large-scale organization.

Example. Software development by distributed teams focuses on work cooperation and resource sharing between physically dispersed team members during the development. Research on such work focuses only on aspects of technique. Human cognitive characteristics are seldom addressed. The following are reasons for incorporating formal knowledge flow into software development by distributed teams:

(1) *Software development is a knowledge-intensive process.* Team members can improve their work not only by using software tools but also through cognitive cooperation.

(2) *Cognitive cooperation cannot be planned.* Team members' development knowledge is gained and gathered as their work proceeds, so cognitive cooperation among them cannot be planned, though it must be encouraged. Cooperation in the form of knowledge flows is essential.

(3) *A distributed team requires effective and low cost communication.* Planned and disciplined knowledge flow can cut the cost of communication and can better reflect the actual work process of project development.

(4) *A development team should be supported by a formal experience accumulation procedure.* All team members can use the experience of their predecessors accumulated while working on previous projects, so that the team can avoid fruitless work and adapt to any change of participants or of roles.

There are five cognitive levels of knowledge in software development, given here from low to high.

(1) *Coding knowledge* helps members to share programming skills. The skills of this level are in the form of problem-solution pairs.

(2) *Reuse knowledge* helps members to reuse code components.

(3) *Knowledge of methods* enables team members to apply known problem solving techniques. Such knowledge is in the form of problem-method pairs, where a method can be a process, a pattern, or an algorithm.

(4) *Rules for development and cooperation* encourage team members to share knowledge and experience, which flow on to others to improve their software development generally. Rules for cooperation can make sharing more efficient, and are very useful for bringing new members successfully into a team.

(5) *Decision and evaluation knowledge* is meta-knowledge gained from developing the knowledge of the other four levels. It reflects the manner of making decisions during the development process, and provides guidance in making new decisions, even in quite new circumstances.

5.4 Knowledge Intensity

Knowledge flows can be used to transfer capability and expertise in an orderly and effective way. The major obstacle is the absence of criteria for assessing the effectiveness of a knowledge flow network and for ensuring its optimal operation. Effectiveness lies in essence in having a good path for needed knowledge to flow from where it resides to where it is needed—across time and space and within and between organizations as necessary.

Knowledge intensity is a critical parameter in this process, whereby a team member with profound knowledge is qualified to occupy a position of very high intensity in the flow network. Good management will keep knowledge flowing from those who are more knowledgeable to those who are less, and so avoid wasted flows.

The notion of intensity reflecting degree of knowledge leads to principles that provide objective laws for the existence and development of effective knowledge flow.

To set up a reasonable scope for research, the following assumptions specify the nature of equality, autonomy, and generosity in a knowledge flow network.

Assumption. *Nodes in a knowledge flow network are able to acquire, use and create knowledge*. It is reasonable to assume that people in an organization all have some ability to generate, use and spread knowledge.

Assumption. *Knowledge nodes share knowledge autonomously*. This limits research to the passing and sharing of knowledge among nodes independently, without outside influence. Then we can just focus on team members' effectiveness and the needs of the task at hand when designing knowledge flow networks.

Assumption. *Nodes share useful knowledge without reserve.*

Knowledge within a team usually covers several areas, classified according to discipline. Knowledge can be also classified into five levels as outlined above (H. Zhuge, "A Knowledge Grid Model and Platform for Global Knowledge Sharing", *Expert Systems with Applications*, 2002, vol.22, no.4, pp.313-320).

Knowledge area and level are two dimensions of knowledge space. An area i and a level j determine a *unit knowledge field* (or unit field for short) denoted by $UFd\,(i, j)$.

Knowledge intensity is a parameter that expresses a node's degree of knowledge and reflects the corresponding person's cognitive and creative abilities in a unit field. The intensity of a knowledge node and its change determine the node's "rank" in a network. It is in direct proportion to the aggregate knowledge held by the node.

A node with superior knowledge and ability to learn, use and create knowledge will be of high intensity. Thus, we estimate the intensity of a node in a unit field by assessing how much knowledge in the unit field is held by the node.

The knowledge intensity of a node will be different in different unit fields. We use the following four-dimensional orthogonal space *KIS* to represent the knowledge intensity of a knowledge node:

$$KIS\ (knowledge\text{-}area,\ knowledge\text{-}level,\ knowledge\text{-}intensity,\ time).$$

Any point in this space represents the knowledge intensity of a node in a certain unit field at certain time. At the given time t, the intensity of node u in unit field $UFd\,(i, j)$ for a given *task* is *KI* (*task, u, i, j, t*).

In every unit field some nodes need to pass knowledge to others. We can define a knowledge flow network for every unit field with flows that avoid unnecessary knowledge passing. Cooperation within a task can involve many networks, one for each unit field.

5.5 Knowledge Flow Principles

Principle. *Knowledge only flows between two nodes when their intensity differs in at least one unit field.*

This can be formally expressed as follows. Let u and v be two knowledge nodes, and $KI\,(task, u, i, j, t)$ and $KI\,(task, v, i, j, t)$ be their intensity in $UFd\,(i,j)$ at time t. If the following formula holds, knowledge will flow between u and v.

$$\exists i \exists j (KI(task,u,i,j,t) - KI(task,v,i,j,t)) \neq 0$$

Principle. *A knowledge flow network is effective if and only if every flow is to a node of lower intensity than its source.*

This can be formally expressed as follows. If u_k is any node in a knowledge flow network, with $u_{k\text{-}1}$ its predecessor, then the network is effective if the following formula holds.

$$\forall k (KI(task,u_{k-1},i,j,t) - KI(task,u_k,i,j,t)) > 0.$$

Just as for water or electricity, knowledge naturally flows from high intensity nodes to low intensity nodes.

Principle. *The intensity difference between any two nodes in a knowledge flow network always tends to zero. That is, the following formula holds*:

$$\forall i \forall j \lim_{t \to \infty} (KI(task,v,i,j,t) - KI(task,u,i,j,t)) = 0.$$

Let nodes u and v be the two ends of a knowledge flow in unit field $UFd\,(i,j)$. If they share their useful knowledge *without reserve*, the one with lower intensity will learn from the other, and the difference in their knowledge intensity in $UFd\,(i,j)$ will become smaller and smaller with the passing of time. This effect will be apparent in a closed environment, one in which there is no flow into the network from outside. In such an environment, all nodes are likely to have similar knowledge in the long term simply from learning together and sharing. All flow could stop. This principle implies that a team will improve its performance more by learning from outside the team than by only exchanging knowledge within the team.

Principle. *If knowledge depreciation is ignored, the intensity in any unit field at any node will never decrease.*

If KI (*task, u, i, j, Δt*) is the change in knowledge intensity of node u in UFd (i, j) in a period of time $\Delta t > 0$, then KI (*task, u, i, j, Δt*) should not be negative. So we have:

$$KI(task, u, i, j, \Delta t) = KI(task, u, i, j, t + \Delta t) - KI(task, u, i, j, t) \geq 0$$

Knowledge depreciation can be ignored if the flow duration is rather short or the depreciation rate in the unit field is quite low.

When the intensity at a node changes, the knowledge flow network should be reformed if it will improve the flow.

In a competitive team, each node will attempt to increase its intensity so as to raise its position and rewards. This incentive inspires team members to learn, create and contribute as much as possible.

5.6 Computational Model of Knowledge Intensity

5.6.1 *Computing knowledge intensity in a closed environment*

We first discuss the simple case where node v is the only predecessor of node u, u is the only successor of v, and the knowledge intensity of node v is a constant. The knowledge intensity of node u in unit field $UFd\,(i,j)$ at time t, $KI_{closed}\,(task,\ u,\ i,\ j,\ t)$, has the following features:

(1) $KI_{closed}\,(task,\ u,\ i,\ j,\ t)$ monotonically increases.
(2) $KI_{closed}\,(task,\ u,\ i,\ j,\ t)$ tends to that of its predecessor in the long term. So the eventual stable value of $KI_{closed}\,(task,\ u,\ i,\ j,\ t)$ is that of its predecessor, that is, $KI_{fs} = KI_{closed}\,(task,\ v,\ i,\ j,\ 0)$.
(3) The rate of increase of $KI_{closed}\,(task,\ u,\ i,\ j,\ t)$ is in direct proportion to two factors; one is its current intensity and the other is the ratio of its difference from its possible stable value of KI_{fs} to the value of KI_{fs}.

From the above analysis, we obtain the following non-linear differential equation, where λ is the proportionality coefficient and KI_{u0} is the initial intensity of u:

$$\begin{cases} \dfrac{dKI_{closed}(task,u,i,j,t)}{dt} = \lambda(\dfrac{KI_{fs} - KI_{closed}(task,u,i,j,t)}{KI_{fs}})KI_{closed}(task,u,i,j,t) \\ KI_{u0} = KI_{closed}(task,u,i,j,0) \end{cases}$$

The following is the solution of above equation:

$$KI_{closed}\,(task,u,i,j,t) = \frac{KI_{fs}}{1 + (\dfrac{KI_{fs}}{KI_{u0}} - 1)e^{-\lambda t}}$$

While the knowledge intensity at the source node v changes with time, consequent intensity change at u comes after that at its predecessor.

Let the intensity of node v in unit field $UFd\,(i,j)$ at time t be $KI_{closed}\,(task,\ v,\ i,\ j,\ t)$. Then we have the following equation:

$$\begin{cases} \dfrac{dKI_{closed}(task,u,i,j,t)}{dt} = \lambda(\dfrac{KI_{closed}(task,v,i,j,t) - KI_{closed}(task,u,i,j,t)}{KI_{closed}(task,v,i,j,t)})KI_{closde}(task,u,i,j,t) \\ KI_{u0} = KI_{closed}(task,u,i,j,0) \end{cases}$$

The following is the general solution of the above equation, where C_1 is a constant:

$$\begin{cases} KI_{closed}(task,u,i,j,t) = \dfrac{1}{C_1 e^{-\lambda t} + \lambda e^{-\lambda t}\displaystyle\int_0^t \dfrac{e^{\lambda t}}{KI_{closed}(task,v,i,j,t)}dt} \\ KI_{u0} = KI_{closed}(task,u,i,j,0) \end{cases}$$

We can get the solution of $KI_{closed}\,(task,\ u,\ i,\ j,\ t)$ by replacing $KI_{closed}\,(task,\ v,\ i,\ j,\ t)$ in the above formula with the appropriate expression.

For example, in a closed team composed of three nodes, let a be the predecessor of b, and b be the predecessor of c. Let $KI_{closed}\,(task,\ a,\ i,\ j,\ t)$ be a constant KI_{a0}. Then we get b's intensity function from the above formula as follows:

$$KI_{closed}(task,b,i,j,t) = \dfrac{KI_{a0}}{1 + (\dfrac{KI_{a0}}{KI_{b0}} - 1)e^{-\lambda t}}.$$

And c's intensity function is

$$KI_{closed}(task,c,i,j,t) = \dfrac{KI_{a0}KI_{b0}}{KI_{b0} + (KI_{a0} - KI_{b0})\lambda t e^{\lambda t} + \dfrac{(KI_{u0} - KI_{c0})KI_{b0}}{KI_{c0}}e^{-\lambda t}}.$$

5.6.2 *Computing knowledge intensity in an open environment*

In an open environment, a knowledge node can learn from the external environment as well as from within its team.

Let $KI_{open}(task, u, i, j, t)$ (in short, $KI(u, t)$) be the knowledge intensity value of node u in $UFd(i,j)$ at time t in an open environment. It is composed of the intensity coming from within the team (denoted by $KI_{in}(u, t)$) and that from the external environment (denoted by $KI_{out}(u, t)$). The overall intensity at node u is thus

$$KI(u,t) = KI_{in}(u,t) + KI_{out}(u,t)$$

In an open environment, the nodes that have higher intensity will absorb knowledge more rapidly than those with lower. The rate of increase of $KI_{out}(u, t)$ is in direct proportion to u's intensity. And when the intensity of predecessor node v is higher than that of u, $KI_{in}(u, t)$ can be computed as described above.

Therefore, we can obtain the following non-linear differential equations, where λ and δ are proportionality coefficients and KI_{u0} is the initial knowledge intensity of u:

$$\begin{cases} \begin{cases} KI(u,t) = KI_{in}(u,t) + KI_{out}(u,t) \\ \dfrac{dKI_{out}(u,t)}{dt} = \delta KI(u,t) \\ \dfrac{dKI_{in}(u,t)}{dt} = \lambda(\dfrac{KI(v,t) - KI(u,t)}{KI(v,t)})KP(u,t) \\ KI_{u0} = KI(task,u,i,j,0) \end{cases} & if\ KI(v,t) - KI(u,t) > 0 \\ \\ \begin{cases} KI(u,t) = KI_{in}(u,t) + KI_{out}(u,t) \\ \dfrac{dKI_{out}(u,t)}{dt} = \delta KI(u,t) \\ KI_{in}(u,t) = 0 \\ KI_{u0} = KI(task,u,i,j,0) \end{cases} & if\ KI(v,t) - KI(u,t) \le 0 \end{cases}$$

Its general solution is as follows, where C_2 is a constant:

$$\begin{cases} \begin{cases} KI(u,t) = \dfrac{1}{C_2 e^{-(\delta+\lambda)t} + \lambda e^{-(\delta+\lambda)t} \displaystyle\int_0^t \dfrac{e^{(\delta+\lambda)t}}{KI(v,t)} dt}, & \textit{if } KI(v,t) - KI(u,t) > 0 \\ KI_{u0} = KI(u,0) \\ KI(u,t) = KI_{u0} e^{\delta t}, & \textit{if } KI(v,t) - KI(u,t) \le 0 \end{cases} \end{cases}$$

By appropriately replacing $KI(v, t)$ in the above formula, we can get the solution for $KI(u, t)$.

Using this approach, we can compute changes in knowledge intensity at nodes of a network in a closed or open environment based on their initial intensities, their learning ability and their predecessor nodes' intensities.

In the following, we will discuss how to estimate the initial knowledge intensity.

5.6.3 *Knowledge intensity evaluation*

Knowledge can be explicit or tacit. Explicit knowledge is expressible, linguistic, and simple to encode. Tacit knowledge comes more from experience and intuition, and is therefore much more difficult to pass on (K.C. Desouza, "Facilitating Tacit Knowledge Exchange", *Communications of the ACM*, 2003, vol.46, no.6, pp.85-88; I. Nonaka, "A Dynamic Theory of Organizational Knowledge Creation", *Organization Science*, 1994, vol.5, no.1, pp.14-37).

Explicit knowledge is easy to assess by using objective methods such as statistics. Tacit knowledge is difficult to assess because it is often at least partly subconscious (M. Mitri, "Applying Tacit Knowledge Management Techniques for Performance Assessment", *Computers & Education*, 2003, vol.4, pp.173-189).

Combining an objective evaluation approach with a subjective one could be a good way to assess knowledge intensity (H. Zhuge, "A Dynamic Evaluation Approach for Virtual Conflict Decision Training",

IEEE Transactions on Systems, Man and Cybernetics, 2000, vol.30, no.3, pp.374-380; H. Zhuge and J. Liu, "A Fuzzy On-line Collaborative Assessment Approach for Knowledge Grid", *Future Generation Computer Systems*, 2004, vol.20, no.1, pp.101-112).

The objective approach uses the quantity and quality of a node's explicit knowledge. The subjective approach uses questionnaires for completion by the node itself and by others, and assessment of achievement. Although the tacit knowledge and the cognitive and creative abilities of a node are hard to assess, they can be inferred subjectively to some extent. The node with more knowledge always emits better data and one with more ability always gets better evaluations.

5.7 Knowledge Spiral Model

Knowledge spirals are formed when knowledge flows in networks. A node can deliver knowledge to its successors either by forwarding knowledge from a predecessor, or by passing on its own.

Fig. 5.1 depicts a knowledge spiral, which consists of nodes with two types of flow: external—knowledge passed between nodes; and internal—knowledge created at a node, for example through abstraction, analogy, synthesis or reasoning.

The knowledge spiral model is very similar to the hypercycle model (K. Oida, "The Birth and Death Process of Hypercycle Spirals", in: R.K. Standish, M.A. Bedau, H.A. Abbass, edd., *Artificial Life VIII, MIT Press*, 2002). The self–replication arc and the catalytic–support arc of the hypercycle correspond to the knowledge passing and the knowledge processing respectively. The differences are twofold: self–replication in a hypercycle is carried out within nodes but knowledge passing is between nodes; and catalytic–support in a hypercycle happens between nodes but knowledge processing happens within nodes.

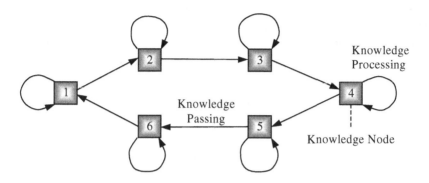

Fig.5.1 Knowledge spiral process model.

An effective knowledge spiral should maintain the intensity differences between nodes and ensure that only needed knowledge is passed between nodes. The processing at a knowledge node can be modeled as an automaton (H. Zhuge, "Conflict decision training through multi-space cooperation", *Decision Support Systems*, 2000, vol.29, pp.111-123).

In general, work and knowledge both flow within a team (H. Zhuge, "Workflow-based cognitive flow management for distributed team cooperation", *Information and Management*, 2003, vol.40, no.5, pp.419-429). A team member can take on one or more roles, and a role can also be part of other roles. Some roles take part in knowledge flow spirals and others carry out the tasks specified in work lists.

A knowledge flow spiral can be in one of the following four states.

(1) *Static*: creating and storing knowledge.
(2) *Active*: fulfilling roles.
(3) *Suspension*: waiting for something.
(4) *Termination*: reaching either the successful or the unsuccessful exit node.

5.8 Knowledge Flow Network Planning

Planning the knowledge flow network for a team means describing and designing a network free of unnecessary flows so that the network is efficient and effective. The success of the planning depends on the experience of the planner. Planning a large network is time consuming and may need a team of planners. Without an agreed abstraction method, planners will find it hard to work together and to bring about a coherent plan. These difficulties are the main obstacles to planning successful large knowledge flow networks.

5.8.1 *Composition operations and principles*

A knowledge flow network can be made from two or more existing networks by using the following composition operations.

(1) *Merge*: overlay common nodes.
(2) *Add flow*: connect nodes between networks.
(3) *Add condition*: add a *join* or *split* to express the relationship between flows related to the same node.
(4) *Embed*: put one network entirely within a node of another.
(5) *Graph operations*: combine networks with union, intersection, or subtraction.

Flows should be added whenever nodes have unit fields in common. Conditions should be added when a node is itself a network.

Composing knowledge flow networks also involves composing their roles. Let Rel_i be the relationship between the roles in $RoleSet_i$, $Roles_1 = <RoleSet_1, Rel_1>$ and $Roles_2 = <RoleSet_2, Rel_2>$ the role models of two networks KFN_1 and KFN_2 of the same team (maybe created by different planners), and KFN the union of KFN_1 and KFN_2 (that is, $KFN_1 \cup KFN_2$). The role model of KFN can be obtained by using the following union operation:

$$Roles = Roles_1 \cup Roles_2 = <RoleSet_1 \cup RoleSet_2, Rel_1 \cup Rel_2>.$$

People, teams and tasks are the three main considerations in building a knowledge flow network. Composition of networks should respect the following principles:

The flow effectiveness principle. Composition of knowledge flow networks should ensure the effectiveness of the composed network. Effectiveness will be achieved if flows in the same chain share the same knowledge space or subspace so that the right knowledge can be delivered to the node in need of it, and so that the content of a flow can be stored at the right node. Where there are intensity differences between nodes, knowledge flow is only effective from the node with higher intensity to that with lower.

The organizational effectiveness principle. Composition of knowledge flow networks will not be effective unless it meets the regulations and targets of the team. If the composition requires that the team expand then the expansion should help meet regulations and targets, for example in respect of profit, security and copyright.

The task relevancy principle. Knowledge gained by the composite team should help the team complete its tasks. If knowledge resulting from the composition does not help task completion, then the composition is ineffective.

The mutual benefit principle. All members of the team should benefit from the composition, for example by gaining helpful knowledge or by increase in some reward. Otherwise, the team may suffer from lessened cooperation in the long run.

The minimum coverage principle. The composite knowledge flow network should be the smallest that includes all the nodes and flows of the original networks. In other words, there must be no redundant flows or nodes. Otherwise effective knowledge sharing cannot be assured in the composite network.

The trust principle. Effective cooperation requires that team members trust each other as much as possible.

5.8.2 *Knowledge flow network components*

A large–scale building block used in the design of knowledge flow networks is the knowledge flow component. It is a knowledge flow network that is *independent, encapsulated,* and *complete.*

Independence. Processing within a component should be relatively independent of that in other components. Consequently the density of knowledge flow paths within a component is usually higher than that between components.

Encapsulation. It can itself be used as a knowledge node. A knowledge flow component can be normalized to have just one initial node and one successful final node. Any external knowledge flow can only use the component through those two nodes.

Completeness. The knowledge flow process is complete in both build–time (definition phase) and run–time (execution phase).

A knowledge flow network component is called *definition complete* if: (1) every internal node has at least one input and one output flow, (2) every internal flow except from the final node goes to an internal node, (3) the final node can be reached from the initial node, and, (4) there is no isolated node or subnetwork.

Execution completeness requires that all restrictions and conditions be met during execution, and that the execution of the knowledge flow component can be treated as that of a single knowledge node.

Components can be used to compose a knowledge flow network. Using known and well-understood patterns of flow can help planners compose effective new networks in the same way that using design patterns leads to effective software engineering (E. Gamma, et al., "Design patterns: elements of reusable object-oriented software", *Pearson Education*, 1995). It can also promote understanding between planners.

A knowledge flow network pattern is an abstraction of a mode of teamwork. In the pattern, every node should be reachable from every other node via a path of nodes and flows under certain constraints. The flow characteristic of the pattern is peer–to–peer.

Further work needs to be done on the following aspects:
(1) Mathematical models for adapting a knowledge flow network to new conditions;
(2) Algorithms for matching patterns and components and for selecting usable ones; and,
(3) Approaches that consider intention, trust and belief (B.J. Grosz and S. Kraus, "Collaborative plans for complex group action", *Artificial Intelligence*, 1996, vol.86, pp.269-357).

5.8.3 *The team organization principle*

Trust between team members is an important factor that affects team cooperation. People more trusted by current team members should be preferred when recruiting.

The distribution of page ranks of the Web obeys the "power-law" and "the rich get richer" rules, and so do aspects of many other networks (L.A. Adamic and B.A. Huberman, "Power-Law Distribution of the World Wide Web", *Science*, 2000, vol.287, no.24, pp.2115).

The distribution of trust levels is somewhat similar to that of Web page ranks because nodes with high trust levels have more opportunities to cooperate than nodes with low trust levels.

However, knowledge differences tend to level off, a "the poor get richer" rule, because a node with less knowledge can gain from nodes with more (that is, knowledge intensity always tends to equilibrium).

The following principle can now be affirmed.

Principle. *A team prefers the recruit who has more knowledge and is highly trusted by more team members.*

5.9 Resource-Mediated Knowledge Flows

Knowledge flows can be also generated and carried out by asking and answering; knowledge flowing from the person/role who answers a question to the person / role who asks the question.

Some relationships between resources reflect knowledge flows between resources' authors. For example, citation relationships between scientific papers reflect knowledge flows from an author of a paper being cited to an author of the paper that cites it. A citing paper is a confluence of incoming knowledge flows and a source of output knowledge flows conveying the innovation of its author(s). So a resource–mediated knowledge flow management tool would be very useful in managing knowledge and in exploring the nature of innovation in scientific research.

Hyperlinks between resources reflect a kind of weak citation relationship. Semantic relationships between resources can be set up to refine the citation relationship by using text–mining approaches (J. Han and M. Kambr, "Data Mining: Concepts and Techniques", *Morgan Kaufmann Publishers*, 2000).

In resource-mediated mode, knowledge flows through four types of links: *question answering links*, *citation links*, *hyperlinks*, and *semantic links,* as shown by the broken lines in Fig. 5.2.

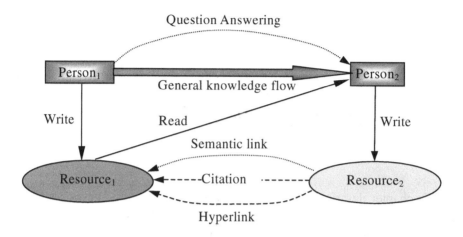

Fig. 5.2 Resource-mediated knowledge flows.

Algorithms for computing the ranks in a knowledge flow network can be designed with reference to the PageRank algorithm (J. Kleinberg and S. Lawrence, "The structure of the Web", *Science*, 2001, vol.294, no.30, pp.1849-1850).

A Knowledge Grid has three flows: *knowledge*, *information* and *service*. Exploring their common features can lead to the design and implementation of a uniform flow model. In-depth investigation of knowledge flow involves interdisciplinary research into management, cognition, psychology and epistemology.

Chapter 6

Exploring Scale-Free Networks

This chapter describes the properties of diverse scale-free networks and reviews the development of methods for modeling such networks, covering random graph theory, small-world effects, the idea of preferential attachment, and the dynamic evolution of these networks. By extending the current scale-free network model, we explore an abstract live network—a possible high-level model for Knowledge Grid development.

6.1 Introduction

Complex networks are common in nature and society. The World Wide Web is a complex network, where nodes are Web pages connected by hyperlinks pointing from one page to another. The Internet is also a complex network, where a large number of routers and computers are linked by various physical and wireless links. Another wonderful example is the brain, which is an enormous network of microscopic nerve cells connected by axons and in many other ways, and the nerve cells are themselves networks of molecules connected by biochemical reactions.

The importance and pervasiveness of complex networks in both natural and artificial fields have drawn the attention of many scientists. But so far, we are still far from uncovering all the rules and principles. The past few years have witnessed dramatic advances: increased computing power allows us to gather, share and analyze data on a scale far larger than before. A variety of complex networks — from information networks (for example, the World Wide Web, citation networks) to biological networks (for example, a cell's metabolic system) to social networks (for example, actors in Hollywood)—have been discovered to share an important property: the systems are dominated overall by relatively few nodes that are linked to relatively many other nodes. Networks containing such dominant nodes are called *scale-free* in the sense that some nodes have a very large number of links, whereas most nodes have relatively very few. It has been shown that such scale-free networks are remarkably robust against accidental failure but vulnerable to coordinated attack.

How then do the distinctive characteristics of such a network come about? (L.A. Adamic, B.A. Huberman, "Power-law Distribution of the World Wide Web", *Science*, 2000, vol.287, p.2115; R. Albert, H. Jeong, A.L. Barabási, "Diameter of the world-wide web", *Nature*, 1999, vol.401, pp.130-131). Several statistical methods for characterizing and modeling network structure will be discussed in this chapter.

Traditionally, complex networks with no specific governing rules have been described as random graphs, proposed as the simplest and most direct realization of a complex network. This idea has its roots in the work of two Hungarian mathematicians, Paul Erdös and Alfréd Rényi. In their model, pairs of nodes to be linked are randomly chosen. The most intriguing question here is whether or not such a simple operation is enough to produce a scale-free structure. If not, we will return to the question posed in the previous paragraph.

One basic measure of the structure of a complex network that has assumed particular importance is its degree distribution, $P(k)$ (D.S. Callaway, et al., "Are randomly grown graphs really random?", *Phys. Rev.*, E64, 041902, 2001; P.L. Krapivsky and S. Redner, "Organization of growing random networks", *Phys. Rev.*, E63, 066123-1-066123014, 2001; W.E. Leland, et al., "On the self-similar nature of Ethernet traffic", *IEEE/ACM Transactions on Networking*, 1994, pp.1-15;

A.L. Barabási and R. Albert, "Emergence of Scaling in Random Networks", *Science*, 1999, vol.286, pp.509-512), defined as the number of nodes that are linked to *k* other nodes. In a network where links are placed randomly, the majority of nodes have approximately the same number of links and the whole system takes on a deeply democratic structure. Therefore its degree follows a Poisson distribution with a peak at some *k* (A.L. Barabási and E. Bonabeau, "Scale-free networks", *Scientific American*, May 2003, pp.50-59; A.L. Barabási, R. Albert and H. Jeong, "Mean-field theory for scale-free random networks", *Physica A*, 1999, vol.272, pp.173-187). Perhaps the most significant advance that promotes the adoption of various modeling measures is the discovery that for most large networks the degree distribution deviates somewhat from a Poisson distribution. For example, a recent project to map the Internet found that its degree distribution follows a power law. Power laws are quite different from the bell-shaped distributions that characterize random networks. In particular, a power law does not have a peak, as the Poisson distribution does, but is instead described by a continuously decreasing function. This discovery allows various scale-free models to be constructed, and could well lead to a universal theory of network evolution.

This chapter reviews theoretical developments in statistical theory used to characterize complex networks, and then describes a scenario and modeling approach for the future interconnection environment.

6.2 The Topologies of Some Real Networks

The rapid development in speed and capability of computers and networks allows us to collect and generate data on a global scale, so the exploration of the underlying architecture of various complex systems has become active and fruitful. We review here the study of some representative networks with structures that are scale-free.

6.2.1 The Internet

The Internet is a net of interconnected nodes: hosts (users' computers), servers (computers or programs providing a network service) that may also be hosts, and routers that direct traffic across the Internet as shown in Fig. 6.1 (M. Faloutsos, P. Faloutsos and C. Faloutsos, "On power law relationships of the Internet topology", *Comput. Commun. Rev.*, 1999, vol.29, pp.251-262; Q. Chen, et al., "The origin of power laws in Internet topologies revisited", in *Proceedings of the 21st Annual Joint Conference of the IEEE Computer and Communications Societies*, IEEE Computer Society, 2002).

Internet

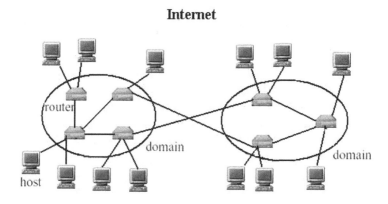

Fig. 6.1 Naive scheme of the structure of the Internet.

The topology of the Internet may be studied at two different levels. At the router level, the nodes are the routers and computers, and the links are the wires and cables that physically connect them. At the domain level, each domain (or autonomous system), composed of very many routers and computers, is considered to be a single node. A link is drawn between two domains if there is at least one route that connects them

(R. Govindan and H. Tangmunarunkit, "Heuristics for Internet Map Discovery", *Proceedings of the 2000 IEEE INFOCOM Conference*, Tel Aviv, Israel, March 2000, pp.1371-1380; S.H. Yook, et al., "Modeling the Internet's large-scale topology", cond-mat/0107417).

At the domain level, the Internet is a relatively small sparse network with the following basic characteristics. In November 1997, it consisted of 3015 nodes and 5156 links, the average degree distribution was 3.42, and the highest degree of a node was 590. In April 1998, there were 3530 nodes and 6432 links, the average degree was 3.65, and the highest degree was 746. In December 1998 there were 4389 nodes and 8256 links, the average degree was 3.76 and the highest degree was 979. The degree distribution of this network was reported to be of power law form, $P(k) \sim k^{-\gamma}$, where $\gamma = 2.2$ (M. Faloutsos, P. Faloutsos and C. Faloutsos, "On power-law relationships of the Internet topology", *Computer Communications Review*, 1999, vol.29, pp.251-262).

At the router level, going by relatively poor data from 1995 (J.J. Pansiot and D. Grad, "On routes and multicast trees in the Internet", *Computer Communications Review*, 1998, vol.28, pp.41-50), the Internet consisted of 3888 nodes and 5012 links, with the average degree 2.57 and the highest degree 39. The degree distribution of this network was fitted by a power law with $\gamma = 2.5$. Note that the estimate based on the highest degree value gives a quite different value, $\gamma = 1 + \ln 3888 / \ln 39 = 3.3$, so that the empirical value of the γ exponent is not very accurate. In 2000, Govindan and Tangmunarunkit found that the Internet had by then about 150,000 routers connected by 200,000 links (R. Govindan and H. Tangmunarunkit, "Heuristics for Internet Map Discovery", *Proceedings of the 2000 IEEE INFOCOM Conference*, Tel Aviv, Israel, March 2000, pp.1371-1380). The degree distribution was found to "lend some support to the conjecture that a power law governs the degree distribution of real networks". If this is true, one can estimate from this degree distribution that its γ exponent is about 2.3.

6.2.2 The World Wide Web

The World Wide Web is the largest network for which topological information is available. The nodes of network are the Web pages and its links are the hyperlinks pointing from one page to another, as shown in Fig. 6.2.

World Wide Web

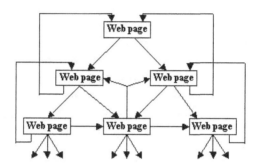

Fig. 6.2 Naive scheme of the structure of the WWW.

The size of this network was close to one billion nodes at the end of 1999 (S. Lawrence and C.L. Giles, "Searching the World Wide Web", *Science*, vol.280, no.5360, 1998, pp.98-100; S. Lawrence and C.L. Giles, "Accessibility of Information on the Web", *Nature*, vol.400, no.8, 1999, pp.107-109). Interest in the World Wide Web as a network boomed after it was discovered that the degree distribution of Web pages followed a power law over several orders of magnitude. Since the links of the World Wide Web are directed, the network is characterized by two degree distributions. That of outgoing links, $P_{out}(k)$, signifies the probability that a Web page has k outgoing hyperlinks. That of incoming links, $P_{in}(k)$, is the probability that k hyperlinks point to a page.

Several studies have established that both $P_{out}(k)$ and $P_{in}(k)$ have power law tails: $P_{out}(k) = k^{-r_{out}}$ and $P_{in}(k) = k^{-r_{in}}$.

Albert et al. studied a subset of the World Wide Web containing 325,729 nodes and have found $\gamma_{out} = 2.45$ and $\gamma_{in} = 2.1$ (R. Albert, H. Jeong, A.L. Barabási, "Diameter of the world-wide web", *Nature*, 1999, vol.401, pp.130-131). Kumar et al. used a 40-million-page crawl by Alexa Inc., obtaining $\gamma_{out} = 2.38$ and $\gamma_{in} = 2.1$. A later survey of the World Wide Web topology by Broder et al. used two Altavista crawls over a total of 200 million pages, obtaining $\gamma_{out} = 2.72$ and $\gamma_{in} = 2.1$ (A. Broder, et al., "Graph structure of the Web", *Proceedings of the 9th WWW conference*, Amsterdam, May 2000, pp.309-320; R. Kumar, et al., "Extracting large-scale knowledge bases from the Web", *Proceedings of the 25th VLDB Conference*, Edinburgh, Scotland, September 1999, pp.639-650). Fig. 6.3 shows the degree distributions of incoming and outgoing links from two different sources: squares stand for the results of Albert et al., and circles for the results of Broder et al. (R. Albert and A.L. Barabási, "Statistical Mechanics of complex networks", *Reviews of Modern Physics*, 2002, vol.74, pp.48-94).

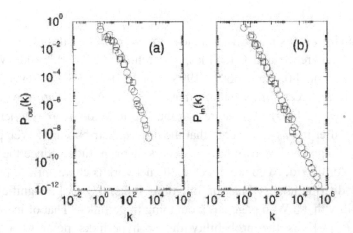

Fig. 6.3 Degree distribution of Web pages.

Adamic and Huberman used a somewhat different representation of the World Wide Web, with each node representing a separate domain name and considering two nodes to be linked if any of the pages in one domain linked to any page in the other. While this method lumped together pages that were in the same domain, a nontrivial aggregation of the nodes, the distribution of incoming links still followed a power law with $\gamma = 1.94$ (L.A. Adamic and B.A. Huberman, "Power-law Distribution of the World Wide Web", *Science*, 2000, vol.287, p.2115).

6.2.3 Networks of citations of scientific papers

In the network defined by citation relationships between scientific papers, nodes stand for scientific papers and directed links from the starting node to the ending node denote the link from the citing paper to the cited paper. There is a sequencing constraint for papers: in general, a paper can only cite papers published before it, though occasionally a citation will specify *in print* or *preprint*. Hence, the citation network takes on a distinctive feature—no closed loops.

The growth of citation networks is very simple. As illustrated in Fig. 6.4, a new node joins the net only if it contains at least one reference to an older node. This is the only way to create new nodes and links. Since citations between old papers will never be updated, new links between old papers will not appear. The number of citations of any paper is the in-degree of the corresponding node of the network.

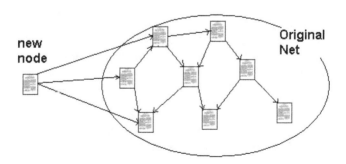

Fig. 6.4 Growth of citation networks.

Render collected and examined numerical data based on two relatively large sets of data. One set was about papers published in 1981 in journals that were catalogued by the Institute for Scientific Information (783,339 papers). The other was about 20 years of publications in Physical Review D, (vols.11-50, 24,296 papers). The main finding of this study was that the asymptotic tail of the citation distribution appears to be described by a power law, $N(k) \sim k^{-\gamma}$, with $\gamma = 3$ (S. Redner, "How Popular is Your Paper? An Empirical Study of the Citation Distribution", *European Physics Journal B*, 1998, vol.4, pp.131-134). This conclusion is reached indirectly by means of a Zipf plot measure (see Fig. 6.5).

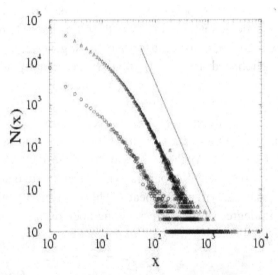

Fig. 6.5. Citation distribution from the 738,339 papers in the ISI data set ($\triangle$) and the 24,296 papers in the PRD data set (o). After Render's paper.

A more recent study by Vazquez extended these studies to the outgoing degree distribution as well, finding that it has an exponential tail (A. Vazquez, "Statistics of citation networks", 2001, cond-mat/0105031).

6.2.4 Networks of collaboration

As an object of scientific study, collaboration networks have a great advantage in their copious and relatively reliable data. The links between collaborators can be vividly depicted by a bipartite graph (see Fig. 6.6) containing two distinct types of nodes—collaborators (denoted by empty circles) and collaborations (denoted by filled circles) (M.E.J. Newman, et al., "Random graphs with arbitrary degree distribution and their applications", *Phys. Rev. E*, 2001, vol.64, no.026118, cond-mat/0007235).

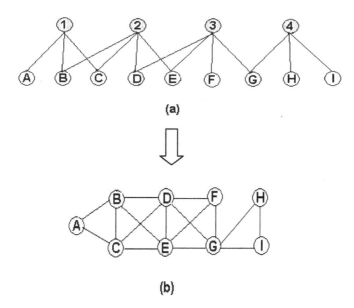

Fig. 6.6 A bipartite graph (a) and its projection (b).

Collaborations are of different sets of collaborators, so the collaboration nodes link to the individual collaborator nodes. Note that the bipartite graph stresses the relation between two roles, not the interactions between collaborators, so direct links between nodes of the same kind are absent and the links are undirected. The bipartite graph can also be transformed into its corresponding network by removing collaborations and linking collaborators that are linked to the same collaboration (see Fig. 6.6 (b)) (M.E.J. Newman, "The structure of scientific collaboration networks", *Proc. Nat. Acad. Sci. U.S.A.*, 2001, vol.98, p.404-409; M.E.J. Newman, "Scientific collaboration networks: I. Network construction and fundamental results", *Phys. Rev. E*, 2001, vol.64, 016131. M.E.J. Newman, "Scientific collaboration networks: II. Shortest paths, weighted networks, and centrality", *Phys. Rev. E*, 2001, vol.64, 016132; M.E.J. Newman, "Who is the best connected scientist? A study of scientific coauthorship networks", *Phys. Rev. E*, 2001, vol.64, 016131, cond-mat/0011144).

A classical and much studied network is the movie actor collaboration network, which is thoroughly documented in the online Internet Movie Database (http://www.imdb.com) (D.J. Watts and S.H. Strogatz, "Collective dynamics of small-world networks", *Nature*, 1998, vol.393, pp.440-442; L.A.N. Amaral, et al., "Classes of small-world networks", *Proc. Nat. Acad. Sci.*, 2000, vol.97, no.21, pp.11149-11152; R. Albert and A.L. Barabási, "Topology of evolving networks: Local events and universality", *Phys. Rev. Lett.*, 2000, vol.85, pp.5234-5237, cond-mat/0005085).

In its bipartite graph, the two types of node are movies and actors respectively. An actor node is linked to a movie node if the actor appeared in the movie. These relationships can be reconfigured by the projection of this graph onto a graph including actor nodes only, where two actor nodes are connected by an undirected link if and only if the actors collaborated in a movie. Since the construction of the actor-node-only network loses data about multiple collaborations contained in the original bipartite network, it is better to model collaboration networks using the full bipartite structure.

Similar examples are the Boards of Directors of companies in which two directors are linked if they belong to the same board (G.F. Davis and H.R. Greve, "Corporate élite networks and governance changes in the 1980s", *Am. J. Sociol.*, 1997, vol.103, pp.1-37), and co-ownership networks of companies in which individuals as co-owners are linked, and collaborations of scientists in which scientists as the co-authors in the same paper are linked (A.L. Barabási, et al., "Evolution of the social network of scientific collaborations", *Physica A*, 2002, vol.311, pp.590-614; V. Batagelj and A. Mrvar, "Some analyses of the Erdös collaboration graph", *Social Networks*, 2000, vol.22, pp.173-186).

The degree distribution in the movie/actor network, with the number of nodes $N = 212,250$ and the average degree $k = 28.78$, was observed to obey a power law form with exponent $\gamma = 2.4$ (A.L. Barabási and R. Albert, "Emergence of Scaling in Random Networks", *Science*, 1999, vol.286, pp.509-512). The degree distribution of mathematical journals containing 70,975 different authors and 70,901 published papers was investigated and described by a power law with exponent $\gamma = 2.4$. *Neuroscience* journal issues from 1991 to 1998, containing 209,293 authors with 3,534,724 citations and 210,750 papers, were scanned in and the degree distribution was fitted by a power law with exponent $\gamma = 2.4$ (A.L Barabási, et al., "Evolution of the social network of scientific collaborations", *Physica A*, 2002, vol.311, pp.590-614; H. Jeong, Z. Neda and A.L. Barabási, "Measuring preferential attachment for evolving networks", *Europhysics letters*, 2003, vol.61, pp.567-572, cond-mat/0104131).

6.2.5 Networks of human language

The human language as a carrier of information can also be thought of as a network made up of word nodes or some other components linked by semantic or other relationships. There are various ways to link such nodes when constructing a network based on a language bank. For instance, one may link neighboring words within sentences. In this case there will be a link between two nodes if and only if the words are next to one another in at least one sentence in the language bank. Or one may also link the second nearest neighbors for each word in a sentence, which gives rise to two types of links.

Ferrer and Sole constructed a Word Web for the English language based on the British National Corpus (R. Ferrer and R.V. Sole, "The small-world of human language", *Working Papers of Santa Fe Institute*, http://www.santafe.edu/sfi/publications/Abstracts/01-03-004abs.htm).
The nodes are English words, and the undirected links are connections between every pair of nodes that have their words as neighbors in sentences of the corpus. Two slightly different networks, called the unrestricted word network (UWN) and the restricted word network (RWN), yielded $N_{UWN} = 478,773$, $N_{RWN} = 460,902$ nodes, and $E_{UWN} = 1.77 \times 10^7$, $E_{UWN} = 1.61 \times 10^7$ links. The two networks, however, gave very similar results for the distribution of degrees after about three quarters of the 10^7 words of the British National Corpus (a collection of text samples of both spoken and written modern British English) had been processed. The degree distribution of the UWN and RWN showed two sections with different power law exponents: $\gamma_1 = -0.15$ for the first and $\gamma_2 = -0.27$ for the second (see Fig. 6.7).

Based on these results, Dorogovtsev and Mendes proposed a simple stochastic theory of the evolution of human language based on the view of language as an evolving network of interacting words (S.N. Dorogovtsev and J.F.F. Mendes, "Language as an evolving Word Web", *Proc. Royal Soc. London B*, vol.268, No.2603, 2001, cond-mat/0105093). To characterize the Word Web, they adopted the idea of preferential attachment: the more links a node acquires, the more likely it is to be linked to subsequently.

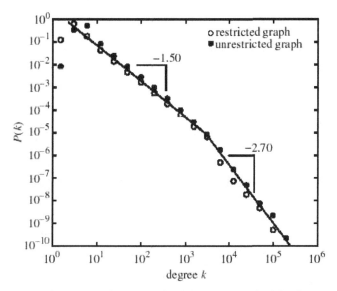

Fig. 6.7 Degree distribution for the word network. After R. Ferrer and R.V. Sole's paper.

The idea can be described as follows. At each time step, a new node (word) is added to the network, and the total number of nodes t plays the role of time. The new node is linked to some old one i with the probability proportional to its degree k_i. In addition, $c\,t$ new links are created between old nodes, where c is a coefficient that characterizes the network. These new links between old nodes i and j are formed with probability proportional to the product of their degrees $k_i k_j$. Note that all the links are undirected.

Dorogovtsev and Mendes concluded that the basic characteristic of the word net structure, namely its degree distribution, does not depend on the rules of the language but is determined entirely by the general principles of the evolutionary dynamics of the word network.

6.2.6 Other networks

Besides the above representative networks, there exist, however, many other kinds of network, which also play important roles in their own fields.

Biological networks, for example, are a useful and valuable kind of network, which recently attracted much attention (H. Jeong, et al., "The large-scale organization of metabolic networks", *Nature*, 2000, vol.407, pp.651-654).

Food webs are useful to quantify the interaction between various species. In a food web the nodes are species and the links represent predator-prey relationships between species (N.D. Martinez, "Artifacts or attributes? Effects of resolution on the Little Rock Lake food web", *Ecological Monographs*, 1991, vol.61, pp.367-392).

A genomic regulatory system can be regarded as an extremely large directed network, where the nodes are the distinct components of the system, and the links point from the regulating to the regulated component (S.A. Kauffman, *The Origins of Order: Self-organization and Selection in Evolution*, Oxford University Press, Oxford, 1993).

Long distance telephone call patterns are another class of large directed graph, which have long been constructed in the telecommunications industry. In these graphs, the nodes are phone numbers and every completed phone call is a link directed from the caller to the receiver (W. Aiello, F. Chung and L. Lu, "A random graph model for massive graphs", *Proceedings of the 32nd ACM Symposium on the Theory of Computing*, New York, 2000, pp.171-180).

The power grid is regarded as a complex network whose nodes are generators, transformers and substations, and whose links are high-voltage transmission lines (D.J. Watts, *Small Worlds*, Princeton University Press, Princeton, 1999).

One interesting study of the class diagram (a notation in software engineering) of the public Java Development Framework 1.2 revealed that its optimization design process turns out to be a scale-free network (S. Valverde, R.F. Cancho and R.V. Sole, "Scale-free Networks from Optimal Design", *Europhysics Letters*, 2002, vol.60, pp.512-517, cond-mat/0204344).

In addition, electronic circuits are also viewed as undirected graphs. Their nodes are electronic components (resistors, diodes, capacitors, and the like, in analog circuits and logic gates in digital circuits) and their undirected links are wires (R. Ferrer, C. Janssen and R.V. Sole, "The topology of technology graphs: Small-world patterns in electronic circuits", *Phys. Rev.*, E, vol.64, no.32767).

6.3 Random Graph Theory

Traditionally, networks of complex topology have been treated as completely random graphs. This paradigm has its roots in the work of two Hungarian mathematicians, Paul Erdös and Alfréd Rényi, who were the first to study the statistical aspects of random graphs by probabilistic methods (P. Erdös and A. Rényi, "On random graphs", *Publications Mathematicæ* 1959, vol.6, pp.290-297; P. Erdös and A. Rényi, "On the evolution of random graphs", *Publications of the Mathematical Institute of the Hungarian Academy of Sciences*, 1960, vol.5, pp.17-61).

In the Erdös-Rényi (ER) graph model:

(1) The total number of nodes N is fixed;
(2) The probability that any two nodes are linked is p.

Consequently the total number of links n is a random variable with the expectation value $E(n) = p N (N-1)/2$. The degree distribution is binomial:

$$P(k) = \binom{N-1}{k} p^k (1-p)^{N-1-k}$$

So the average degree is $k = p (N-1)$. For large N, the distribution takes the Poisson form with a bell shape, $P(k) = e^{-k} \overline{k}^k / k!$. The clear prediction of the ER model is that, because of the random placement of links, the resulting system will be deeply democratic: most nodes will have approximately the same number of links and it will be extremely rare to find nodes that have significantly more or fewer links than the average.

What's more, the ER model demonstrates that many properties of diverse random graphs appear quite suddenly at a threshold value of $p_c \sim c/N$. That is, for $p < p_c$ the graph is composed of many isolated clusters, while at p_c large clusters form, which towards the limit become a single cluster.

Fig. 6.8 shows the graph evolution process for the ER model. As illustrated in Fig. 6.8 (a), we start with $N = 10$ isolated nodes. Then pairs of nodes are linked with probability p. Figures (b), (c) and (d) show three results for $p = 0.1, 0.15$ and 0.2 respectively. We notice the emergence of clusters with increasing p. In this context, a linked cluster unites half of the nodes at $p = 0.15$. In the limit $p = 1$, the graph becomes fully linked.

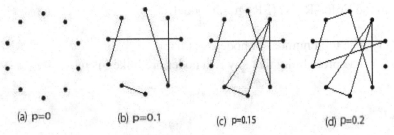

(a) p=0   (b) p=0.1   (c) p=0.15   (d) p=0.2

Fig. 6.8 An example of graph evolution for the ER model.

6.4 The Small-World Theory

The small-world phenomenon (D.J. Watts, "Networks, dynamics, and the small-world phenomenon", *Am. J. Sociol.*, 1999, vol.105, pp.493-592; D.J. Watts, *Small Worlds*, Princeton University Press, Princeton, 1999) is common among networks in nature. "Small" means that almost every node in such a network is to some degree "close" to every other, even to those that are perceived as likely to be far away. Thus "small" describes the global property of such networks: remarkably short path lengths. Also, in such networks there is fairly high clustering locally.

To facilitate description, we introduce here a clustering coefficient giving the extent to which nodes link together locally. The clustering coefficient is defined as the probability that the immediate neighbors of one node are also neighbors of one another. Interestingly enough, small-world networks simultaneously possess the features of random networks —short path length; and of ordered lattices—high clustering.

Watts and Strogatz studied the inherent relationships between these three systems and developed a one-dimensional link-rewiring process that can interpolate between regular and random networks (D.J. Watts and S.H. Strogatz, "Collective dynamics of 'small-world' networks", *Nature*, 1998, vol.393, pp.440-442). The Watts-Strogatz (WS) model begins with a one-dimensional lattice of n nodes with each linked to its k nearest neighbors by undirected links (for example, in Fig. 6.9 (a) $n = 20$ and $k = 4$). And then with probability p each link is rewired until every link in the original lattice has been treated once. Rewiring here means moving one endpoint of the link away to a new node chosen at random over the entire lattice but such that no node is linked to itself. Networks of different topology are obtained by tuning the probability p within the range [0, 1]. As illustrated in Fig. 6.9, for one extreme $p = 0$, the original lattice is unchanged; but as p increases, the graph becomes increasingly disordered until at $p = 1$, it becomes a random graph. In this sense, random graphs are small worlds as well. Fig. 6.10 shows the clustering coefficient $C(p)$ as circles, and the path length $L(p)$ as squares, both

The Knowledge Grid

functions of the rewiring probability p. For clarity, both C and L are divided by their maximum value which is taken as $C(0)$ and $L(0)$ respectively. As p increases smoothly from 0 to 1, the path length drops rapidly, though clustering declines relatively slowly, but when p is near 0, clustering is almost stable. This result suggests that the rewiring of a few links can have a great influence on the local property, but little on the global property. According to Watts and Strogatz, small-world networks are those having large clustering and short path length. Besides rewiring, adding links uniformly at random on an ordered lattice can also lead to a small-world network (see Fig. 6.9 (b)).

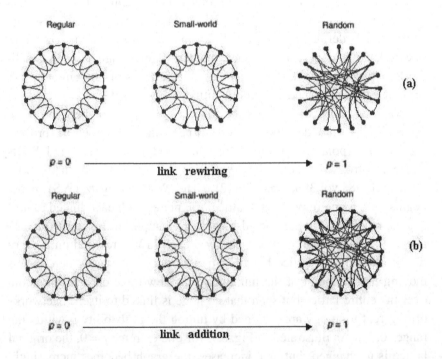

Fig. 6.9 Small-world networks realized through interpolating between a regular lattice and a random network.

The degree distribution of the WS model depends strongly on p (A. Barrat and M. Weigt, "On the properties of small-world networks", *Eur. Phys. J. B*, 2000, vol.13, pp.547-560). When $p = 0$, each node has the same degree k, and the degree distribution is a delta function centered at k, $P(k) = \delta(k - z)$ where z is the coordination number of the lattice, while for $0 < p < 1$, $P(k)$ becomes broader but is still peaked around z. Ultimately, as p approaches 1, the degree distribution $P(k)$ approaches that of a random graph.

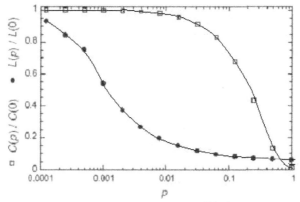

Fig. 6.10 The clustering coefficient $C(p)$ and the path length $L(p)$ as a function of rewiring probability p.

From the above, we can see that the degree distribution of the small-world model does not match most real-world networks very well. This is not surprising. However, the small-world model is concerned with clustering and path length properties, not with degree distribution. Certainly, many real networks simultaneously display the features of both scale-free and small-world networks. These observations pose the challenge of developing a more suitable model to describe real networks in all their aspects.

6.5 Modeling Measures for Live Scale-Free Networks

Over the past few years, scientists have discovered that various complex networks, both natural and artificial, share an important property—some nodes have very many links to other nodes, while most nodes have just a handful—which exhibits a pronounced power law scaling. The dominant nodes can have hundreds, thousands, or even millions of links. In this sense, the networks appear to have no scale.

Scale-free networks have some important characteristics. They are, for instance, remarkably resistant to accidental failure but extremely vulnerable to coordinated attack. We review here some of the main modeling measures for scale-free systems and attempt to gain an insight into the actual rules that govern the growth of such systems.

6.5.1 The Barabási-Albert model

The power law degree distribution was first observed in networks by Barabási and Albert, who proposed an improved version of the Erdős-Rényi (ER) theory of random networks to account for the scaling properties of a number of systems, including the link structure of the Web (A.L. Barabási, R. Albert and H. Jeong, "Mean-field theory for scale-free random networks", *Physica A*, 1999, vol.272, pp.173-187; A.L. Barabási and R. Albert, "Emergence of Scaling in Random Networks", *Science*, vol.286, 1999, pp.509-512). They argued that the key factor in capturing the topological evolution of scale-free networks is the hypothesis that highly linked nodes increase their connectivity faster than less linked peers, a phenomenon called preferential attachment.

The scale-free BA model introduced by Barabási and Albert, incorporating growth with preferential attachment, leads naturally to the observed scale invariant distribution. The model is defined in the following two aspects:

(1) Growth: Starting with a small number (m_0) of nodes, at each time step we add a new node with m ($\leqslant m_0$) links that will be linked to the nodes already present in the system.

(2) Preferential attachment: When choosing the nodes to which the new node links, we assume that the probability Π that a new node will be linked to node i depends on the connectivity k_i of that node, and will be $\Pi\left(k_i\right) = k_i / \sum_j k_j$.

Then at time step t the expected total number of nodes and links are $t + m_0$ and mt respectively. Barabási and Albert developed a mean-field method to calculate $p(k) = 2m^2 t / (k^3 \times (m_0 + t))$ with $\gamma = 3$. Simulations were carried out validating this result. Fig. 6.11 (a) shows degree distributions $p(k)$ with $N = m_0 + t = 300,000$ and $m_0 = m = 1$ (circles), $m_0 = m = 3$ (squares), $m_0 = m = 5$ (diamonds) and $m_0 = m = 7$ (triangles). The slope of the dashed line is $\gamma = 2.9$. Fig. 6.11 (b), for $m_0 = m = 5$, and system sizes $N = 100,000$ (circles), $N = 150,000$ (squares) and $N = 200,000$ (diamonds) shows that $p(k)$ is independent of time, and consequently independent of the system size.

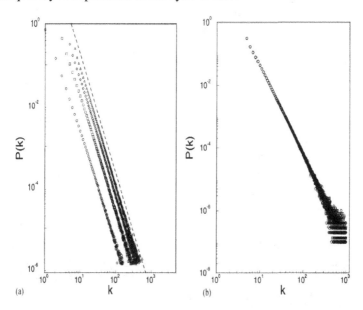

Fig. 6.11 Numerical simulations of the BA model. After Barabási and Albert's paper.

The BA model is successful in explaining the emergence of power law statistics in the link structure of growing networks. However, when applied to the Web, it fails to predict a scaling exponent that agrees with the observed value. But we should emphasize that the preferential attachment mechanism proposed by Barabási and Albert is the basic idea of the modern theory of evolving networks.

6.5.2 Generalizations of the Barabási-Albert model

6.5.2.1 Link rewiring

Because the measured and predicted exponents disagreed, Albert and Barabási later introduced an extended model of network evolution that gives a more realistic description of the Web, incorporating the addition of new nodes, new links, and the rewiring of links. They made some modifications to the rules of growth. The starting conditions of the extended model were the same, but it was revised to have three phases instead of the previous two phases ("Topology of Evolving Networks: Local Events and Universality", *Phys. Rev. Lett.*, 2000, vol.85, pp.5234-5237):

(1) With probability p, the network adds m ($\leqslant m_0$) new links:

$$\left(\frac{\partial k_i}{\partial t}\right) = pm\frac{1}{N} + pm\frac{(k_i+1)}{\sum_j(k_j+1)}$$

where N is the size of the system. A node is randomly selected as the starting point of the new link that corresponds to the first term in the equation above (for example, a web developer decides to add a new hyperlink to a page). To reflect the second term, the other end of the link is selected with the following probability:

$$\Pi(k_i) = \frac{k_i + 1}{\sum_j (k_j + 1)}$$

because new links prefer to point to popular nodes, those with a high number of links. The process is repeated m times.

(2) With probability q, m links are rewired:

$$\left(\frac{\partial k_i}{\partial t}\right) = -qm\frac{1}{N} + qm\frac{k_i + 1}{\sum_j (k_j + 1)}.$$

Here we randomly select a node i and a link l_{ij}. Then we remove this link with probability given by the first term and replace it with a new link l_{ij}' that connects i to node j' chosen with the probability given by the second term. Here m has the same significance as in rule (1).

(3) With probability $1 - p - q$, a new node is added:

$$\left(\frac{\partial k_i}{\partial t}\right) = (1 - p - q)m\frac{k_i + 1}{\sum_j (k_j + 1)}.$$

The new node, together with m new links connected to it is added into the system.

In the model, the probabilities p and q can be varied within the intervals $0 \leqslant p < 1$ and $0 \leqslant q < 1 - p$. Note that Albert and Barabási chose the probability $\Pi(k_i)$ to be proportional to $(k_i + 1)$ to ensure that all the nodes in the network can acquire links, even isolated nodes ($k_i = 0$). We also note that for $p = 0$ and $q = 0$, the model is reduced to the first one discussed above with the prediction of $\gamma = 3$.

By combining the contribution of the three processes, the network model evolves according to

$$\partial k_i / \partial t = (p - q)m / N + m(k_i + 1) / \sum_j (k_j + 1).$$

The total number of nodes $N(t) = m_0 + (1 - p - q)t$ and the total number of links $\sum_j k_j = (1 - q)2mt - m$, indicating that for large t, the initial condition for the constants m_0 and m is irrelevant. Its theoretical resolution has the following form:

$$P(k) = \left[k + \kappa(p,q,m) \right]^{-\gamma(p,q,m)},$$

which predicts for $q < q_{max} = \min\left\{ 1-p, (1-p+m)/(1+2m) \right\}$ the degree distribution follows a generalized power law, while for $q > q_{max}$, however, the equation is not valid, but numerical simulations indicate that $P(k)$ approaches an exponential. In addition, the exponent $\gamma(p,q,m)$ characterizing the tail of $P(k)$ for $k \gg \kappa(p,q)$ changes continuously with p, q, and m, predicting a range of exponents between 2 and ∞. From this result, we can see that this model offers a more realistic description of various real networks.

6.5.2.2 *Node attractiveness*

Dorogovtsev et al. modified the BA model by specifying that the probability that a new link points to a given k-degree node is proportional to the following characteristic of the node: $A_k = A^{(0)} + k$, called attractiveness (S.N. Dorogovtsev, J.F.F. Mendes, A.N. Samukhin, "Structure of growing networks with preferential linking", *Phys. Rev. Lett.*, 2000, vol.85, pp.4633-4636). All nodes are added with some initial attractiveness $A^{(0)}$ but its attractiveness increases later, proportionally to its degree k.

In the particular case of the BA model, $A^{(0)} = m$. The calculations indicate that the degree distribution follows $P(k) \sim k^{\gamma}$ with $\gamma = 2 + A^{(0)}/m$. Consequently the initial attractiveness does not destroy the scale-free nature of the degree distribution, but only changes the degree exponent. What is more, this exponent value is consistent with the empirical value of the exponent of the distribution of incoming links provided $A^{(0)}/m$ is sufficiently small.

In response to S. Bornholdt and H. Ebel ("World Wide Web scaling exponent from Simon's 1955 model", *Phys. Rev. E*, 2001, vol.64, 035104(R)), Dorogovtsev et al. further proposed a more generalized model and showed that this model is essentially the same as the Simon model (S.N. Dorogovtsev, J.F.F. Mendes, A.N. Samukhin, "WWW and Internet models from 1955 till our days and the 'popularity is attractive' principle", *Condensed Matter Archive*, 2000, cond-mat/0009090). The only mismatch is in the definitions of the time scales, and the differences in these do not influence the result. The model they considered is a combination of a preferential component (denoted by n_r) and a non-preferential component (denoted by m). The expression for the degree exponent thus is $\gamma = 2 + (n_r + n + B)/m$.

The Bornholdt-Ebel model is the particular case of $n_r = 0$, $n = 1$ and $B = 0$ with probability $\alpha = 1/(1+m)$, while the BA model is in fact the case of $n_r = 0$ and $n + B = m$.

6.5.3 The idea of random fraction for Web growth

While highly diverse information is added to the Web in an extremely complex and undisciplined manner, there may be certain rules hidden in the Web. Huberman and Adamic determined the distribution of site sizes based on two databases, Alexa and Infoseek, which covered 259,794 and 525,882 sites respectively (B.A. Huberman and L.A. Adamic, "Growth dynamics of the World-Wide Web", *Nature*, 1999, vol.401, p.131). Both data sets displayed a power law over several orders of magnitude. They used a simple stochastic growth model to explain this distribution.

Their assumption is that the day-to-day fluctuation in site size is proportional to the size of the site. One would not be surprised to find that a site with a million pages has lost or gained a few hundred pages on any given day. On the other hand, finding an additional hundred pages within a day on a site with just ten pages would be unusual, to say the least. Thus, they assume that the number n of pages on the site on a given day is equal to the number of pages on that site on the previous day, plus or minus a random fraction of n.

Two additional factors they considered are: first, sites appear at different times and grow at different rates; second, the number of Web sites has been growing exponentially since its inception, which means that there are many more young sites than old ones. When factoring the age of each site into the Web growth process, $P(n)$, the probability of finding a site of size n, obeys a power law. Thus, Huberman and Adamic draw the conclusion that considering sites with a wide range of distributions in growth rates yields the same result: a power law distribution in site size.

6.5.4 The Krapivsky-Redner model

Krapivsky et al. studied three models to investigate the evolution rules of the World Wide Web (P.L. Krapivsky and S. Redner, "Organization of growing random networks", *Phys. Rev. E*, 2001, vol. 63, 066123; P.L. Krapivsky and S. Redner, "Rate equation approach for growing networks", *Lecture Notes in Physics*, Springer, Berlin, 2003; P.L. Krapivsky, S. Redner and F. Leyvraz, "Connectivity of growing random networks", *Phys. Rev. Lett.*, 2000, vol.85, pp.4629-4632; P.L. Krapivsky, G.J. Rodgers and S. Redner, "Degree distributions of growing networks", *Phys. Rev. Lett.*, 2001, vol.86, pp.5401-5404). They quantified the structure of Web growth by the rate equation approach. These models are:

(1) The GN (growth network) model. At each time step, one node is added and immediately linked to an old node according to an attachment probability $A_k \sim k^\gamma$ that depends only on the degree of the "target" node.

(2) The WG (Web graph) model. This extends the GN model and allows link directionality that leads to independent in-degree and out-degree distributions. Network growth occurs by two distinct processes that are meant to mimic how hyperlinks are created in the Web:

① With probability p, a new node is introduced and it immediately links to an earlier target node. The linking probability depends only on the in-degree of the target.

② With probability $q = 1 - p$, a new link is created between already existing nodes. The choices of the originating and target nodes depend on the out-degree of the former and the in-degree of the latter.

(3) The MG (multi-component graph) model. Nodes and links are introduced independently.

① With probability p, a new unlinked node is introduced.

② With probability $q = 1 - p$, a new link is created between existing nodes. As in the WG model, the choices of the issuing and target nodes depend on the out-degree of the former and in-degree of the latter. Step ① allows for the formation of many clusters.

Note that very different behaviors arise for $\gamma < 1$, $\gamma = 1$, and $\gamma > 1$. Krapivsky et al. focus only on the strictly linear kernel $A_k \sim k$.

For a homogeneous GN model, $P(k) \sim k^{-3}$, while for a heterogeneous GN model, where each node is endowed with an intrinsic and permanently defined "attractiveness" η, the attachment rate is modified to be $A_k(\eta) = \eta k$ and the degree distribution is no longer a strict power law, but exhibits a logarithmic correction: $P(k) \sim k^{-(1+m(\eta))} (\ln k)^{-\omega}$.

As for the WG and MG models, the attachment rate $A(i, j)$, defined as the probability that a newly introduced node links to an existing node with i incoming and j outgoing links, depends only on the in-degree of the target node, $A(i, j) = A_i = i + \lambda_{\eta n}$, while the creation rate $C(i_1, j_1 \mid i_2, j_2)$, defined as the probability of adding a new link from $a(i_1, j_1)$ node to $a(i_2, j_2)$ node, depends only on the out-degree of the issuing   node   and   the   in-degree   of   the   target   node, $C\left(i_1, j_1 \mid i_2, j_2\right) = C\left(j_1, i_2\right)$. The parameters λ_{in} and λ_{out} are stochastic factors. By tuning model parameters to reasonable values, Krapivsky et al. obtain distinct power law forms for the in-degree and out-degree distributions with exponents that are in good agreement with current data for the Web.

6.5.5 The Simon model

Simon proposed a class of stochastic models that resulted in a power law distribution function, which was originally described in terms of the underlying process leading to the distribution of words in a piece of text (H.A. Simon, "On a class of skew distribution functions", *Biometrika*, 1955, vol. 42, pp.425-440; H.A. Simon, T. Van Wormer, "Some Monte Carlo estimates of the Yule distribution", *Behavioral Sci.*, 1963, vol.8, pp.203-210). Simon's stochastic process was essentially a birth process, which had the following algorithm: consider a text that is being written and has reached a length of N words. $f(i)$ denotes the number of different words that have each occurred exactly i times in the text. Thus $f(1)$ denotes the number of different words that have occurred only once. The text is continued by adding another word. With probability p this is a new word, while with probability $1-p$ this word is already present. In this case, Simon assumes that the probability that the $(N+1)$th word has already appeared i times is proportional to $i \times f(i)$, that is, the total number of words that have occurred i times.

As described above, the Simon model was originally proposed without any relation to networks. However, it is possible to formulate the Simon model for networks in terms of nodes and directed links. Bornholdt and Ebel first addressed the problem of WWW growth by sketching a simple stochastic process of adding new nodes and links, based on the Simon model (S. Bornholdt and H. Ebel, "World Wide Web scaling exponent from Simon's 1955 model", *Phys. Rev. E*, 2001, vol.64, 035104(R)). The following steps are iterated:

(1) With probability α, a new node is added with a link pointing to it from a node chosen in an arbitrary way.

(2) Otherwise (with probability $1 - \alpha$) a new link is added into the network between two existing nodes; The issuing node chosen randomly, the target node chosen with probability proportional to its degree, that is, for *k*-degree nodes, the probability is $p_k = \dfrac{kf(k)}{\sum\limits_i if(i)}$.

Note that this model does not specify where the links originate, so it does not include modeling out-degree statistics. The Simon model represents a form of the "rich-get-richer" phenomenon, but it does not imply the preferential attachment used in the BA model, whose node-chosen-probability is only proportional to node's degree *k*. In addition, from the viewpoint of Bornholdt and Ebel, the linking process is in two distinct parts: first, finding a node that has obeyed the rule (2), and second, deciding whether to link this page or not. This process depends, however, on many other variables such as contents and age. In the models discussed above, for example, the BA model, both steps occur at once, and link a page with a probability proportional to its popularity.

6.5.6 An example from software engineering

Software architecture graphs can be conceived as complex networks where blocks are software components and links are relationships between software components. Communication between these components drives program functionality. After analyzing the class diagram of the public Java Development Framework 1.2 and a computer game, Valverde et al. discovered that, apart from preferential attachment, local optimization design in a software development process could also lead to scale-free or small-world structures (S. Valverde, R.F. Cancho and R.V. Sole, "Scale-free Networks from Optimal Design", *Europhysics Letters*, 2002, vol.60, pp.512-517, cond-mat/0204344). Scale-free topology originates from a simultaneous minimization of link density and path distance, while small-world structure takes shape only if link length is minimized.

6.5.7 Other growth models with constraints

For many real networks, either nodes or links have a finite life time (for example, biological networks) or links have a finite capacity (Internet routers or nodes in the electrical power grid). The concept of finite life span in such models means nodes and links are not only added to the network, but may also be removed from the network.

6.5.7.1 *Decaying networks*

In real networks, for example, the Internet, links are not only added but may break from time to time. That certainly changes the structure of such networks. Dorogovtsev and Mendes proposed a decaying network model with undirected links based on the BA model (S.N. Dorogovtsev and J.F.F. Mendes, "Scaling behavior of developing and decaying networks", *Europhys. Lett.*, 2000, vol.52, pp.33-39). The model evolves for the following reasons. Firstly, it grows as in the BA model, that is, at each time step a new node is added and is undirectedly linked to an old node with a probability proportional to its connectivity k. In addition, a new parallel component of the evolution is introduced—the removal of some old links. At each time step, $|c|$ links between old nodes are removed with equal probability. c (≤ 0) may be also non-integer and it can be regarded as the probability for removing links. The resultant degree exponent is $\gamma = 2 + 1/(1+2c)$. The limiting value of c is -1, since the rate of removal of links cannot be higher than the rate of addition of new nodes and links, leading to $\gamma \rightarrow \infty$.

6.5.7.2 *Aging networks*

Dorogovtsev and Mendes studied the growth of a reference network with aging of sites defined in the following way (S.N. Dorogovtsev and J.F.F. Mendes, "Evolution of reference networks with aging", *Phys. Rev. E.*, 2000, vol.62, pp.1842-1845). Each new site of the network is linked to some old site with probability proportional (i) to the connectivity of the old site, as in the BA model, and (ii) to power law $\tau^{-\alpha}$, where τ is the age of the old site and the parameter α is in the interval $[0, \infty]$. Rule (ii) expresses the concept of aging in real reference networks as papers or actors will gradually lose their ability to attract attachment.

Both numerical and analytical results show that the structure of the network depends on α. When α increases from $-\infty$ to 0, the exponent γ of the degree distribution ($P(k) \sim k^{\gamma}$ for large k) grows from 2 to the value for the network without aging, that is, to 3 for the BA model. The following increase of α to 1 makes γ grow to ∞. For $\alpha > 1$, the scaling disappears and $P(k)$ becomes exponential, and the network has a chain structure.

6.5.7.3 *Fitness networks*

In the first version of BA model, older nodes increase their connectivity at the expense of newer ones, as older nodes have more time to acquire links and they gather links at a faster rate than newer nodes. In reality, however, a node's degree and growth depend not only on age, but also on content, advertisement, and so on.

For example, on the WWW, some documents acquire a large number of links in a very short time through good content, successful marketing, and other factors. Bianconi and Barabási attributed this phenomenon to an inherent competition mechanism working with some intrinsic quality of the nodes in the network (G. Bianconi and A.L. Barabási, "Bose-Einstein condensation in complex networks", *Phys. Rev. Lett.*, 2001, vol.86, pp.5632-5635; G. Bianconi and A.L. Barabási, "Competition and multiscaling in evolving networks", *Europhys. Lett.*, 2001, vol.54, pp.436-442). To address this phenomenon, they offered a fitness model, in which nodes have differing ability (fitness) to compete for links. Each node i is endowed with a fitness and unchanged factor η_k since its inception. Initially, there are few nodes in the network. At each step, a new node k is added with fitness η_k, where η is chosen from the distribution $\rho(\eta)$. Each node k is linked to m already existing nodes in the network. The probability of linking to a node i is proportional to the degree and the fitness of node i,

$$\Pi_i = \frac{\eta_i k_i}{\sum_j \eta_j k_j}$$

This combines preferential attachment with the fitness factor, that is, even a relatively new node with few links can acquire links at a high rate if it has high fitness. The continuum theory predicts the degree distribution is

$$P(k) \sim \frac{k^{-C-1}}{\ln(k)},$$

(where C is a constant), that is, a power law with a logarithmic correction. While the fitness model allows for recently added nodes with high fitness to take a central role in the network topology, the price paid is a large number of free parameters in the model.

6.5.7.4 *Age or cost constrained networks*

Amaral et al. studied a variety of real world networks and divided them into three classes: scale-free networks, broad-scale networks and single-scale networks (L.A.N. Amaral, A. Scala et al., "Classes of Small-World Networks", *Proceedings of the National Academy of Sciences*, 2000, vol.97, pp.11149-11152).

They further attributed the source of this classification to certain constraints on preferential attachment that resulted in free scale behavior and added two factors to the model: aging of the nodes and imposing a cost on the adding of links to the nodes or on increasing the link capacity of a node. In the movie actor network, for example, every actor's career lasts a limited time, which implies that in such a network, no matter how many links a node has received, sooner or later it will receive no new links at all. An example of the second factor is in the network of world airports. Constrained in space and time, airports must limit the number of landings or departures per hour and the number of passengers in transit. Therefore, the physical cost of adding a link (flight) and the limited capacity of a node (airport) will limit the number of possible links attaching to a given node.

Amaral et al. then consider a network in which nodes have two states: active and inactive, with inactive nodes refusing new links. All nodes are initially active but become inactive. Two factors were considered to lead to inactivity:

(1) The time a node may remain active decays exponentially, which is called aging.
(2) A node becomes inactive when it reaches a maximum number of links, which is called cost.

There may have certain critical values of degree k which distinguish the three classes of networks mentioned above. Near the critical point k, the degree distribution follows a power law. A little away from the critical point, the distribution becomes broad in scale. Far from the critical point, the distribution becomes singular in scale.

6.6 Modeling Actual Scale-Free Networks

The large and rapidly increasing number of Web pages, the use of HTML, the characteristics of Web structure and the mode of Web information services have made it hard to support effective, efficient and intelligent services. To get past the shortcomings of the Web, scientists are working towards a future interconnection environment (T. Berners-Lee, J. Hendler and O. Lassila, "Semantic Web", *Scientific American*, vol.284, no.5, 2001, pp.34-43; I. Foster, C. Kesselman, J.M. Nick, and S. Tuecke, "Grid Services for Distributed System Integration", *Computer*, June 2002, vol.35, pp.37-46).

Computer scientists are exploring the fundamental issues of the future interconnection environment. For example, what ideal computing model goes beyond the scope of the client/server, Grid and peer-to-peer computing models? And what resource organization model gives the advantages of both autonomy and normalization?

One vision of the future interconnection environment is described as a platform-independent *Virtual Grid* environment of requirements, roles and resources. With machine-understandable semantics, resources can dynamically cluster and fuse to provide on-demand and appropriate services by understanding the requirements and functions of each other. Services based on a uniform resource model can access all resources through a single semantic entry point. Through virtual roles, a resource can intelligently help people accomplish complex tasks and solve problems by participating in versatile resource flow cycles to use appropriate knowledge, information, and computing resources (H. Zhuge, "Semantics, Resource and Grid", *Future Generation Computer Systems*, 2004, vol.20, no.1, pp.1-5).

The future interconnection environment needs networks of diverse design to cooperate in supporting complex and intelligent applications. Fig. 6.12 depicts a four-layer network architecture, where the Social Web, Service Web, Knowledge Web and Information Web work in cooperation. The research objective here is to abstract the four networks: semantically rich and living networks of "live" resource nodes with semantic links between the nodes. Every node has a life span from birth (addition to the network) to death (removal from the network). Nodes can represent versatile resources including live sub-networks. Investigating the rules of evolution of such a network will reveal useful implications for developing the future interconnection environment.

A node's life is determined by the number of links to it. When all the links to a node have been deleted it "dies" because it is can no longer be reached from other nodes, and hence it can itself be removed from the network.

A network with add and delete operations can better support a *competitive environment*: the more robust a node (having many more links with its environment), the more likely it is to survive; conversely, the less robust, the more likely it is to be deleted. By investigating the abstract life network, we can better predict the distributions of other special Webs as shown in Fig. 6.12, and also provide evidence for evaluating and selecting the experimental data set to be used to simulate the future interconnection environment.

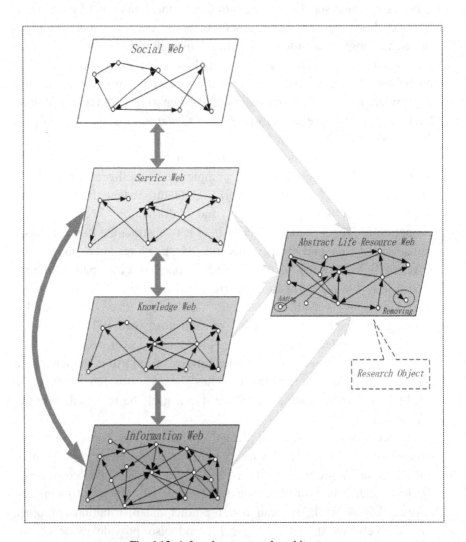

Fig. 6.12 A four-layer network architecture.

6.6.1 An urn transfer model for a live scale-free network

In our model, the inter-resource semantic relationships are reflected by a variety of semantic links such as *cause-effect links, implication links, subtype links, similar-to links, instance links, sequential links,* and *reference links* (H. Zhuge, "Active e-document framework ADF: model and tool", *Information & Management,* 2003, vol.41, no.1, pp.87-97; chapter 2). We can consider the distribution of these different types of semantic link separately but in a similar way. The differences between the seven types of link lie in the values of their parameters. We can use an asymptotic formula to describe their respective distributions.

In our urn transfer model, urns contain balls with pins attached to them. In representing the semantic link network, urns stand for sets of resource nodes with the same number of semantic links, their balls standing for resource nodes, and their pins standing for semantic links. We assume a countable number of urns: urn_k ($k = 0, 1, 2, 3, ...$), where each ball in urn_k has k pins attached to it.

Initially, at time step $t = 0$, all the urns are empty except urn_0 which has one ball in it. Let $F_k(t)$ be the number of balls in urn_k at time step t, thus $F_0(0) = 1$, $F_k(0) = 0$, $k \neq 0$, and let p, p' and α be parameters, with $0 < p < 1$, $0 < p' < 1/2$ and $\alpha > 0$. Note that p is the expectation of adding a new ball into urn_0 each time step, p' is the delete factor and α is the non-preferential factor. Then, at each time step one of following behaviors may occur in this model: add a new ball having no pins attached into urn_0 or add/remove one pin to/from a selected ball, then transfer the ball into the urn containing balls with its number of pins. To be more precise, a new ball is added to urn_0 with the probability:

$$P_{t+1} = 1 - \frac{(1-p)\sum_{k=0}^{t}(k+\alpha)F_k(t)}{t[(1-p)(1-2p')+\alpha p]+\alpha(1-p)}, \text{ where } 0 \le p_{i+1} \le 1 \qquad (6.1)$$

and urn_k being chosen with the following probability:

$$\frac{(1-p)(k+\alpha)F_k(t)}{t[(1-p)(1-2p')+\alpha p]+\alpha(1-p)} \qquad (6.2)$$

Note that the denominator is the expected value of $\sum_{k=1}^{t}(k+\alpha)F_k(t)$. Thus, one ball from urn_k is transferred to urn_{k-1} (that is to say, one pin is removed from the ball) with probability p, $k > 0$; or transferred to urn_{k+1} (one pin is added) with probability $1-p$, that is,

$$P_{transdown} = \frac{p'(1-p)(k+\alpha)F_k(t)}{t[(1-p)(1-2p')+\alpha p]+\alpha(1-p)} \quad \text{and}$$

$$P_{transup} = \frac{(1-p')(1-p)(k+\alpha)F_k(t)}{t[(1-p)(1-2p')+\alpha p]+\alpha(1-p)} \qquad (6.3)$$

In the boundary case, $k = 0$, one ball is either removed from the urn_0 with probability $P_{transdown}$ or transferred to urn_1 with probability $P_{tran\,sup}$ after attaching a pin to it.

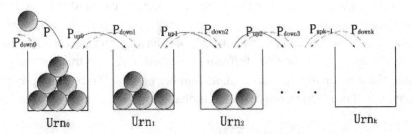

Fig. 6.13 The urn-transfer process.

To show this more clearly, we illustrate the urn transfer process in Fig. 6.13. An arrow denotes a ball being chosen and transferred, with the probability shown alongside. The placement of the arrow shows the urns involved. Solid arrows denote pins or balls being added, while dashed arrows denote pins or balls being removed. For example, the figure shows the number of balls in urn_1 changing with both a probability of increase (that is, $p_{transup0} + p_{transdown2}$), and a probability of decrease (that is, $p_{transup1} + p_{transdown1}$).

For $k > 0$, we have the following expected value of $F_k(t+1)$ at time step t.

$$E_t(F_k(t+1)) = F_k(t) + \frac{(1-p')(1-p)(k-1+\alpha)}{t[(1-p)(1-2p')+\alpha p] + \alpha(1-p)} F_{k-1}(t)$$

$$- \frac{(1-p)(k+\alpha)}{t[(1-p)(1-2p')+\alpha p] + \alpha(1-p)} F_k(t)$$

$$= F_k(t) + \beta_t((1-p')(k-1+\alpha)F_{k-1}(t)$$

$$+ p'(k+1+\alpha)F_{k+1}(t) - (k+\alpha)F_k(t)) \tag{6.4}$$

where $\beta_t = (1-p)/[t((1-p)(1-2p') + \alpha p) + \alpha(1-p)]$. Equation (6.4) gives the expected number of balls in urn_k ($k > 0$) as the previous number of balls in that urn plus the probability of increasing the number of balls in urn_k. This is equal to the probability of choosing urn_{k-1} to add a pin plus that of choosing urn_{k+1} to remove one pin with the probability of choosing urn_k subtracted. In the boundary case $k = 0$, we have

$$E_t(F_0(t+1)) = F_0(t) + p_{t+1} + p'\beta_t(1+\alpha)F_1(t) - \beta_t\alpha F_0(t) \tag{6.5}$$

Equation (6.5) gives the expected number of balls in urn_0, and it equals the previous number of balls in the urn_0 plus the probability of inserting a new ball into urn_0 and the probability of transferring a ball (removing one pin from it first) from urn_1 to urn_0, with the probability of choosing urn_0 subtracted: the probability of adding one pin to a ball and that of deleting one ball in urn_0.

Let $\quad \beta = \dfrac{1-p}{(1-p)(1-2p') + \alpha p}$,

We have $t\beta_t \approx \beta$ for large t. Indeed, for $t \ge 1$, $\beta - t\beta_t = \alpha\beta\beta_t$.

We prove that $E(F_k(t))/t$ tends to a limit f_k as t tends to infinity in section 6.6.5. As a direct result of this, $\beta_t E(F_k(t))$ tends to βf_k as t tends to infinity. Moreover, if the convergence is fast enough, $E(F_k(t+1)) - E(F_k(t))$ will tend to f_k as t tends to infinity, and we can use these facts to obtain the value of f_k. Let

$$E(F_k(t)) = t(f_k + \varepsilon_{k,t}) \tag{6.6}$$

where $\varepsilon_{k,t}$ tends to zero as t tends to infinity. So, by letting t tend to infinity, we can get the following from equation (6.4):

$$f_k = \beta[(1-p')(k-1+\alpha)f_{k-1} + p'(k+1+\alpha)f_{k+1} - (k+\alpha)f_k] \tag{6.7}$$

and the following equation from equation (6.5):

$$f_0 = p + \beta p'(1+\alpha)f_1 - \beta\alpha f_0 \tag{6.8}$$

by virtue of $E(p_t) = p$. But it is difficult to solve equation (6.7) to obtain a perfect analytic expression directly without some simplification. Because p' as a parameter should generally be small in comparison with $1 - p'$, we could make an approximation as follows:

$$f_k \approx \beta[(1-p')(k-1+\alpha)f_{k-1} - (k+\alpha)f_k], \quad f_0 \approx p - \beta\alpha f_0$$

Consequently

$$f_k \approx \frac{\beta(1-p')(k-1+\alpha)f_{k-1}}{1 + \beta(k+\alpha)}, \quad f_0 \approx \frac{p}{1+\alpha\beta}.$$

Recursively we obtain:

$$f_k \approx (1-p')^k \frac{p}{1+\alpha\beta} \times \frac{\Gamma(k+\alpha)\Gamma(^{(1+\beta+\alpha\beta)}\!/\!_\beta)}{\Gamma(\alpha)\Gamma(^{(1+\beta+\alpha\beta+k\beta)}\!/\!_\beta)}$$

$$= (1-p')^k \frac{p\Gamma(k+\alpha)\Gamma(\rho+\alpha+1)}{(1+\alpha\beta)\Gamma(\alpha)\Gamma(k+1+\rho+\alpha)} \qquad (6.9)$$

where Γ is the Gamma function and $\rho = 1/\beta$. Through the asymptotic behavior of the Gamma function when x is large, we have:

$$\Gamma(x) = \sqrt{2\pi} x^{x-1/2} e^{-x+u(x)} \qquad (6.10)$$

$$u(x) = \sum_{n=0}^{\infty} (x+n+1/2)\ln(1+\frac{1}{x+n}) - 1 = \frac{\theta}{12x}, \ 0 < \theta < 1$$

By virtue of (6.10), equation (6.9) can be turned into:

$$f_k \approx \frac{p}{1+\alpha\beta}(1-p')^k \times$$

$$\frac{\Gamma(\rho+\alpha+1)(k+\alpha)^{k+\alpha-0.5} e^{-(k+\alpha)+u(k+\alpha)}}{\Gamma(\alpha)(k+1+\rho+\alpha)^{(k+1+\rho+\alpha)-0.5} e^{-(k+1+\rho+\alpha)+u(k+1+\rho+\alpha)}}$$

By only retaining the most influential part of the approximating equation above, we can get the following asymptotic formula:

$$f_k \sim Ck^{-(1+\rho)}(1-p')^k \qquad (6.11)$$

where C is a constant and $\sim$ stands for asymptosis. Thus we can use f_k, a function of k with p, α and p' as parameters, to describe the distribution of resource nodes with the same number of semantic links.

Obviously, we can also conclude that $f_k > f_{k+1}$, that is, asymptotically there are more balls in urn_k than that in urn_{k+1}. Without the deletion of semantic links, that is, when $p = 0$, the extended model reduces to the stochastic model proposed in M. Levene, et al. ("A stochastic model for the evolution of the Web", *Computer Networks*,

2002, vol.39, pp.277-287).   Thus when $\alpha = 0$ and $p' = 0$ the extended model reduces to Simon's original model.

6.6.2 A directed evolving graph for a live scale-free network

Now we further pursue our research objective by using a different approach to the urn transfer model. We employ the rate equation method to describe Web growth in light of the evolution characteristic. At each time step, the state of the network is given by a directed evolving graph $G = (N, E)$, where N is the node set and E is the link set. For simplicity, we use the following notations:

$F_{i,j}(t)$: the expected number of nodes with i incoming semantic links (that is, in-degree) and j outgoing semantic links (that is, out-degree) at time step t;

$F(t)$: the expected total number of nodes in the graph at time step t;

$I(t)$ and $J(t)$: the expected in-degree and out-degree of the entire graph at time step t respectively;

α_{in} and α_{out} : the non-preferential factors for in-degree and out-degree respectively.

At each time step of the evolution, one of two kinds of operation for nodes and links may occur:

(1) with probability p, a new unlinked node is introduced,

(2) with probability $(1 - p)(1 - p'')$, a node is chosen to receive a new link, and with probability $(1 - p)p'$, a node is chosen to have an existing link deleted.

In addition, the probability of link addition/deletion from an issuing node to a target node is proportional to $(k + \alpha)$, which is a combination of a preferential component k and a non-preferential component α. For the issuing node, k stands for its out-degree and α stands for α_{out}, while for the target node, k stands for its in-degree and α stands for α_{in}.

Since the long-term behavior is most significant, we look only at the asymptotic regime $(t \rightarrow \infty)$ where the initial condition is irrelevant. Therefore, the expected total number of nodes $F(t) = \sum_k F_k(t) = pt$.

Further, the expectation of the total number of incoming/outgoing links $E(\sum kF_k(t)) = (1-p)(1-p')t -(1-p)p't = (1-p)(1-2p')t$.

Consequently,

$$E\left(\sum_k (k + \alpha)F_k(t) \right) = \left[(1-p)(1-2p') + \alpha p \right]t.$$

According to the rules of evolution outlined above, the rate equation for the joint degree distribution $F_{i,j}(t)$ is

$$\frac{dF_{i,j}}{dt} = (1-p')(1-p)\frac{(i-1+\alpha_{in})F_{i-1,j}-(i+\alpha_{in})F_{i,j}}{\left[(1-p)(1-2p')+\alpha_{in}p\right]t}$$

$$+(1-p')(1-p)\frac{(j-1+\alpha_{out})F_{i,j-1}-(j+\alpha_{out})F_{i,j}}{\left[(1-p)(1-2p')+\alpha_{out}p\right]t}$$

$$+p'(1-p)\frac{(i+1+\alpha_{in})F_{i+1,j}-(i+\alpha_{in})F_{i,j}}{\left[(1-p)(1-2p')+\alpha_{in}p\right]t}$$

$$+p'(1-p)\frac{(j+1+\alpha_{out})F_{i,j+1}-(j+\alpha_{out})F_{i,j}}{\left[(1-p)(1-2p')+\alpha_{out}p\right]t} + p\delta_{i,0}\delta_{j,0} \qquad (6.12)$$

The first group of terms on the right side relates to the changes in the in-degree of target nodes by creation of a new link between already existing nodes (probability $1 - p'$). For instance, the creation of a new link to a node with in-degree $i - 1$ leads to a gain in the number of i in-degree nodes. This occurs with rate $(1 - p')(1 - p)(i - 1 + \alpha_{in}) F_{i-1}$, divided by the appropriate normalization factor

$\Sigma_{i,j}(i + \alpha_{in}) \, F_i(t) = i + \alpha_{in} \, F$. The second group of terms describes the same cases for out-degree changes, but the normalization factor is replaced by $\Sigma_{i,j}(j + \alpha_{out}) \, F_j(t) = i + \alpha_{out} \, F$. The third and fourth groups relate to deletion processes for in- and out-degrees respectively. Hence, the prefixed factor is $p'\,(1 - p)$. The last term relates to the contribution of new nodes. In the boundary case for the isolated nodes in the network described here, that is, $F_{0,0}$, the link deletion behavior might be regarded as isolated nodes being removed from the network.

For clarity, we resolve the joint distribution $F_{i,j}(t)$ straightforwardly into separate in-degree and out-degree distributions by means of summing i and j respectively:

$$\sum_j \frac{dF_{i,j}}{dt} = \frac{dI_i}{dt}, \quad \sum_i \frac{dF_{i,j}}{dt} = \frac{dO_j}{dt}$$

Thus, the in-degree distribution $I_i(t)$ satisfies:

$$\frac{dI_i}{dt} = (1 - p')(1 - p)\frac{(i-1+\alpha_{in})I_{i-1} - (i+\alpha_{in})I_i}{\left[(1-p)(1-2p') + \alpha_{in}\,p\right]t}$$

$$+ p'(1-p)\frac{(i+1+\alpha_{in})I_{i+1} - (i+\alpha_{in})I_i}{\left[(1-p)(1-2p') + \alpha_{in}\,p\right]t} + p\delta_{i,0}$$

And the out-degree distribution $O_j(t)$ satisfies:

$$\frac{dO_j}{dt} = (1 - p')(1 - p)\frac{(j-1+\alpha_{out})O_j - (j+\alpha_{out})O_j}{\left[(1-p)(1-2p') + \alpha_{out}\,p\right]t}$$

$$+ p'(1-p)\frac{(j+1+\alpha_{out})O_{j+1} - (i+\alpha_{out})O_j}{\left[(1-p)(1-2p') + \alpha_{out}\,p\right]t} + p\delta_{j,0}$$

Therefore, the in- and out-degree distributions evolve in the same manner except for the difference between the factors α_{in} and α_{out}, which reflects the fact that the governing rules of this model are symmetric. Hence it is safe to say that both the incoming and outgoing links share the same evolutionary trend in their degree distribution and the only difference lies in the values of non-preferential factors. In what follows, we therefore employ α to represent α_{in} or α_{out} and F_k to represent I_i or O_j. Thus we only need to consider $F_k(t)$.

$$\frac{dF_k}{dt} = (1-p')(1-p)\frac{(k-1+\alpha)F_{k-1}}{\left[(1-p)(1-2p')+\alpha p\right]t}$$

$$+p'(1-p)\frac{(k+1+\alpha)F_{k+1}}{\left[(1-p)(1-2p')+\alpha p\right]t}$$

$$-(1-p)\frac{(k+\alpha)F_k}{\left[(1-p)(1-2p')+\alpha p\right]t} + p\delta_{k,0} \qquad (6.13)$$

Although equation (6.13) is an exact differential equation for the generating function of degree distribution $F_k(t)$, it is quite difficult to solve it exactly. Using measures like those adopted in simplifying the urn transfer model, we simplify equation (6.13) as follows:

$$\frac{dF_0}{dt} = p - \frac{(1-p)\alpha F_0}{\left[(1-p)(1-2p')+\alpha p\right]t}$$

$$\frac{dF_k}{dt} = \frac{(1-p')(1-p)(k-1+\alpha)F_{k-1}-(1-p)(k+\alpha)F_k}{\left[(1-p)(1-2p')+\alpha p\right]t} \qquad (6.14)$$

The exact solution to equation (6.14) can be obtained.

$$F_0(t) = \frac{p\left[(1-p)(1-2p')+\alpha p\right]}{\left[(1-p)(1-2p')+\alpha\right]}t + C_0$$

If $F_0(0) = 0$, then $C_0 = 0$. As a result, the solution to the above recursion may be expressed in terms of the following ratios of gamma functions:

$$F_k = (1-p')^k F_0 \frac{\Gamma(k+\alpha)\Gamma\left(\alpha/(1-p) + 2(1-p')\right)}{\Gamma\left(k + \alpha/(1-p) + 2(1-p')\right)\Gamma(\alpha)} \qquad (6.15)$$

with

$$F_0(t) = \frac{p\left[(1-p)(1-2p')+\alpha p\right]}{\left[(1-p)(1-2p')+\alpha\right]} t$$

It is clear from equation (6.15) that we can substitute $F_k(t)$ for $f_k * t$, that is $F_k = f_k * t$. We then get the same asymptotic formula as that of the urn transfer model:

$$f \sim Ck^{-(1+\rho)}(1-p')^k.$$

which resembles a power law.

We now compare the two modeling measures. Firstly, they are based on different mechanisms. In the urn transfer model, we use operations on balls and pins in each urn to stand for the evolution, while the directed evolving graph model more clearly reflects the addition and removal of nodes and links. In this sense, the urn transfer model is more abstract. Secondly, in the urn transfer model, pins denote either incoming links or outgoing links but don't distinguish between them. In fact the main difference between the two kinds of link lies in the values of the parameters. In the directed evolving graph, however, the addition or deletion of a link can have an effect on both the incoming and outgoing link distributions.

6.6.3 Experiments and analysis

For the purpose of validating the feasibility of our models, we designed and ran a simulation program with 10^6 time steps to mimic the dynamic evolution. Due to the similarity of the results between the urn transfer model and the directed evolving graph model, we need consider only the latter. The values of the parameters are based on the empirical data from the current hyperlink Web because of course data from the future interconnection environment is not available. We chose an initial condition for the evolving graph in which there is only a single node, although the asymptotic long-term behavior does not depend on this initial condition. Furthermore, an accurate solution for the original equation (6.13) can be iteratively produced using mathematical tools. Note that the only difference between in- and out-degree distributions lies in the different values for α, which will be illustrated in the figures below.

Fig. 6.14 (a) shows the in-degree distribution on a double logarithmic scale as derived from the *Web graph* model (P.L. Krapivsky, S. Redner, "A statistical physics perspective on Web growth", *Computer Networks*, 2002, vol.39, pp.261-276) with $p = 0.125$, $\alpha = 0.75$ and $p' = 0.01$. Points are results from numerical simulations and the solid lines are precise results from equation (6.13). The two curves are basically consistent. Fig. 6.14 (b) is an amplified illustration, which is the same as (a) except for being on a linear scale.

We need further to check the validity of our revision of equation (6.13). Fig. 6.15 compares equations (6.13) and (6.15) for in-degree distribution. The x coordinates stand for the number of incoming links, that is, in-degree, and y coordinates for the number of nodes that have the same in-degree. The solid lines are the results from iteration, that is, equation (6.13), while the dotted ones are for the revised version, that is, equation (6.15). In Fig. 6.15 (a), $p = 0.125$, $\alpha = 0.75$ and $p' = 0.1$, and for clarity a portion of the graph is shown as a magnified inset. Note that the insets in subsequent figures are of a similar nature. Fig. 6.15 (b) is for

$p = 0.125$, $\alpha = 0.75$ and $p' = 0.2$. It becomes clear that the smaller the value of link deleting factor p', the more similar the two curves.

As far as outgoing links are concerned, Fig. 6.16 shows the out-degree distribution for $p = 0.125$, $\alpha = 3.55$ and $p' = 0.01$ on both a double logarithmic scale (a) and a linear scale (b), which evolves in a fashion similar to the in-degree distribution.

Again, we compare equation (6.13) and equation (6.15) for out-degree distribution in Fig. 6.17, where the x coordinates stand for the number of outgoing links, that is, out-degree, and y coordinates for the number of nodes with the same out-degree. Fig. 6.17 (a) is for $p = 0.125$, $\alpha = 3.55$ and $p' = 0.1$, while Fig. 6.17 (b) is for $p = 0.125$, $\alpha = 3.55$ and $p' = 0.2$. Comparing these, we arrive at the same conclusion as for the in-degree distribution.

From all these comparisons we can therefore draw a conclusion: the evolution of the in- and out-degree distributions of our model is in agreement with the revised analytical solution. The discrepancy between the numerical simulations and the precise iterations may partly be a result of inadequate numbers of iterations. Thus running the simulations for a much larger number of iterations might give more satisfying results.

In the following, we make a further comparison between the current hyperlink distribution in the Web graph model and the semantic link distribution in our model. Fig. 6.18 (a) shows the in-degree distribution, while Fig. 6.18 (b) illustrates the out-degree distribution. We can clearly see the offset between the current Web model and our model. The key reason may be both node and link removal behaviors in our model. Obviously, the bigger the deletion value is, the larger the offset. In addition, the value of the slope for our model is always smaller in magnitude than that of the current hyperlink Web.

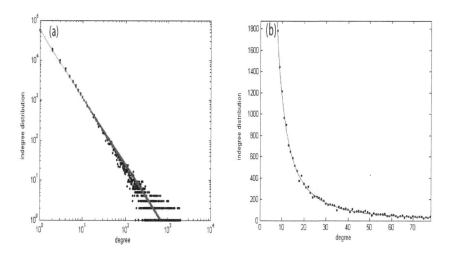

Fig. 6.14 In-degree distribution for simulation and precise iteration

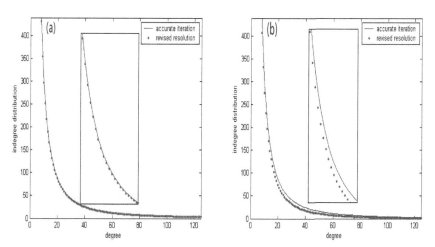

Fig. 6.15 In-degree distributions for precise iteration and revised analytical resolution.

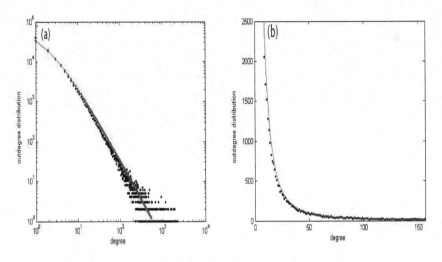

Fig. 6.16 Out-degree distribution for simulation and accurate iteration.

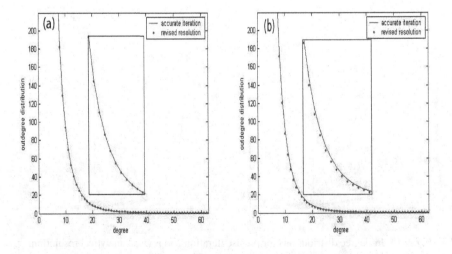

Fig. 6.17 Out-degree distribution for precise iteration and revised analytical resolution.

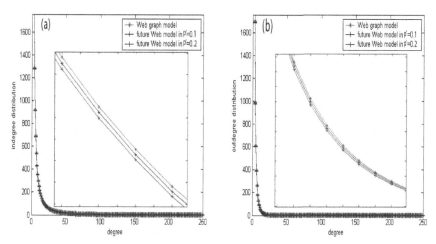

Fig. 6.18 Comparisons between the previous model and our model.

6.6.4 Further consideration and comparisons

In the live scale-free network, resource nodes may be deleted directly rather than by deleting links step by step. That means that not only isolated nodes may be deleted. In this case, we employ the following urn transfer model.

Using the same terms as in section 6.6.1, we can describe the model in this way: while at stage $k+1$ of the stochastic process for $k \geq 1$, for urn_i, $i > 0$, one of two kinds of operation may be carried out at each time step: add one pin to a selected ball with probability $p_{tran\sup}$, then transfer the ball into urn_{i+1}, or delete the selected ball with probability $p_{transdown}$ rather than transferring it to urn_{i-1}; in the limiting case, one more operation is performed: add a new ball having no pin attached into urn_0

with probability p_{k+1}. Thence we get the expected value of $F_i(k+1)$ at stage k for $i > 0$ in the following equation:

$$E_k(F_i(k+1)) = F_i(k) + \beta_k((1-p')(i-1+\alpha)F_{i-1}(k) - (i+\alpha)F_i(k)) \quad (6.16)$$

In the boundary case, we have

$$E_k(F_0(k+1)) = F_0(k) + p_{k+1} - \beta_k \alpha F_0(k) \quad (6.17)$$

Using a method similar to that of section 6.6.1, we can derive the following equation from equation (6.16) as k tends to infinity

$$f_i = \beta[(1-p')(i-1+\alpha)f_{i-1} - (i+\alpha)f_i] \quad (6.18)$$

and from equation (6.13) as k tends to infinity we derive:

$$f_0 = p - \beta\alpha f_0 \quad (6.19)$$

Making use of the characteristic of the Gamma function as shown in equation (6.10), we can solve equation (6.18) to obtain an asymptotic formula with equation (6.19) as an initial condition.

$$f_i \sim Ci^{-(1+\rho)}(1-p')^i$$

which could also be used to describe the distribution of future resource nodes with the same number of incoming or outgoing links.

Though the asymptotic formula is the same as the formula deduced in section 6.6.1, the delete probability in this urn transfer strategy could be large. In contrast, the asymptotic formula in section 2 could apply only when the delete probability p' is small compared to $1-p'$.

We can also compare the link distributions between the empirical data (denoted by *previous*) of the current hyperlink Web and the asymptotic formula (denoted by *revised*) derived from our growth model using the delete mechanism proposed in this section when the delete probability is relatively large. We show the comparison in Fig. 6.19.

Another possibility for the live scale-free network is to control the rich/poor gap (this term is employed to describe the gap between nodes with very different numbers of links), since the preferential attachment mechanism will certainly lead to the 'rich get richer' phenomenon. Here we attempt a simulation as follows: if the number of links coming in to a node reaches a certain value, no further incoming links will be attached to it. As expected, the distribution as in Fig. 6.20 no longer obeys a power law, and its tail in fact rises a little. This observation indicates that "wealth" has been shared among relatively rich nodes.

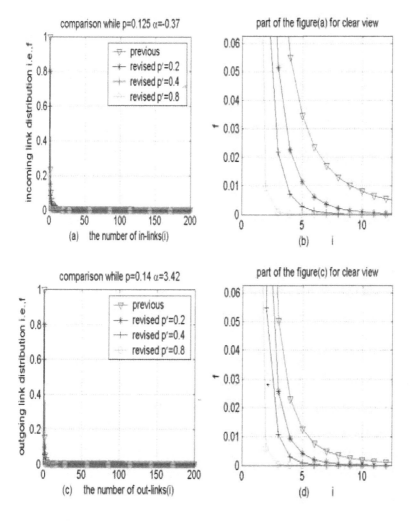

Fig. 6.19 Distributions of the previous model and our model with new delete mechanism.

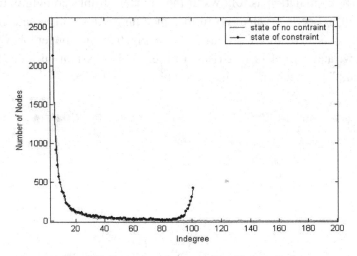

Fig. 6.20 Power law changes with added constraints.

6.6.5 *Proof of the proposition*

Proposition. *For all* $k \geq 0$, $\lim_{t \to \infty} E(F_k(t))/t = f_k$

Proof. Using (6.6) to rewrite (6.4) and (6.5), we obtain: for $k > 0$,

$$(t+1)(f_k + \varepsilon_{k,t+1}) = t(f_k + \varepsilon_{k,t}) + t\beta_t[(1-p')(k-1+\alpha)(f_{k-1} + \varepsilon_{k-1,t})$$

$$+p'(k+1+\alpha)(f_{k+1} + \varepsilon_{k+1,t}) - (k+\alpha)(f_k + \varepsilon_{k,t})] \tag{1}$$

and for $k = 0$,

$$(t+1)(f_0 + \varepsilon_{0,t+1}) = t(f_0 + \varepsilon_{0,t}) + p'' - t\beta_t\alpha(f_0 + \varepsilon_{0,t})$$

$$+t\beta_t p'(1+\alpha)(f_1 + \varepsilon_{1,t}), \tag{2}$$

Equations (6.7) and (6.8) may be written in a similar form as

$$(t+1)f_k = tf_k + \beta(1-p')(k-1+\alpha)f_{k-1}$$
$$+\beta p'(k+1+\alpha)f_{k+1} - \beta(k+\alpha)f_k, \tag{3}$$

and $(t+1)f_0 = tf_0 + p - \beta\alpha f_0 + \beta p'(1+\alpha)f_1,$ (4)

For $k>0$, subtracting (3) from (1) yields:

$$(t+1)\varepsilon_{k,t+1} = t\varepsilon_{k,t} + t\beta_t[(1-p')(k-1+\alpha)\varepsilon_{k-1,t}$$
$$+p'(k+1+\alpha)\varepsilon_{k+1,t} - (k+\alpha)\varepsilon_{k,t}]$$
$$+(t\beta_t-\beta)[(1-p')(k-1+\alpha)f_{k-1}+p'(k+1+\alpha)f_{k+1}-(k+\alpha)f_k]$$

using (6.7) and $\beta - t\beta_t = \alpha\beta\beta_t$, this equation simplifies to

$$(t+1)\varepsilon_{k,t+1} = (1-\beta_t(k+\alpha))t\varepsilon_{k,t} + \beta_t(k-1+\alpha)(1-p')t\varepsilon_{k-1,t}$$
$$+\beta_t p'(k+1+\alpha)t\varepsilon_{k+1,t} - \alpha\beta_t f_k \tag{5}$$

Similarly, for $k=0$, using (6.8), subtracting (4) from (2) we obtain:

$$(t+1)\varepsilon_{0,t+1} = (1-\alpha\beta_t)t\varepsilon_{0,t} + \beta_t p'(1+\alpha)t\varepsilon_{1,t} + \alpha\beta_t(p-f_0) \tag{6}$$

From (5), by virtue of $0 < \beta_t < 1/(t/C_0+\alpha)$ for $t \geq 1$ and $0 < \beta < C_0$ where C_0 is a constant for definite parameters, and the fact that $f_k < 1$, $0 \leq p' < 1/2$, $0 < p < 1$ and $\alpha > 0$, we have: for $0 < k \leq t$, (where t may tends to infinity and k should have the upper bound in reality)

$$(t+1)\left|\varepsilon_{k,t+1}\right| \leq (1-\beta_t(k+\alpha))t\left|\varepsilon_{k,t}\right| + \beta_t(1-p')(k-1+\alpha)t\left|\varepsilon_{k-1,t}\right|$$
$$+\beta_t p'(k+1+\alpha)t\left|\varepsilon_{k+1,t}\right| + \alpha\beta_t \tag{7}$$

for $k=0$, from (6) we have:

$$(t+1)\left|\varepsilon_{0,t+1}\right| \leq (1-\alpha\beta_t)t\left|\varepsilon_{0,t}\right| + \beta_t p'(1+\alpha)t\left|\varepsilon_{1,t}\right| + \alpha\beta_t(p-f_0) \tag{8}$$

We now define $\delta_t = \max_{k\geq 0}\left|\varepsilon_{k,t}\right| = \max_{0\leq k\leq t+1}\left|\varepsilon_{k,t}\right|$ (9)

Let $C = \max\left\{\dfrac{\alpha}{(\alpha - p'(1+\alpha))(1+\alpha\beta)}, \dfrac{\alpha}{1-2p'}, 1\right\}$ (In reality, the first element will be positive), we will show by induction on t that

$$t\delta_t \leq C \tag{10}$$

From (9) and (6.6), we obtain that $\delta_1 = \max\{1 - f_1, f_2) < 1$, so (10) holds for $t = 1$.

Now we assume that (10) holds for some $t \geq 1$, so for $k = 0$, from (8) we get

$$(t+1)\left|\varepsilon_{0,t+1}\right| \leq (1 - \alpha\beta_t)C_1 + \beta_t p'(1+\alpha)C_1 + \alpha\beta_t(p - f_0)$$

$$\leq (1 - \alpha\beta_t)C_1 + \beta_t p'(1+\alpha)C_1 + \alpha\beta_t p(1 - \dfrac{1}{1+\alpha\beta})$$

(since $f_0 > p/(1+\alpha\beta)$)

$$\leq C_1 \quad \text{where } C_1 = \dfrac{\alpha}{(\alpha - p'(1+\alpha))(1+\alpha\beta)}$$

For $0 < k \leq t$, from (7) we obtain:

$$(t+1)\left|\varepsilon_{k,t+1}\right| \leq (1 - \beta_t(k+\alpha))C_2 + \beta_t(1 - p')(k - 1 + \alpha)C_2$$

$$+ \beta_t p'(k + 1 + \alpha)C_2 + \alpha\beta_t$$

$$\leq (1 - (1 - 2p')\beta_t)C_2 + \alpha\beta_t$$

$$\leq C_2 \quad \text{where } C_2 = \dfrac{\alpha}{1-2p'}$$

Therefore, $(t+1)\delta_{t+1} \leq C$.

In conclusion, as t tends to infinity, δ_t tends to 0 for all k. So far, we have proved that

$$\lim_{t \to \infty} E(F_k(t))/t = f_k, \text{ for } k \geq 0.$$

6.7 Summary and Implications

Studies of real-world complex networks relate to the Internet, the World Wide Web, social networks, collaboration networks, citation networks, and a variety of biological networks. Statistical data revealed that most networks are scale-free. Models have been proposed to explain how such networks organize themselves and what the expected effects of the resulting structure will be. R. Albert and A.L. Barabási have given an extensive pedagogical review from physics literature. They have proved the simplicity and the power of statistical physics for characterizing evolving networks. ("Statistical mechanism of complex networks", *Reviews of Modern Physics*, 2002, vol.74, pp.48-94). Another review of models of growing networks that uncovered some generic topological and dynamical principles was "Evolution of networks" (S.N. Dorogovtsev and J.F.F. Mendes, *Advances in Physics,* 2002, vol.51, pp.1079-1187).

Starting with a brief description of these representative networks, we have provided a broader view of network growth. The large discrepancy between scale-free networks and random networks is a big challenge to classical graph theory. The preferential attachment mechanism (preferential linking to nodes with a higher number of links) indeed produces a desired property: the scale-free structure of real networks. However, the models created by it can be applied to real networks only at a macroscopic and qualitative level. These simple models are far from reality. Therefore, the actual rules and complex relations behind real scale-free networks deserve further investigation.

We have studied an instance of the future interconnected environment: an abstract overlay where nodes stand for versatile resources having lifespans, and links imply certain semantic relationships between nodes. By defining and investigating two types of models, a stochastic growth model and a directed evolving graph model, we have obtained the same scale-free distribution rule. Simulations and comparisons validate the proposed models.

An important obstacle encountered in the investigation of the future interconnection environment is the lack of proper experimental data. Besides introducing the growth rule of the live scale-free network, the proposed models can also provide the evidence for evaluating and selecting experimental data that can simulate the future interconnection environment.

Many application models and overlays can be built to describe a complex network. For example, different infection models can be used for the same contact network to study disease propagation (H.Zhuge and X.Shi, "Fighting Epidemics in Knowledge and Information Age", *Computer*, 2003, vol.36, no.10, pp.114-116). To apply these models we must try to find the complete evolution rules of these complex networks. For example, it could help us to answer the question: Is there any degeneration phase in the evolution of these networks? We believe there is, because the development of anything real is essentially limited. But the keys to the answer are the degeneration rule and the modeling of the degeneration phase.

On the other hand, different semantic views can be taken of the one network to meet the needs of different applications (H.Zhuge, "Semantic Grid: Scientific Issues, Methodology, and Practice in China", Keynote at *the 2ⁿᵈ International Conference on Grid and Cooperative Computing, GCC 2003*, Shanghai, China, December 7-10, 2003). An important growth characteristic of a semantically rich network is that a new node is likely to link to the most semantically relevant nodes rather than to the highly linked ones, which is not at all what preferential attachment models. Does this characteristic influence the growth of the networks, and to what extent?

Many interesting issues challenge current theories and techniques (H.Zhuge, "Future Interconnection Environment — Dream, Principle, Challenge and Practice", keynote at *the 5ᵗʰ International Conference on Web-Age Information Management, WAIM 2004*, Dalian, China, July, in LNCS 3129, pp.13-22).

Bibliography

Adamic, L. A. and Huberman, B. A. (2000). Power-law distribution of the World Wide Web, *Science*, 287, No.24, pp.2115.

Aiello, W., Chung, F. and Lu, L. (2000). A random graph model for massive graphs, *Proc. 32nd ACM Symposium on the Theory of Computing*, New York, pp.171-180.

Albert, R., Jeong, H. and Barabási, A. L. (1999). Diameter of the World-Wide Web, *Nature*, 401, pp.130-131.

Albert, R. and Barabási, A. L.(2000). Topology of evolving networks: local events and universality, *Phys. Rev. Lett.*, 85, pp.5234-5237.

Albert, R. and Barabási, A. L. (2002). Statistical mechanics of complex networks, *Rev. Mod. Phys.*, 74, pp.48-94.

Allan, J. (1997). Building hypertext using information retrieval, *Information Processing and Management*, 33, No.2, pp.145-159.

Amaral, L.A.N. et al. (2000). Classes of small-world networks, *Proc. Nat. Acad. Sci.*, 97, No.21, pp.11149-11152.

Barabási, A. L. and Albert, R. (1999a). Emergence of scaling in random networks, *Science*, 286, pp. 509-512.

Barabási, A. L., Albert, R. and Jeong, H. (1999b). Mean-field theory for scale-free random networks, *Physica A*, 272, pp.173-187.

Barabási, A. L., Jeong, H., Neda, Z., Ravasz, E., Schubert, A. and Vicsek, T. (2002). Evolution of the social network of scientific collaborations, *Physica A*, 311, pp.590-614.

Barabási, A. L. and Bonabeau, E. (2003). Scale-free networks, *Scientific American*, May, pp.50-59.

Barrat, A. and Weigt, M. (2000). On the properties of small-world networks, *Eur Phys. J. B*, 13, pp.547-560.

Batagelj, V. and Mrvar, A. (2000). Some analyses of the erdös collaboration graph, *Social Networks*, 22, pp.173-186

Beckwith, R., Fellbaum, C., Gross, C. and Miller, G. (1991). WordNet: a lexical database organized on psycholinguistic principles, lexical acquisition: exploiting on-line resources to build a lexicon, U.Zernik, ed., *Lawrence Erlbaum*, pp.211-231.

Berners-Lee, T., Hendler, J. and Lassila, O. (2001). Semantic Web, *Scientific American*, 284, No.5, pp.34-43.

Bianconi, G. and Barabási, A. L. (2001a). Bose-Einstein condensation in complex networks, *Phys. Rev. Lett.*, 86, pp.5632-5635.

Bianconi, G. and Barabási, A. L. (2001b). Competition and multiscaling in evolving networks, *Europhys. Lett.*, 54, pp.436-442.

Bocy, R. et al. (1975). Specifying queries as relational expressions, *Communications of the ACM*, 18, No.11, pp.621-628.

Booch, G., Rumbaugh, J. and Jacobson, I. (1999). The unified modeling language: user guide. Reading, Mass. *Addison-Wesley*.

Bornholdt, S. and Ebel, H. (2001). World Wide Web scaling exponent from Simon's 1955 model, *Phys. Rev. E*, 64, 035104(R).

Bradshaw, J. M., Greaves, M. and Holmback, H. (1999). Agents for the masses? *IEEE Intelligent Systems*, 14, No.2, Mar./Apr., pp.53-63.

Broder, A. et al. (2000). Graph structure of the Web, *Proc. of the 9th WWW Conf.*, Amsterdam, May, pp.309-320.

Broekstra, J. et al, (2001). Enabling knowledge representation on the Web by extending RDF schema, *Proc. 10th International WWW Conf.*, Hong Kong, pp.467-478, available at http://www.cs.vu.nl/~frankh/abstracts/www01.html.

Bush, V. (1945). As we may think. *The Atlantic Monthly*, 176, No.1, pp.101-108.

Callaway, D. S. et al. (2001). Are randomly grown graphs really random? *Phys. Rev. E.*, 64, cond-mat/0104546.

Cascia, M. L., Sethi, S. and Sclaroff, S. (1998). Combining textual and visual cues for content-based image retrieval on the worldwide web. *Proc. IEEE Workshop on Content-based Access of Image and Video Libraries*, pp.24-28.

Cass, S. (2004). A fountain of knowledge. *IEEE Spectrum*, 41, No.1, pp.60-67.

Chakrabarti, S., Dom, B., Gibson, D., Kleinberg, J., Raghavan, P. and Rajagopalan, S. (1998). Automatic resource list compilation by analyzing hyperlink structure and associated text, *Proc. 7th International WWW Conf.*, pp.65-74.

Chen, Q. et al. (2002). The origin of power laws in Internet topologies revisited, *Proc. of the IEEE INFOCOM Conf.*, pp.608-617.

Codd, E. F. (1970). A relational model of data for large shared data banks, *Communications of the ACM*, 13, No.6, pp.377-387.

Davenport, T. H., Jarvenpaa, S. L. and Beer, M. C. (1996). Improving knowledge work process, *Sloan Management Review*, 34, No.4, pp. 53-65.

Davis, G. F. and Greve, H. R. (1997). Corporate élite networks and governance changes in the 1980s, *Am. J. Sociol.*, 103, pp.1-37.

Dean, J. and Henzinger, M. R. (1999). Finding related pages in the World Wide Web, *Proc. 8th International WWW Conf.*, pp.1467-1476.

Decker, S., et al. (2000). The Semantic Web: the roles of XML and RDF, *IEEE Internet Computing*, 4, No. 5, pp.63-74.

Desouza, K. C. (2003). Facilitating tacit knowledge exchange, *Communications of the ACM*, 46, No.6, pp.85-88.

Dieng, R. (2000). Knowledge management and the Internet, *IEEE Intelligent Systems*, 15, No.3, May/June, pp.14-17.

Dorogovtsev, S. N. and Mendes, J. F. F. (2000a). Scaling behavior of developing and decaying networks, *Europhys. Lett.*, 52, pp.33-39.

Dorogovtsev, S. N. and Mendes, J. F. F. (2000b). Evolution of reference networks with aging, *Phys. Rev. E.*, 62, pp.1842-1845.

Dorogovtsev, S. N., Mendes, J. F. F. and Samukhin, A. N. (2000c). Structure of growing networks with preferential linking, *Phys. Rev. Lett.*, 85, pp.4633-4636.

Dorogovtsev, S. N., Mendes, J. F. F. and Samukhin, A. N. (2000d). WWW and Internet models from 1955 till our days and the "popularity is attractive" principle, *Condensed Matter Archive*, cond-mat/0009090.

Dorogovtsev, S. N. and Mendes, J. F. F. (2001). Language as an evolving word Web, *Proc. Royal Soc. London B*, 268, No.2603, cond-mat/0105093.

Drucker, P. F. (1998). Harvard business review on knowledge management, Boston, *Harvard Business School Press*.

Faloutsos, M., Faloutsos, P. and Faloutsos, C. (1999). On power law relationships of the Internet topology, *Comput. Commun. Rev.*, 29, pp.251-262.

Fensel, D., et al. (2001). OIL: an ontology infrastructure for the Semantic Web, *IEEE Intelligent Systems*, 16, No.2, Mar./Apr., pp.38-45.

Ferrer, R., Janssen, C. and Sole, R. V. (2001b). The topology of technology graphs: small-world patterns in electronic circuits, *Phys. Rev.E.*, 64, No.32767.

Ferrer, R. and Sole, R. V. (2001a). The small-world of human language, *Working Papers of Santa Fe Institute*, http://www.santafe.edu/sfi/publications/Abstracts/01-03-004abs.htm.

Fikes, R. and Farquhar, A. (1999). Distributed repositories of highly expressive reusable ontologies, *IEEE Intelligent Systems*, 14, No. 2, Mar/April, pp.73-79.

Foster, I. (2000). Internet computing and the emerging Grid, 408, No.6815, *Nature*, http://www.nature.com/nature/webmatters/grid/grid.html.

Foster, I., Kesselman, C., Nick, J. M. and Tuecke, S. (2002). Grid services for distributed system integration, *Computer*, 35, pp.37-46.

Gevers, T. and Smeulders, A. W. M. (1999). The PicToSeek WWW image search system, *Proc. IEEE International Conf. on Multimedia Computing and Systems*, pp.264-269.

Govindan, R. and Tangmunarunkit, H. (2000). Heuristics for Internet map discovery, *Proc. of the IEEE INFOCOM Conf.*, Tel Aviv, Israel, March, pp.1371-1380.

Gray, J. (2003). What next? A dozen information-technology research goals, *Journal of the ACM*, 50, No.1, pp.41-57.

Green, S. J. (1999). Building hypertext links by computing semantic similarity, *IEEE Trans. On Knowledge and Data Engineering*, 11, No.5, pp.713-730.

Grosz, B. J. and Kraus, S. (1996). Collaborative plans for complex group action, *Artificial Intelligence*, 86, pp.269-357.

Gupta, A. and Jain, R. (1997). Visual information retrieval, *Communications of the ACM*, 40, No.5, pp.71-79.

Han, J. and Kambr, M. (2000). Data mining: concepts and techniques, *Morgan Kaufmann Publishers*.

Harmandas, V., Sanderson, M. and Dunlop, M. D. (1997). Image retrieval by hypertext links. *Proc. 20th Annual International ACM SIGIR Conf. on Research and Development in Information Retrieval*, pp.296-303.

Heflin, J. and Hendler, J. (2001). A portrait of the Semantic Web in action, *IEEE Intelligent Systems*, 16, No.2, Mar./Apr., pp.54-59.

Hendler, J and McGuinness, D. (2000). The DARPA agent markup language, *IEEE Intelligent Systems*, 15, No.6, Nov./Dec., pp.72-73.

Hendler, J. (2001). Agents and the Semantic Web, *IEEE Intelligent Systems*, 16, No.2, Mar./Apr., pp.30-37.

Henzinger, M. R. (2001). Hyperlink analysis for the Web, *IEEE Internet Computing*, 5, No.1, Jan./Feb., pp.45-50.

Heylighen, F. (1992). A Cognitive-systemic reconstruction of maslow's theory of self-actualization, *Behavioral Science*, 37, pp.39-58.

Huberman, B. A. and Adamic, L. A. (1999). Growth dynamics of the World-Wide Web, *Nature*, 401, 131p

Jeong, H., Tombor, B., Albert, R., Oltvai, Z. N., Barabási, A. L. (2000). The large-scale organization of metabolic networks, *Nature*, 407, pp.651-654.

Jeong, H. Neda, Z. and Barabási, A. L. (2003). Measuring preferential attachment for evolving networks, *Europhysics letters*, 61, pp.567-572.

Kanth, K., Agrawal, D. and Singh, A. (1998). Dimensionality reduction for similarity searching in dynamic databases, *Proc. ACM SIGMOD International Conf. on Management of Data*, 75, pp.166-176.

Klein, M. (2001). XML, RDF, and relatives, *IEEE Internet Computing*, 16, No.2, Mar./Apr., pp.26-28.

Kleinberg, J. M. (1999). Authoritative sources in a hyperlinked environment. *Journal of the ACM*, 46, No.5, pp.604-632.

Kleinberg, J and Lawrence, S. (2001). The structure of the Web, *Science*, 294, No.5548, pp.1849-1850.

Krapivsky, P. L. Redner, S. and Leyvraz, F. (2000). Connectivity of growing random networks, *Phys. Rev. Lett.*, 1.85, pp.4629-4632.

Krapivsky, P. L. and Redner, S. (2001a). Organization of growing random networks, *Phys. Rev. E.*, 63, cond-mat/0011094.

Krapivsky, P. L., Rodgers, G. J. and Redner, S. (2001b). Degree distributions of growing networks, *Phys. Rev. Lett.*, 86, pp.5401-5404.

Krapivsky, P. L. and Redner, S. (2002). A statistical physics perspective on Web growth, *Computer Networks*, 39, pp.261-276.

Kumar, R. et al. (1999). Extracting large-scale knowledge bases from the Web, *Proc. 25th VLDB Conf.*, Edinburgh, Scotland, September, pp.639-650.

Lawrence, S. and Giles, C. L. (1998). Searching the World Wide Web, *Science*, 280, No.5360, pp.98-100.

Lawrence, S. and Giles, C. L. (1999). Accessibility of information on the Web, *Nature*, 400, No.8, pp.107-109.

Leland, W. E. et al. (1994). On the self-similar nature of Ethernet traffic, *IEEE/ACM Transactions on Networking*, 2, No.1, pp.1-15.

Lempel, R. and Moran, S. (2000). The stochastic approach for link-structure analysis (SALSA) and the TKC effect. *Proc. 9th International WWW Conf.*, No.33, pp.387-401.

Lempel, R. and Soffer, A. (2001). PicASHOW: pictorial authority search by hyperlinks on the Web, *Proc. 10th International WWW Conf.*, pp.438-448.

Levene, M., Fenner, T., Loizou, G. and Wheeldon, R. (2002). A stochastic model for the evolution of the Web, *Computer Networks*, 39, pp.277-287.

Leymann, F. and Roller, D. (1997). Workflow-based applications, *IBM Systems Journal*, 36, No.1, pp.102-122.

Liu, Z. Q. and Satur, R. (1999). Contextual fuzzy cognitive maps for decision support in geographic information systems, *IEEE Transactions on Fuzzy Systems*, 7, No.10, pp.495-502.

Mack, R., Ravin, Y. and Byrd, R. J. (2001). Knowledge portals and the emerging knowledge workplace, *IBM Systems Journal*, 40, No. 4, pp. 925-955.

Maedche, A. and Staab, S. (2001). Ontology learning for the Semantic Web, *IEEE Intelligent Systems*, 16, No.2, Mar./Apr., pp.72-79.

Marchionini, G., Dwiggins, S., Katz, A. and Lin, X. (1990). Information roles of domain and search expertise, *Library and Information Science Research*, 15, No.1, pp.391-407.

Martin, P. and Eklund, P. W. (2000). Knowledge retrieval and the World Wide Web, *IEEE Intelligent Systems*, 15, No.3, May/June, pp. 18-25.

Martinez, N. D. (1991). Artifacts or attributes? Effects of resolution on the Little Rock Lake food web, *Ecological Monographs*, 61, pp.367-392.

Maybury, M. (2001). Collaborative virtual environments for analysis and decision support, *Communication of the ACM*, 14, No.12, pp. 51-54.

McHraith, S. A., Son, T. C. and Zeng, H. (2001). Semantic Web services, *IEEE Intelligent Systems*, 16, No.2, Mar./Apr., pp. 46-53.

Miao, Y., et al. (2001). Dynamic cognitive network, *IEEE Transactions on Fuzzy System*, 9, No.5, pp. 760-770;

Mitri, M. (2003). Applying tacit knowledge management techniques for performance assessment, *Computers & Education*, 4, pp.173-189.

Mok, W.Y. (2002). A comparative study of various nested normal forms, *IEEE Trans. on Knowledge and Data Engineering*, 14, No.2, pp. 369-385.

Nasukawa, T. and Nagano, T. (2001). Text analysis and knowledge mining system, *IBM Systems Journal*, 40, No. 4, pp. 967-984.

Newman, M. E. J. et al.(2001a). Random graphs with arbitrary degree distribution and their applications", *Phys. Rev. E*, 64, No.026118, cond-mat/0007235.

Newman, M. E. J. (2001b). The structure of scientific collaboration networks, *Proc. Nat. Acad. Sci. U.S.A.*, 98, pp.404-409.

Newman, M. E. J. (2001c). Scientific collaboration networks: I. Network construction and fundamental results, *Phys. Rev. E*, 64, No.016131.

Newman, M. E. J. (2001d). Scientific collaboration networks: II. Shortest paths, weighted networks, and centrality, *Phys. Rev. E*, 64, No.016132.

Newman, M. E. J. (2001e). Who is the best connected scientist? A study of scientific coauthorship networks, *Phys. Rev. E*, 64, No.016131.

Ng, W.S. et al. (2003). PeerDB: A P2P-Based system for distributed data sharing, *Proc. of International Conf. on Data Engineering*, ICDE2003, Bangalore, India.

Nissen, M. E. (2002). An extended model for knowledge-flow dynamics, *Communications of the Associations for Information Systems*, 8, pp. 251-266.

Nonaka, I. (1994). A dynamic theory of organizational knowledge creation, *Organization Science*, 5, No.1, pp. 14-37.

Oida, K.(2002). The birth and death process of hypercycle spirals, in: R.K. Standish, M.A. Bedau, H.A. Abbass, edd., Artificial Life VIII, *MIT Press*.

O'Leary, D. E. (1998). Enterprise knowledge management, *Computer*, 31, No.3, pp.54-61.

Ozsoyoglu, Z. M. and Yuan, L. Y. (1987). A new normal form for nested relations, *ACM Trans. Database Systems*, 12, No.1, pp.111-136.

Pansiot, J. J. and Grad, D. (1998). On routes and multicast trees in the Internet, *Computer Communications Review*, 28, pp.41-50.

Parise, S. and Henderson, J. C. (2001). Knowledge resource exchange in strategic alliances, *IBM Systems Journal*, 40, No. 4, pp.908-924.

Redner, S. (1998). How popular is your paper? An empirical study of the citation distribution, *European Physics Journal B*, 4, pp.131-134.

Ritter, F. E., Baxter, G. E., Jones, G and Young, R.M. (2000). Supporting cognitive models as users, *ACM Trans. on Computer-Human Interaction*, 7, No.2, pp.141-173.

Schoder D. and Fischbach, K. (2003). Peer-to-peer prospects, *Communications of the ACM*, 46, No.2, pp.27-29.

Simon, H. A. (1955). On a class of skew distribution functions, *Biometrika*, 42, pp.425-440.

Simon, H. A. and Van Wormer, T. (1963). Some Monte Carlo estimates of the Yule distribution, *Behavioral Sci.*, 8, pp.203-210.

Srihari, R. K., Zhang, Z. and Rao, A. (2000). Intelligent indexing and semantic retrieval of multimodel documents, *Information Retrieval*, 2, No.2, pp. 245-275.

Stoica, I. et al., (2003). Chord: A scalable Peer-to-Peer lookup protocol for Internet applications, *IEEE/ACM Transactions on Networking*, 11, pp. 17–32.

Tari, Z., Stokes, J. and Spaccapietra, S. (1997). Object normal forms and dependency constraints for object-oriented schemata, *ACM Trans. Database Systems*, 22, No.4, pp.513-569.

Thistlewaite, P. (1997). Automatic construction and management of large open Webs, *Information Processing and Management*, 33, No.2, pp. 145-159.

Thomas, J. C., Kellogg, W. A. and Erickson, T. (2001). The knowledge management puzzle: Human and social factors in knowledge management, *IBM Systems Journal*, 40, No. 4, pp.863-884.

Tudhope, D. and Taylor, C. (1997). Navigation via similarity: automatic linking based on semantic closeness, *Information Processing and Management*, 33, No.2, pp.233-242.

Ullman, J. D. (1988). Principles of database and knowledge-base systems, *Computer Science Press, Inc.*,

Valverde, S., Cancho, R. F. and Sole, R. V. (2002). Scale-free networks from optimal design, *Europhysics Letters*, 60, pp.512-517.

Watts, D. J. and Strogatz, S. H. (1998). Collective dynamics of "Small-world" networks, *Nature*, 393, pp.440-442.

Watts, D. J. (1999). Networks, dynamics, and the small-world phenomenon, *Am. J. Sociol.*, 105, pp.493-592.

Yook, S. H. et al. (2002). Modeling the Internet's large-scale topology, *Proc. the National Academy of Sciences*, pp. 13382-13386, cond-mat/0107417.

Zhuge, H. (1998). Inheritance rules for flexible model retrieval, *Decision Support Systems*, 22, No.4, pp. 383-394.

Zhuge, H. (2000a). Conflict decision training through multi-space co-operation, *Decision Support Systems*, 29, No. 5, pp.111-123.

Zhuge, H., Cheung, T. Y. and Pung, H. K. (2000b). A timed workflow process model, *Journal of Systems and Software*, 55, No.3, pp.231-243.

Zhuge, H. and Shi, X. (2000c). A dynamic evaluation approach for virtual conflict decision training, *IEEE Transactions on Systems Man and Cybernetics*, 30, No.3, August, pp.374-380.

Zhuge, H. (2002a). A Knowledge Grid model and platform for global knowledge sharing, *Expert Systems with Applications*, 22, No.4, pp.313-320.

Zhuge, H. (2002b). A knowledge flow model for peer-to-peer team knowledge sharing and management, *Expert Systems with Applications*, 23, No.1, pp.23-30.

Zhuge, H. (2002c). Clustering soft-device in the Semantic Grid, *IEEE Computing in Science and Engineering*, 4, No.6, Nov./Dec., pp.60-62.

Zhuge, H. (2003a). An inexact model matching approach and its applications, *Journal of Systems and Software*, 67, No.3, pp.201-212.

Zhuge, H. (2003b). China e-science Knowledge Grid Environment, *IEEE Intelligent Systems*, 19, No.1, Sep./Oct., pp. 13-17.

Zhuge, H. (2003c). Workflow-based cognitive flow management for distributed team cooperation, *Information and Management*, 40, No.5, pp.419-429.

Zhuge, H. (2003d). Active e-Document Framework ADF: model and tool, *Information and Management*, 41, No.1, pp. 87-97.

Zhuge, H. and Shi, X. (2003e). Fighting epistemology in knowledge and information age, *Computer*, 36, No.10, pp.114-116.

Zhuge, H. (2003f). Semantic Grid: Scientific Issues, Methodology, and Practice in China, Keynote at *the 2nd International Conf. on Grid and Cooperative Computing*, GCC2003, Shanghai, China, December 7-10, 2003.

Zhuge, H. (2004a). Resource Space Model, its design method and applications, *Journal of Systems and Software*, 72, No.1, pp. 71-81.

Zhuge, H. (2004b). Semantics, resources and Grid, Future Generation Computer Systems, Special issue on *Semantic Grid and Knowledge Grid: the Next-generation Web*, editorial, 20, No.1, pp.1-5.

Zhuge, H. (2004c). Fuzzy resource space model and platform, *Journal of Systems and Software*, 73, No.3, pp.389-396.

Zhuge, H. (2004d). Resource Space Grid: model, method and platform, *Concurrency and Computation: Practice and Experience*, 16, No.13.

Zhuge, H. (2004e). Retrieve images by understanding semantic links and clustering image fragments, *Journal of Systems and Software*, 73, No.3, pp.455-466.

Zhuge, H. (2004f). Toward the eco-grid: a harmoniously evolved interconnection environment, *Communications of the ACM*, 47, No.9, pp.78-83.

Zhuge, H. (2004g). Semantics, Resource and Grid, *Future Generation Computer Systems*, 20, No.1, pp.1-5.

Zhuge, H. (2004h). Future Interconnection Environment — dream, principle, challenge and Practice, keynote at *the 5th International Conf. on Web-Age Information Management*, WAIM 2004, Dalian, China, July, in LNCS 3129, pp.13-22.

Index

263